Communicating Christ
in Asian Cities:
Urban Issues in Buddhist Contexts

Communicating Christ
in Asian Cities:
Urban Issues in Buddhist Contexts

Edited by Paul H. De Neui

WILLIAM CAREY
LIBRARY

Communicating Christ in Asian Cities: Urban Issues in Buddhist Contexts
Copyright © 2009 by SEANET
All rights reserved.

Unless otherwise indicated, all biblical quotations are taken from the Holy Bible, New International Version © 1973, 1978, 1984 by the International Bible Society. Used by permission of Hodder and Stoughton Ltd. All rights reserved.

Naomi Bradley, Editorial Manager
Johanna Deming, Assistant Editor
Jonathan Pon, Graphic Designer

Published by William Carey Library, an imprint of William Carey Publishing
10 W. Dry Creek Circle
Littleton, CO 80120 | www.missionbooks.org

William Carey Library is a ministry of Frontier Ventures
Pasadena, CA 91104 | www.frontierventures.org

Library of Congress Cataloging-in-Publication Data

Communicating Christ in Asian cities : urban issues in Buddhist contexts / edited by Paul H. De Neui.

p. cm. -- (SEANET ; v. 6)
Includes bibliographical references and index.
ISBN 978-0-87808-007-6
1. Missions to Buddhists. 2. Christianity and other religions--Buddhism. 3. Buddhism--Relations--Christianity. 4. City missions--Asia. I. De Neui, Paul H.

23 22 21 20 19 Printed for Worldwide Distribution

Contents

i

INTRODUCTION

Where cross the crowded ways of life,
Where sound the cries of race and clan
Above the noise of selfish strife,
We hear your voice, O Son of Man.

A Christian concern for ministry in urban contexts has been the focus of evangelistic mission long before Frank North penned the words above in 1903. God's mission to lost people began in a garden (Gen. 3:9) but ends in a city (Rev. 21:2). God's intervention in one urban project halted construction of that city (Gen. 11:8) yet resulted in the construction of dozens more (Gen. 10:10-11). God established cities of refuge whose protective embrace included even foreign aliens (Joshua 20:9). Yet God also brought judgment and destruction upon cities that were depraved, unjust, and disobedient, not excluding God's chosen city on Mt. Zion (2 Kings 25:8-11). God's promised future would one day become a human baby born in one of the smallest cities of Asia (Micah 5:2, Matt. 2:5-6).

Throughout scripture we can see that God's mission of love reaches into the promises and the paradoxes of urban life. Cities can protect and restore hope (Neh.12:43) while they can also exploit and demoralize (Job 24:12). As centers of power, cities can enrich and unite (Gen. 11:4) while also impoverishing and dividing (Amos 6:1-8). As centers of achievement, cities display the authority and splendor of this world (Luke 4:6) while also clearly demonstrating enslavement and human depravity (Gen. 19:4, Jud.19:22). Urban centers present a veneer of domestic tranquility (Jer. 7:4) while at the same time producing internal violence and injustice (Ps. 55:9-11). Cities are human constructions that tend to dehumanize (Ecc. 9:15). In the midst of all this, it is within the boundaries of cities that

God provides opportunities for humans to encounter the divine (Acts 17:26-27), come to a knowledge of God (I Kings 8:41-43) and also to repent (Gen.18:23-32, Jer. 5:1, Jon. 3:10). But the very nature of unified urban establishments, with fortifications physical, military, or economic, also breeds self-sufficiency, invulnerability, and an idolatry of security that ultimately disavows God's authority (Is. 36:15, Psalm 127:1). Above the noise of urban ethnocentrism, how and where do we, as mission-minded followers of Christ, still hear the voice of the Son of Man?

This volume attempts to address that question. *Communicating Christ in Asian Cities: Urban Issues in Buddhist Contexts* developed from a keen awareness that certain urban concerns for evangelistic mission must be addressed in a unique way when viewed within the myriad and complex cultures found within Asian Buddhism. All authors included here write from many years of experience as Evangelical mission theologians, scholars, pastors, and practitioners working within Asian urban Buddhist contexts. This book is divided into three sections. The first focuses on foundational issues of ministry within the framework of Asian Buddhist cities. The second section includes four chapters addressing several contextual issues specific to peoples within Asian Buddhist cities. The final section includes three chapters on the topic of strategic means of evangelization found useful in specific Asian urban Buddhist contexts.

Communicating Christ in Asian Cities: Urban Issues in Buddhist Contexts is the sixth volume in a series produced from the annual SEANET Missiological Forum held in Chiang Mai, Thailand. Along with those contributors listed here with whom it has been my privilege to partner in this work, this volume represents the collective input of over one hundred conferees from fifteen countries who participated in the entire conference event. Many thanks to Alan Johnson who assisted me in facilitating the forum. Recognition should be given to Alex Smith, David Lim, and all members of the SEANET steering committee who coordinated the SEANET conference. Special thanks to Alan Johnson and Zachary Lovig in editing the articles and to Dan

Larson for creating the index table. SEANET owes a debt of gratitude to our friends at William Carey Library for allowing us to publish these very important documents as an annual volume. Special recognition to Naomi Bradley and Johanna Deming for their work on finishing the manuscript and to artist Jon Pon for work on the design.

May God's kingdom come and God's will be done beginning in ourselves and in our cities.

Paul H. De Neui, Ph.D., editor
Chicago, Illinois, USA

CONTRIBUTORS

SANTHA LAL DE ALWIS from Sri Lanka comes from a Buddhist background. He studied his General Certificate/Advanced Level at the Department of Examination in Sri Lanka, finishing in 1986, and later pursued a D/Th at the Assembly of God Bible College in 1991 and a B/Th in 1998. He is the senior Pastor of the Assembly of God Church in Kurunegala, a member of the central Regional Presbytery, and serves as a Bible School teacher teaching Buddhism. He is married and has three children. His church is located in an urban, predominantly Buddhist area and plants churches in urban and rural areas.

A. STEVEN EVANS was born in the United Sates and is a Christian. He holds a BA degree in Bible and Journalism from Howard Payne University in Brownwood, Texas and did graduate studies at Southwestern Baptist Theological Seminary in Ft. Worth, Texas. He is currently a graduate student at East Tennessee State University and is a candidate for the MA degree in storytelling. Steve is a cross-cultural and oral communications specialist, doing research and consulting in Asia. He lives in India, is married, and has three adult children.

DAVID S. LIM from Manila, Philippines, shares leadership in the house church networks there and in the house church multiplication movement in Asia. He holds a M.Div. from Asian Theological Seminary (Quezon City, Philippines), a Th.M. from Asian Center for Theological Studies (Seoul, Korea) and a Ph.D. in Theology (N.T.) from Fuller Theological Seminary (California, USA). He is President of China Ministries International-Philippines, Inc. which deploys Filipino missionaries to China. He is also President of the Asian School for Development and Cross-cultural Studies, Inc. (ASDECS) which offers graduate degrees in Transformational Development and Missions, mainly in

Southeast Asia at present. He facilitates the Filipino church's mission to the gateway cities of the Buddhist world through SEANET and the Bridges to Buddhists (B2B) of the Philippine Missions Mobilization Movement (PM3). He is single with two children.

J.N. Manokaran is a civil engineer by profession from urban Tamil Nadu, South India, Madurai. When God called him to be a mission leader he and his family served in the cities of Jagadhir and Chanidgarh in North India as cross cultural missionaries for eleven years. Since 1997 they have served back in Tamil Nadu and are based in Chennai to help missionaries and pastors build their capacities by teaching, training, and writing. Manokaran completed his B.D. from Immanuel Theological Seminary, Georgia as an external student, received his M.Th. at Hindustan Bible Institute, Chennai and earned his Ph.D. from International Institute of Church Management. Presently, he serves as Managing Director of Trainers of Pastors International Coalition (TOPIC) – India, Director of Glocal Leaders Network, and provides consultancy services to several organizations In addition he mentors several leaders and contributes to several magazines and journals. He has authored three books *Christ and Cities, Christ and Missional Leaders* and *Christ and Transformational Missions*. He has had the privilege of ministering in over 135 cities in India and over thirty five cities outside of India. His wife Rosy is a constant encourager in ministry and counsels many people. Dr. Manokaran has one daughter and one son.

Alex Garnett Smith is from Australia. He earned his D.Miss. and M.A. degrees at Fuller Theological Seminary; and his M.Div. is from Western Evangelical Seminary. Alex is a veteran Missionary to Thailand, co-founder and coordinator/chairperson of SEANET (South, East, Southeast, and North Asia Network), and presently he serves as minister-at-large for OMF International. Author, Trainer, Lecturer, he resides with his American wife Faith, three sons, and four grandchildren in the USA. Most of his life, Alex lived in urban contexts in Australia, Asia, and America.

CONTRIBUTORS

GPV Somaratna from Sri Lanka earned his Ph.D. in South Asian History at the University of London. He is now senior research professor at Colombo Theological Seminary in Colombo, Sri Lanka. He has been serving from 1964 in an urban area and since 1966 worked in the university of the Metropolitan city. He has jointly supervised a Ph.D thesis on Urban Missiology.

Stephen Spaulding is the grandson of L. E. Maxwell, founder of Prairie Bible Institute (PBI), and son of missionaries to Japan and Brazil. Steve attended PBI, graduated from Simpson College (BA), and Fuller Theological Seminary (MA, Missiology). His ministry career began in the inner-city of San Jose, CA with City-Team Ministries. Later he joined the staff of a large church in San Jose, and then was involved in urban ministry in Los Angeles. After graduation from Fuller, Steve joined DAWN Ministries where he served for sixteen years, the last ten as regional coordinator for Southeast Asia based in Manila. In 1999 Steve, Alex Smith, and a few others formed SEANET. Since 2006 Steve has served with OC International. Steve lives with his wife and three teenage children in the Colorado Springs area and is considering the possibilities of moving back to Asia in the future.

Michael Solomon Vasanthakumar is from Sri Lanka. He has a BTh., an MA, a MPhil, and a DMin degree. He has been involved in Christian ministry for the past twenty-four years. He has been teaching and training Christian ministers and lay people at Lanka Bible College, Sri Lanka and editing a Tamil Christian magazine for the Back to the Bible Broadcast Ministries in Sri Lanka until he formed the Tamil Bible Research Centre at London in 2005 to write and publish biblical commentaries and study materials in the Tamil language. In addition to this he is involved in teaching and pastoral ministry among the Sri Lankans in London. He has written more than forty books and study materials in the Tamil language and contributed numerous scholarly articles to Tamil magazines and English journals.

DAVID VON STROH was born in Kansas City, Kansas but grew up throughout the southern United States, living in Atlanta, Georgia and the border region of south Texas. He grew up in a Christian family, in fact his family moved around due to his father's service as a pastor in the Lutheran church. David graduated from the Massachusetts Institute of Technology with an S.B in Urban Studies and Planning. For the past five years, he has lived among the urban poor in the slum communities of Bangkok, Thailand. He is on staff with Servant Partners, a Pasadena, CA based agency focused on holistic church planting and community transformation among the world's urban poor. For the past year, he has served as the acting team leader for the Bangkok site. David is presently in an M.Div. program at Mars Hill Graduate School, in Seattle, WA but plans to return to Thailand after his studies. David is currently unmarried.

SECTION ONE

FOUNDATIONAL ISSUES

CHAPTER ONE

Some Historical Views on Asian Urban Extension: Complexities of Urban and Rural Relationships

ALEX G. SMITH

The 21st Century opened with at least 460 major cities scattered across the globe, each with more than one million inhabitants. Many of them are in Asia, though they are found on all continents, except for Antarctica. Some of these urban concentrations have as many as five, ten and in a few cases, over twenty million residents. These modern giants dwarf the ancient cities of Sodom and Gomorrah or even Nineveh and Babylon, and those of the time of the Buddha such as Rajagaha of Magadha, Vaisali, Kosala, and Pataliputra (Patna today).

This analysis will focus on strategic challenges in Asian urban contexts. Discussion will center around three dimensions including 1) the meaning and description of significant elements in urban cultures, 2) historical examples of urban extension, using the Thai as a typical illustration of Asian peoples, and 3) crucial sociological and missiological issues with practical applications and recommendations.

The Modern Challenge of Mega-cities and Their Urban Sprawl

Since the end of the1800s, the burgeoning number of occupants in the cities of the Earth has multiplied exponentially. With the advances of medical science, better health care, and a new emphasis in the

Third World on growing super foods of high nutritional value, the population across the globe has literally exploded. The general move to more productive mechanized agricultural methods of farming, as well as the demands of the postwar industrialization in the developing nations of the world, have contributed significantly to this massive growth of urban centers worldwide. There seems to be no end in sight.

Furthermore in the last quarter of a century, extreme rural famines and unbelievable genocidal warfare in Africa, Asia and elsewhere have forced millions of people to become refugees—often seeking their own survival by migration into the cities. In spite of the scourge of death from famine, war and AIDS, the numbers surge. Therefore, the challenge of current urban centers looms formidably before many governmental and church workers. They face issues pressing them to find almost impossible solutions to the urgent demands of massive problems. These new dimensions of the modern urban challenge confront them in social, moral, economic, health and even religious areas. Under these conditions urban life can be advantageous or it can be disastrous, depending on the kinds of crises one faces in the daily dilemmas of life. City living can be great, but it can also be fraught with dangerous pitfalls, heartaches and frustrations.

Theological and Biblical Perspectives: God's Concern for Urban Dwellers

Cities are obviously important to God. Old Testament references to the city appear almost 1,100 times, and over 1,200 times in the New Testament. This high occurrence indicates a considerable amount of interest in spotlighting cities and is much more than that on many other significant theological issues of importance in the Bible. Does this not indicate that God has a great concern for cities? For more insights on the city noted in Scripture, read Raymond Bakke's *A Theology as Big as the City* (1997). Remember God's urgent concern for Nineveh and Christ's great compassion for the inhabitants of His own capital of Israel, when He wept over Jerusalem (Luke 19:41-42).

In the light of God's mercy to Israel and the aliens in their midst, the Lord ordered Moses to set aside six "cities of refuge" out of the forty-eight cities of the Levites, as safe havens for those people involved in accidental manslaughter (Num. 35:6-15). That is one city in eight.

The Lord God has His special city, "the city of the living God" (Ps. 46:4; Heb 12:22). It was prophesied that after their rescue from exile, Israel and the other nations would make their way back to the mountain of the Lord—that is Zion. Here the peoples of the earth will also return to Jerusalem. The prophets spoke of this and of the time when in that great city all nations and peoples will recognize the God of Israel as the God of all nations (Isa. 2:1-4; Mic. 4:1-4; Jer. 3:17; Isa. 25:6-9, 60:1f; Zech. 8:20ff; Ps. 87:3-6). On Christ's return from the heavens to Jerusalem, that city will be called "the City of Truth" (Zech 8:1-10). At the end of the ages, the holy city, the New Jerusalem, will come down from heaven in those last days, after the first heaven and the first earth have passed away (Rev. 21:1-2, 10f). The nations will bring their glory into it (Rev. 21:26). David Lim writes "The city is one of the key biblical visions of humanity's final destiny, and thence the meaning of human history. Urbanization is, therefore, the apparent consequence of obedience to God's cultural mandate" (1989:22).

Profoundly, one of the early Church Fathers, Augustine of Hippo, wrote *City of God* (413-427) showing that it "is radically distinct from any human city or society in this fallen world" and that it "belongs to a redemptive process above ordinary history" (McManners 1990:2, 127). He used the image of the city as a symbolic substitute for the kingdom of Christ, "outlining the emergence of the divine order through the dissolution" of Rome (Kauffman 1967:52, 121). Strangely, from the author's observation, in the development of Buddhism, the Buddha is mostly silent about the city. Though he tells stories of kings and rulers in the Jataka tales which tell of his rebirths or reincarnations, he does not seem to teach particularly regarding the city or solutions to urban problems, dilemmas and crises.

While the key monasteries of Buddhism were initially in cities, one clue to the success of its spread and adoption among rural peoples was the multiplication of *Wats* (temples) and monasteries locally throughout the country regions. Temples multiplied in the cities under sponsorships and also sprang up like mushrooms after a spring rain in the rural areas. In provincial capitals and district administrative towns multiple *Wats* arose. Many had powerful or wealthy patrons and exerted considerable influence on the rural communities surrounding them.

Historical View: Cities Existed from Antiquity

Cities are no new phenomena. They have been around since ancient times as far back as the beginnings of humanity in Genesis—Babel, Nineveh, and Babylon. Other great ancient civilizations developed immense cities—Egypt, China, Mayan, Aztec and Inca kingdoms, as well as the Greek and Roman empires. In many cases in the past, powerful individual cities controlled key urban centers and surrounding territories. These were called "city states."

Cities became the concentrations of populations, the centers of commerce, business and trading, the crux of government, the chief focus of politics and power, the concerted source of conflict and control, and the central organization of law and order, including police and military forces. Cities became centers for major religious activities. They often extended their sway over the rural regions too. Urban centers significantly affect and influence the whole nation, including the complexities of rural peoples and tribal groups living within the boundaries of the land.

Cities portray the epitome of contrasts between the haves and the have-nots, between the rich and the poor, between the advantaged and the disenfranchised. The urban problems also include concentrations of rabble crowds, pollution, poverty, slums, suffering, sin and slavery. "The city is a place of paradox. Historically, cities are the centers of economic and trading functions. Yet they are also the locations where great poverty co-exists with great wealth" (Ellison 1974:11). By 1980, Bangkok had over 300 identifiable slum areas. Today that number has more than doubled and closer to tripled over the last three decades.

Such is the effect of growth in cities and of the influence of urban pressure on social, economic and moral values.

Valuable infrastructure arose within and around cities to provide essentials for survival, means for convenience and comfort, and solutions to deal with ecological problems like pollution. Thus cities developed adequate means to facilitate the delivery of water, systems of roads and transportation, communications (telephones, internet), power facilities (later electricity), garbage and sewerage disposal, schools for education, and health services for the control of diseases and epidemics.

What Jared Diamond calls "the crowd diseases" relates specifically to urbanization. Significant diseases affecting large segments of humanity "could have arisen only with the buildup of large, dense human populations. That buildup began with the rise of agriculture starting about 10,000 years ago and then accelerated with the rise of cities starting several thousand years ago." He points out that the first attested dates for many of the infectious diseases are quite recent: smallpox – around 1600 B.C.; mumps – 400 B.C.; leprosy – 200 B.C.; epidemic polio – 1840; AIDS – 1959 (1999:205).

Epidemic diseases like cholera, typhoid, and smallpox decimated the populations of crowded cities. In the 1800s Bangkok's water born diseases wiped out tens of thousands in a few months annually (Smith 1982:36). Old city-states were well defended and ancient walled cities caused enemies to lay sieges for years. These cities were virtually impregnable. Sometimes the attackers would catapult dead, diseased bodies over the walls of the city to spread disease, an early form of germ warfare. In the 1300s the Mongols did this at Caffa, a port city located north on the Black Sea. This act contributed to the spread of the Plague across Europe, killing half the population of the continent. Rampant diseases and also famines sometimes caused cannibalism within cities. Mostly cities fell from the inside, through traitors opening the gates to the enemy. City populations rose and fell. Enemies often slaughtered all within the walls or took the whole city captive to their own lands, thus depopulating the cities.

Cities also developed as paragons of education, the bases of universities and training institutions. Thus for major education, especially at tertiary levels, students moved into the cities from their rural homes, at least for periods of time. In earlier times the Buddhist temples were the primary venue for education. Until the end of the 19th century, *only* boys were taught. Girls were considered unworthy of being educated and no girls in those days attended the Temple schools. After all, according to Buddhism, women as a lower form of rebirth, needed to be reborn as men first in order to be able to attain *nirvana*. In Thailand, similar to other lands of that era, primary education for girls was unknown. Concerned about this social inequality, the missionaries often adopted local girls and began educating them. At first they even paid the reticent parents as well as the reluctant girls to attend their small schools, usually set up on the mission station. Over time schools for girls were established, as well as those for boys. Usually these schools were boarding schools (Smith 1982:37-38).

Growth of Thai Cities in Asia

Let us consider the Thai as an illustration of the long history of cities in Asia. The Thai are typical of Asian peoples. Cities have long been a strong feature in Asian civilizations.

Quoting from Khun Vichit Matra's *The Thai Race*, M.L. Manich Jusmai sketches the history of the Thai. He suggests that from around 3000 B.C. the Thai resided in the Altai Mountains of northern Mongolia, from which they migrated east, probably as early as 1450 B.C., into the fertile valleys of the Yellow River of today's China. Later, as the Chinese arrived from the west, many Thai migrated south and set up major cities at Lung and Pa in northern Szechuan (Sichuan). From these cities they migrated eastward into the Yangtze River area, where the Thai founded another kingdom with Ngio (or Yio) as its capital city. The Thai were already organized administratively into a strong country. The Chinese called them T'ai, meaning glorious or great (Jusmai 1972:1-3).

When the Tartars attacked and conquered Lung around 843 B.C., many more Thai were forced to flee south to Pa and Ngio. Then in 215 B.C., when the Chinese occupied these Thai cities, another wave of migration south occurred (Jusmai1972:1-3). Thus from the time of the birth of Gautama until the birth of Jesus Christ, massive migrations of Thai peoples took place as they left their existing city states only to set up new cities elsewhere. Around these cities they planted and farmed the surrounding rich alluvial river basins.

The Thai Kingdom, then known as Ai-Lao (or Mung), divided into three streams (Jusmai 1972:4):

First, two branches of the same kingdom were located east in mid-Hunan (Thai Ai-Lao) and south in Szechuan (Thai Ngai-Lao). They developed different independent city states with the main capital of the south at Pe-Ngai, which was founded around 122 B.C.

Second, another stream was established in Tongking, now North Vietnam, likely by Thai migration from Hunan. The Thai established the forerunners of cities like Hanoi.

Third, was the Shan or Ngios (the bigger Thai) who moved into the river basins of the Irrawaddy and Salween. They established their capital at Muang Pong (Mogaung) in 80 A.D.

By 68 A.D. the Thai has espoused Buddhism, likely en masse. In the early Christian era Thai migration from Szechuan and Yunnan continued, as again the Chinese forces encroached southward across the Yangtse (Government of Thailand 1964:11). After the Chinese occupation of Thai Ngai-Lao, the Thai set up their independence in six smaller kingdoms during the period 221-265. But through repeated, constant attacks over time, the Chinese eventually defeated all six. "The period about 345 witnessed an emigration of the Thai on a very big scale" (Jusmai 1972:5-7). During the Nan Chao Kingdom in Yunnan (679-1253) more Thai city centers arose including Meng-sui, Yueh-hsi, Lang-Ch'iung, Teng-Shan (Teng-lo), Shih Lang, and Meng-sha (or Nong-seh now Talifu). In 756 one of the sons of Khun Borom built the city of Yonok, whose people were the ancestors of the modern Thai. At the height of its power Nang Chao held sway over Annam, Tongking, Pyu (Burma), and Sibsong-Chutai (kingdom of twelve princes—now Laos). At times Nan Chao even extended into Tibet and Szechuan. When, in 1253, Kublai Khan's forces from the north conquered Nan Chao, more Thai migrations took place (Jusmai1972:5-13).

The mobility of the Thai race increased at this time, particularly among the Tai Yai (Shan), who flooded south and west across northern Siam, Burma and, from 1229, into the Brahmaputra delta of northeast India where they became known as the Ahom (Jusmai1972:14; Wyatt 1982:41). Several small Thai-Lao kingdoms such as Chiangsen (773), Chiangtong (Luang Prabang), Chiangrai and Chiangmai (1296) were established under Thai lords.

In 1080 the Khmer seized Chiengsen. From that time they continued to oppress and dominate the Thai lords and their people, who became vassals of the Khmer rulers. Each kingdom had its own "chief walled city" administrating these city-states. After the Thai gained independence from the Khmer in 1238, they established a large kingdom with its capital in Sukhothai. Famous King Ram Kham Haeng, who invented the Thai script, encouraged the widespread acceptance of Buddhism throughout Siam (Smith 1977:68). In 1351 King Rama Tipodi moved the Thai capital to Ayuthaya where, in the early 16th Century, Siam made contact with the West. From the beginning of the seventeenth century, the Chinese began coming to Siam for commerce as traders and as laborers, particularly in the cities (Graham 1924:115). After the Burmese attacked and destroyed Ayuthaya in 1767, General Taksin escaped with many Siamese and re-established the capital in Thonburi, where he became the new monarch (Blanchard 1958:33). Thonburi is on the south bank of the Menam Chao Phraya River. Bangkok on the opposite north bank was already a busy port where Chinese junks plied up and down the coast from China. Following the assassination of Taksin on April 6, 1782, the capital was moved across the river to Bangkok, where it has remained under the Chakri Dynasty until present times. Thus cities have always played a significant role within the various Thai peoples throughout their long history, as they have in other Asian Buddhist nations.

Analysis of Populations in Thailand and Bangkok

In his *Description du Royaume Thai ou Siam* published in 1854, Catholic Vicar Apostolic, Bishop Pallegoix (1841-1861) estimated the population of Siam to be about six million (Graham 1924:113). In 1857 Sir John Bowring suggested the kingdom's population was possibly up to "five million of souls" (Bowring 1857:81). The first census was attempted in 1909. Various people estimated the population then to be between five and twelve million, including over 500,000 in Bangkok "and its suburbs." By 1920 the Census declared the population of Siam was about ten million with 345,000 people in the "city proper," likely meaning within the walled inner city (Graham 1924:113-114). In the intervening sixty-six years (1854 -1920) Thailand's population increased almost fifty nine percent. Both Pallegoix and Graham give broad though helpful numbers of ethnic groupings for comparison.

Ethnic Populations of Siam (Thailand) 1854 and 1920

Ethnic Group	1854	1920
Siamese Proper (T'hai)	1,900,000	3,800,000 [1]
Chinese	1,500,000 [2]	500,000 [3]
Lao	1,000,000	3,650,000
Malays	1,000,000	400,000
Cambodians	500,000	450,000
Peguans (Mon)	50,000	60,000
Karen, Xong etc	50,000	60,000
Lawa, Kache, Lu (Shan)	-	600,000
Total Population	**6,000,000**	**9,520,000**

1) Probably included Sino-Thai offspring in 1920. Skinner (1957) says the Chinese in Siam in 1910 numbered 800,000 (Blanford 1975:11). See also note (3).
2) Probably included Sino-Thai offspring in 1850. Skinner says Chinese in 1850 numbered 300,000 (Blanford 1975:11).
3) Probably mostly pure-blooded Chinese in 1920, as King Rama VI (1910-1925) had pressured the Chinese in Bangkok to assimilate and integrate more completely into Siam and not

maintain their own distinctive Chinese style dress, language, and culture. Many returned to China, many conformed (Smith 1982:54-56, 191-192).

In the late 18th Century Bangkok was a city of maybe less than half a million, or less than ten percent of the country's population. (Though some researchers suggest that back then, the Thai only counted men, excluding women and children). By 1970 fair estimates suggested four million residents lived in the capital. While the whole country was growing at approximately three percent per annum, the capital was increasing at five percent per annum (Smith 1977:74). Within another fifteen years, by 1985, Bangkok surpassed the six million mark. By 2000 it exceeded ten million. Projections for 2010 are closer to sixteen million, which accounts for more than twenty-three percent of the projected total population for the whole country. From 1909 to 1970 the nation's population increased 388% while Bangkok, its capital, grew a phenomenal 700% in those sixty-one years. Thailand, between 1970 and 2000 grew eighty percent but Bangkok increased 150% in the same thirty years. Urbanization and its challenges are not going away, but are speedily increasing decade by decade. This future concentrated urban growth poses major challenges to city churches in the coming century.

Comparative Population Growth: Thailand and Bangkok 1854 on

Year	Thailand	Bangkok	Source & notes
1854	6 million	?	Pallegoix, Bowring 1857:81f.
1909	5 to12 mil.	0.5 million	Graham1924:113-114 "including suburbs"
1920	9.5 million	0.345 mil.	Graham1924:113f. "city proper" =(within walls?)
1959	22 million	?	Hanoi had 3 million, Catholic Directory 1967:24
1970	34.2 mil.	4 million	NSO 1970:1, 7, Smith 1977:72, 74
1985	53.7 mil.	6 million	Operation World, P Johnstone 1986:405

1990	55.7 mil.	6.45 mil.	Operation World, P Johnstone 1993:530
2000	61.4 mi.	10 million	Operation World, P Johnstone 2001:530
2010	66.5 mil.	15.5 mil.	Operation World, P Johnstone 2001:530 Projected
2025	72.7 mil.	?	Operation World, P Johnstone 2001:530 Projected

Intertwined Relationships of City and Country, Urban and Rural

The magnitude of the big cities adds complications to ministry. Though urban centers influence and affect rural regions, modern cities are also impacted and affected by the rural areas. The city is to the rural areas and country communities as a head is to a body's functioning. Urban institutions become the brain centers for activities, the nerve centers that directed actions nationwide, the volitional forces of making significant decisions, and even the emotional support for arts and aesthetics, sports and entertainment. The rural districts provide necessary food and resources for the functioning of the cities. There is a mutual linking or interdependence between urban and rural that is frequently overlooked or at least underestimated.

"Cities differ from villages in their monumental public works, palaces of rulers, accumulation of capital from tribute or taxes, and concentration of people other than food producers" (Diamond 1999:279). He explains later, "Advanced technology, centralized political organization, and other features of complex societies could emerge only in dense sedentary populations capable of accumulating food surpluses"(1999:89). This shows the mutual vital relationship between rural and urban populations.

One key link between country and city is food production and its consequent storage of surpluses. Anyone who has seen thousands of transport trucks coming daily into Bangkok from the rural areas attests to this. Much of the produce comes from rural areas, but through transportation to urban centers most is consumed in cites and towns because of the concentrated populations there. This was not always so, particularly among the hunter-gatherers (Diamond 1999:104-113). But over the years this interdependence on food production and its distribution changed the loci of consumption as the urban areas swelled into burgeoning populations, often at the expense of the rural ones. Gradual mechanization of food production since the Industrial Revolution, as well as massive industrialization in and around the exploding cities, escalated this trend.

Urbanism Reflects Many Rural Values: Similarities and Congruencies

The Thai, like many Asian populations, have followed folk Buddhism for about two millennia. They had contact with that religion likely more than a century before Christ's birth. Certainly in 68 A.D. Chinese Emperor Meng-Te sent an embassy to Khun Luang Mao of the Thai city of Ngai-lao within the Ai-Lao kingdom. The Chinese succeeded in influencing more than half a million of these Thai males to initiate a Buddhist people movement by persuading "553,711 men to profess Buddhism" (Jusmai 1972:4-5). With the addition of women and children that movement was probably in excess of two million! Down through history to present times, the various branches of the Thai/Dai/Lao race have solidly espoused Buddhism.

Like other major religions, Buddhism saturates the worldview and value systems of the people as it infiltrates and permeates the cultures and mentalities of many Asian peoples. Buddhism becomes the dominant driving force behind the thinking and actions of urban folk as much as it does among rural populations in much of Asia. Thus many similarities and congruencies exist commonly among urbanites and rural dwellers. The same is true for hybrid "rurban" populations too, bridging and blending both.

First are the common religious cultures of many forms of Buddhism in much of East and North Asia, including China, Mongolia, southern

Russia and Japan, as well as parts of South Asia like Sri Lanka, India, Nepal, Bhutan and Tibet. Interest in Buddhism and Eastern religions in general is a growing trend in the West. In many large cities of the East, Buddhist influence is advancing and Buddhist lay movements increasing in renewed vigor. In Singapore, China, Taiwan, London and across American cities virile interest and practice of the Buddha's dharma (teaching) is popularly taking root.

Sasana is the Buddhist word for religion, and a full blown religion it is, with its own codified scriptures, temples, priesthood, lay followers, propagation, missions, social outreach, congregational preaching, religious instruction, Sunday Schools and even prayers and worship through devoting donations, offering gifts and burning of incense. Chinese scholars declare that incense burning is a clear sign of worship. While some, especially in the West, blindly think of Buddhism as only a philosophy, millions upon millions throughout Asia especially, consider it their personal and even national religion. The challenges facing the Church of the 21st Century are many. But the greatest and most subtle one, which modern day churches mostly disregard, is Buddhism. Churches often overlook its growing influence as non-threatening. Like the rising tide, Buddhism is affecting urban populations, particularly throughout Asia and the West. The present, popular Wat Dhammagaya movement centered in the Rangsit area of northern Bangkok is a good example. This rapidly growing group is in the process of building a worship hall to seat a million devotees.

Second, the animism prevalent as part of rural Buddhism, is no less pervasive among urban Buddhists. Fear of the ancestors is also as strong for both groups. The upcountry farmer or fisherman uses amulets to protect himself from demonic forces or his enemies. The urban business man or city laborer likewise employs the same kinds of practices. Merchants and shop keepers openly display Buddhist images and use various talismans to attract business, to influence customers and to make money. A town dweller boasted that his amulets were so strong that even if he was shot at in the city his charms would ward off the attack. To prove his point he called for a sharp knife and slashed his wrists, after invoking the resident power of his charms hanging around his neck. Unfortunately he had to be rushed to the hospital because he was bleeding to death. But this did not lessen his strong belief in his occult Buddhism. Around thirty years ago in Bangkok lived a Buddhist priest, who meditated every afternoon. In the middle thereof his mind became covered with a "green" cloud in which he was daily possessed of a spirit, which claimed to be Jesus. Under the power of this Jesus spirit, the priest would perform miracles of healing and fortune telling. Truly animism is alive and well in both urban and rural settings. The cities of the world are likewise hotbeds for animism and eclectic folk religion.

Third, family relationships are of paramount importance among Asian Buddhists whether in Korea or in Laos, both in rural and in urban communities. Relatives provide long term connectedness to the individual within the context of the extended family. Often migrant workers coming from rural areas into the cities, do so because they already have a relative or close friend there in the city. When they get settled, other family members tend to follow them. Among the slum dwellers, a high level of family interdependence exists. In his book *Slum as a Way of Life* (1975) Filipino anthropologist Landa Jocano emphasizes and describes at length the vital significance of the family in the slums of Manila. "One cannot hope to understand why slum dwellers behave the way they do and not otherwise, unless he has a good grasp of the structure and function of the slum family" 1975:153). Slums are not made up of a bunch of individuals, but usually of groups of families and extended networks over several generations. "Within the neighborhood, it is the entire family, not its individual members, which often decides on the resolution of important matters" (Jocano1975:157). According to anthropologist Oscar Lewis, the slums and societies of other poor people develop their own "culture of poverty." Working with slum peoples requires a different mentality and approach than working with middle class folk. Working in the slums is not necessarily easier. This "culture of poverty" reinforces a mindset of acceptance of the existing conditions as normative for those peoples, especially with the strong belief in Buddhist *karma.*

CHAPTER ONE

Complexity of Urban Social Structure: Demographics and Ethnicities

Urban concentrations do not consist of one kind of people or one homogeneous unit, though the term urban often gives that impression. In reality city populations comprise myriads of different people groups and many social classes and strata. Cities have a complex plethora of variegated kinds of peoples, including tribal in-migrants. This is not a new phenomenon, but it has increased in modern times. Several years ago an intertribal church was started in Chiang Mai to provide a meeting place for folk from various tribal backgrounds. This church was like a bridge between the rural tribal cultures and the dominant urbanized contexts.

In 1972 Chulalongkorn University's Institute of Population Studies conducted detailed research among the urban population in Bangkok. They found that by admitting to one of eight Chinese characteristics, such as having a Chinese altar or reading Chinese newspapers, thirty-one and a half percent of the capital's households had direct connection to Chinese ancestry. The research also unveiled that over thirty-two percent of the households surveyed spoke only Chinese or a combination of Chinese and Thai. At least a third of the Bangkok-Thonburi households of the 1970s were primarily Chinese, not counting the Sino-Thai descendants (Smith 1982:291). The changing dynamics of the burgeoning capital today suggests that the Chinese in Bangkok may have a lower percentage than in the 1970s, but their influence has not waned. Strategically, this type of sociological challenge cries out for the churches to know and understand the ethnic composition of their urban areas, so that they can hone effective strategies to reach each segment of the population, especially those which indicate greater receptivity, as did the Chinese.

Just a few years ago, the city of Portland, Oregon, had more than 250 different identifiable ethnic minorities among its million inhabitants. Now it is closer to 500. Today's cities and mega-cities are a colorful cosmopolitan mixture of many ethnicities, religions, cultures and sub-cultures. The modern urban conglomerates are not really a melting pot as much as they are a stew pot of a multitude of multi-cultural multi-ethnic peoples. They do, however, feel some common needs, mutual concerns and reciprocal aspirations.

In America where churches incorporate an Asian tribal group like Mien, Lao or Hmong into the existing congregation, some problems have been observed. *First* is the well meaning, though often patronizing, attitude of the Westerners, who frequently overly care for the tribal immigrants. *Second,* the tribal youth do not seem to fit well into western church life and are often lost to the Christian communities. I remember one concerned Lao leader on the west coast discussing this problem with me. A church in America had sponsored his group. He complained that his people were isolated into a Sunday School class, but the western teachers were not sensitive to or knowledgeable enough about the Lao culture or their deep felt needs. Sadly their young people also felt they were not being understood in this western church, and consequently were being lost to the Lao families and the Church. The Lao leaders asked permission to start their own church as a Lao congregation, primarily because they wanted to preserve and protect their children and teenagers. However, the senior pastor denied the parents' request, saying he would rather they stay in his congregation to receive his teaching each Sunday. This well meaning response was neither affirming to the teenagers nor comforting to their parents. Pastors and elders would do well to encourage church multiplication among tribal and ethnic groups, particularly in cities. This can be accomplished effectively through their own motivated ethnic lay leaders.

The conglomerate church or the gathered church of mixed peoples is becoming a trend in the West, to the detriment of the growth and extension of people group churches, which McGavran called homogeneous churches (1970:85-87). In America and elsewhere throughout the world, the Chinese, Japanese, Koreans, Filipinos and Russians usually plant indigenous congregations of their own kind wherever they move. They do not exclude others who wish to join in, but the majority culture is their own. Urban centers are replete with many different kinds of people groups, each one having dynamics that make them feel a common identity, a social connectedness and an affinity with one another in the group. That is why, particularly in pioneer unchurched urban situations, multiple kinds of churches are needed and should be developed. These in turn should become agents for extensive daughter church planting and multiplication.

Current Sociological and Missiological Urban Headaches

First, effectively evangelizing whole families and their networks in urban centers demands churches to develop a whole new set of strategies and tactics. Wisdom is needed. Working throughout Asia, the Mormons for many decades aimed to approach the head of the family. They believed that once the head converts the rest of the family will follow. While their strategy might have some merit, their tactic of visiting city homes in the early evening right when the family is having dinner, or early Saturday morning when the family head needs to sleep in, is flawed. Frequently, at that inappropriate time the Mormons are not received into homes in the city, and are rejected by the servants, house-help or the children, without having any contact with the head of the household. Their timing is badly off. Christian churches and evangelical missionaries must grapple with the urban condition and its dynamics. How can entry into urban homes be accomplished when high fences obstruct access, security guards or systems block the way, half a dozen wild barking dogs scare the living daylights out of visitors, and only servants or children answer the gate-bell?

One of the major exceptions to this scenario is the slum dwellers. They are easily approached with no barriers, gates or walls. Is that why so many agencies and churches focus on the poor and the slums? However, church workers must grapple with the urban challenge of finding more effective ways to access and reach the families of the majority population that hold influence and power within these nations. How can believers develop prior relationships, which would more readily afford access to the whole family, including those who hold the power and authority in it? Furthermore how can churches be better oriented to interact sensitively with them and incorporate such people into the home fellowships of believers, so that those in the upper classes or middle classes or government officer classes feel more at home in house congregations or in even larger Christian groups? How can the intelligentsia and upper echelons of society feel at home in churches where they sense that they are among "our kind of people" who happen to be thoroughly loving and accepting believers in Christ? Maybe this is the place to concentrate on catalyzing insider movements, rather than extracting high profile converts out of their native urban cultures to incorporate them into existing gathered churches.

Kevin Higgins defined Insider Movement as "A growing number of families, individuals, clans, and/or friendship-webs becoming faithful disciples of Jesus within the culture of their people group, including their religious culture. This faithful discipleship will express itself in culturally appropriate communities of believers who will also continue to live within as much of their culture, including the religious life of the culture, as is biblically faithful. The Holy Spirit, through the Word and His people will also begin to transform His people and their culture, religious life, and worldview" (2004:156). As the present writer applies the above definition, an insider movement therefore means a sometimes rapidly multiplying indigenous movement of family networks and social webs within a people group, whereby a growing faith in Jesus Christ accompanies the general retention of much of the existing culture, social structure, family dynamics and religious heritage without their necessarily calling themselves "Christian" or wholly rejecting their indigenous cultural or religious heritages. This quiet life-changing process initiates a scripturally based transformation in all areas of life, perception and values as the movement extends throughout the entire people group. The fellowships of believers that arise in this context (often not called churches) will fit appropriately within the culture of the people group, but will also be changed over time through the obedience of the believers to the Bible and the Holy Spirit. An inherent present danger in this approach is that the existing religious leaders might sooner or later proscribe and reject this movement as heretical, like the Jewish hierarchy did the early Christians of the first century, *unless* the insider movement occurs so swiftly and sweepingly that a total conversion and/or renewal of the culture and society is effectively generated.

Second, church multiplication in urban areas must therefore take seriously the discussion of the sociological dimension of the homogeneous church movement noted in the earlier section above. The task of evangelistic outreach to whole families and individuals, as well as to church planting in urban centers, is more complicated because of the current climate of the surrounding pluralistic world of today. Different approaches employing sensitivity in methods and message demands a more genuine, loving and gentle advance. This does not mean advocating a watered down or compromised Gospel, but it calls for a greater sensitivity to cultural, sociological and compassionate means to better communicate that Gospel. Such means and methods must be carefully researched, implemented through experiments, seriously tested and carefully and humbly evaluated. There is little room or excuse normally for forceful evangelism in today's pluralistic world. Nor do Christians need to be ashamed of or compromise the clear unique message of Christ. But they do need to couch it with kindness and love, and to deliver it with gracious compassion and honest humility. Arnold Toynbee suggested in *Christianity Among the Religions of the World* that "we can have conviction without fanaticism, we can have belief and action without arrogance or self centeredness or pride" (1957:110).

Third, a significant socio-religious headache that faces urban Buddhism in the present age relates to the status of women in the Sangha. This is still somewhat of a residual problem among Christian circles too, at least among some groups. Churches need to address this and especially provide training in awareness to their members, preparing them to reach out lovingly to women in the community who, according to the Bible, do not need to be reborn as men first in order to gain salvation or liberation. The fundamental Buddhist concept on the status of women has been referred to earlier in regards to their ignoring the educating of girls in the past. While their attitude to educating girls no longer is an issue with Buddhists, the ordaining of women as monks or priests (*bhikku*) still is. The Buddha accepted women to serve in *Wats* as *bhikkuni*, or orders of nuns, usually in white robes (called *mae chi* in Thai). The *Bangkok Post* Sunday July 20, 2003, highlighted the life of Mae Chi Sansanee Sthirasuta as a fine example of a Buddhist nun (2003:8).

However, the full ordination of women into the saffron robed priesthood or inner Sangha has lagged far behind. This is a sensitive issue among the Buddhist hierarchy. Some exceptions have been observed, specifically among Mahayana Buddhists. In Mongolia and Taiwan there have been a few cases of the ordination of women, usually related to orders of women, monasteries exclusively for women, or for some who have high profile in social action and compassion services. In about 2004 a Thai woman went to Sri Lanka where she was ordained as a Buddhist priest. It does not seem that, on her return to Thailand, she was accepted to function as a monk, and her papers were withdrawn. Nevertheless the 21st Century may well see a change in this issue of the ordination of Buddhist women into the Buddhist Sangha, priesthood, even in Theravada Buddhism. The urban scene where women already exercise their voice, position and power in their homes and in businesses is likely to be the stage for this movement.

A *fourth* issue of modern urbanization is growing radical Buddhism among some groups. In recent years, especially in South and Southeast Asia, Buddhist activist's social actions, known as Protestant Buddhism or Engaged Buddhism, have increased. For example on September 25, 2007 many Buddhist Monks marched with protestors against the Military Junta in Yangon, Myanmar. Also in 2007 two thousand Thai Buddhist priests marched before Parliament House in Bangkok, in an open show of force, calling for Buddhism to be made the State Religion in the Constitution of Thailand. In early 2004 the *Bangkok Post* (Mon. Feb 9, 2004) reported that Buddhist priests dressed in their yellow robes were among angry activists openly attacking Christian philanthropic aid agencies in Sri Lanka. In *Zen at War* (1997) and *Zen War Stories* (2003), author Brian Daizen Victoria concluded that during World War II, Buddhist Zen Masters supported Japan's national military machine to dominate Asia and then the West through their Buddhist teaching of *sunyata* (emptiness or no self) which contributed to a lack of moral conscience towards those who were not Japanese. The Buddhist hierarchy also elevated the Emperor of Japan as the Buddha Incarnate on earth (a compatible parallel to Shinto identifying the Emperor of that era as the representative of their Sun Goddess). These kinds of actions portray Buddhism in a different light. They questioned the general concept that Buddhism is only a "passive" and pacifistic religious system. Do examples like these indicate possible increased aggressive Buddhist approaches on social action as the 21st Century advances? Most of these kinds of actions occur in urban settings.

Fifth, competition for the hearts of men, women and families in the pluralistic world is no longer a concern only of the Church. Most current major religions including Buddhism and even minority groups like the Wiccans, Satan worshippers, atheists and others, actively and sometimes aggressively propagate their forms of belief. An evidence of this open approach to spreading Buddhism was the significant gathering of prominent *Sangha* leaders from seventeen Asian countries, including the Dalai Lama. This First International Buddhist Propagation Conference was held in Kyoto, Japan on April 8-13, 1998 (Dhammananda 1998:207). Several years ago in China, the Buddhist Falun Gong made headline news worldwide as the communist government proscribed them because of their growing power in society and their outspokenness on social issues.

Another fast expanding movement of Buddhism is connected to Kwan Yin (Guan Yin), which was an ancient male image from India known as Avalokitesvara. Kwan Yin is the Chinese name for him, which gradually became feminized in form in China as the bodhisattva of compassion or mercy. Burnett says that the feminine Kwan Yin "served Confucian family values and was adopted into every home" (2003:196). Actually in the religion of the Buddha all Buddhist images and bodhisattvas are male only. But this feminine aspect seems to appeal to Asian Buddhists just as the image of the Virgin Mary did among South American peoples who became Roman Catholics. The Kwan Yin aggressive renewal movement was initiated largely in recent decades from Taiwan. Its revival quickly spread to Japan, Korea, China, Southeast Asia and even the West. Well known and rooted in Chinese Buddhism for centuries, Kwan Yin today is closely associated and compatible with the largest form of Mahayana Buddhism, namely Pure Land, which also concentrates belief in the Bodhisattva Amida in Japan (or Amithaba in China). Kwan Yin features strongly in Tibetan Buddhism, Zen and other branches. It also has been introduced and integrated even into Theravada forms. In the Tibetan Buddhist tradition the Dalai Lama is believed to be the reincarnation of Kwan Yin. A few years ago a Nazarene Church around the corner from my home was sold. Within three months it was converted into a Kwan Yin Buddhist Temple. I personally watched as they cast this image on site. Soon after that a second Kwan Yin temple was built only a few miles away.

The expansion of Buddhism into Africa and India during this past decade is also significant. The energetic Soka Gakkai form of Nichiren Buddhism seems to be at the forefront of this expansion. Zen Buddhism along with adaptations of Tibetan Buddhism has expanded popularly in the West. Powerful testimonies of Buddhists in London, Bangkok, and elsewhere are now available on DVDs. In recent years, radio and television coverage on Buddhism has increased dramatically, to say nothing of Hollywood's inclusion of it in many films. In a November 2007 satellite television program out of Los Angeles, a Buddhist woman called Ching Hai, claimed to be a Grand Master in her program "Positive News for a Better World." As I travel I have occasionally been given Buddhist literature and books, in airports or on the street. Propagation is the thrust of most religions today, including Buddhism. But the current pluralistic climate seems to put pressure on Christians only, not to propagate their faith.

CHAPTER ONE

Mobility and Receptivity:
Possibility for Insider Movements

Earlier in this chapter reference was already made to the repeated migrations of the Thai during the last two millennia. Today this kind of mobility is common among many peoples and nations. So much so, that the decade of the 1980s was known as the Decade of the Refugee. One phenomenon linking rural with urban, particularly in recent decades revolves around university students who come to the cities for further education. In Thailand during the early 1980s, the "open university" of Ram Kham Haeng was started in Bangkok for students unable to gain entrance into other universities. This stimulated increased mobility of rural students coming in droves into the capital. Multitudes of students from up country flocked to Bangkok to take courses, some coming as transients for the week and returning home on the weekends; others travelling in and out from their rural homes or small towns daily to take their classes at Ram Kham Haeng University. The same pattern has been true of some High School students as well, especially those from nearby towns or farming communities. Some stay with their relatives during the week; others commute by train or bus.

The volatile economics of farming, and the shrinking of land passed on generation after generation force many rural folk to seek employment in the urban areas. One reason is the broader availability of jobs in cities; another is the ability to provide a consistent cash flow for the family back home in the rural situation; another is to supplement the income in times of dwindling resources for a variety of reasons including inflation or the rising cost of just about everything.

Over the years I have personally studied this among the taxi drivers of Bangkok. In the 1960s and 1970s, most who drove taxis or samlos (motorized three wheelers) were of Chinese extraction (Sino-Thai). Then in the 1980s a trend of migration from Isaan Northeast Thailand shifted this cheaper labor force from Chinese to Isaan drivers. More recently a new move has included migrants from the northern tribal areas of Thailand. Two years ago when I asked the taxi driver where he came from, I was surprised that he answered, "I am a Lahu from Chiang Rai. I married a Thai Christian woman here when I came down to find work."

A variation of this migration pattern from the rural regions to the urban ones is the contracted laborers who go overseas to work in construction in Saudi Arabia and other lands, such as Singapore or Japan. This has been a pattern from the Philippines, Thailand, Malaysia, and other parts of Southeast Asia, as well as Central and South America. These categories of workers leave their families in the rural areas or small towns for work in distant places. They send as much of their wages as they can afford back home to help care for their families and relatives. After the end of the 1980s especially, many of these Thai families have built substantial brick or concrete homes in their upcountry regions, a major step up from their more primitive roughly sawn timber and thatch roofed quarters of years ago. A voluntary movement began within the Asian Church. Christian professionals from Singapore have, for decades, gone to places like Myanmar and China in bi-vocational ministries. Similarly the recent goal of the Philippine churches and missions is to train and place 100,000 active witnesses cross-culturally within the next ten years. The book *Scattered: The Filipino Global Presence* (2004) describes that amazing phenomenon.

In recent years China has been in a constant process of depopulating their rural regions with massive moves to the urban centers as labor forces for their new manufacturing industries. Much of this movement has not only been for personal economic reasons but also through governmental policy of multiplying factories for mass production of goods for export. The majority in the phenomenal Christian movement or from revival in China are from rural regions, possibly as high as seventy percent. Many of these Christians have joined this massive movement of populations moving into the cities all across China. Therefore they likely are the best potential instigators of planting new churches in those cities to which they have migrated. Meanwhile, *Business Week*'s Asia Insider (January 14, 2008) declared that a revival of Buddhism among the Chinese elite and urban professionals is currently occurring also.

Mobility often provides an open door to increased receptivity. In the city, rural in-migrants are somewhat incognito. No one knows them like the familiar village folk do back home. Social dislocation or *anomie*, "the feeling of being lost or rootless," often accompanies this anonymity (Greenway 1973:43). The restraints of the close rural community, the influence of the Buddhist temple, and the familial tight farming society are no longer controls in the city. Suddenly more choices are available in the urban contexts, both for good and bad. This allows for a more open mindedness to a multitude of influences and options, including religious mores. This would not be possible back home in the villages. So at least for a time, increased receptivity may accompany this human mobility. Churches need to be alert to this always.

In Myanmar much movement of different ethnic peoples from all over the country into the big cities, particularly Yangon, has been going on for several decades. In recent years this has escalated because of economic aspirations or political frustrations, as well as a basic hopelessness that has been engendered there under current repressive conditions. Already a land of seething cultures and variegated ethnic folk, this mobility has produced growing urban ferment and desperation particularly in the largest cities, where, under the current military rulers, tertiary education was basically halted to the masses for several decades. Has the church really capitalized on the opportunities for potential receptivity that this mobile in-migration presents? In some tribal concentrations in urban areas good advantage of this has occurred, but not as much among the dominant Buddhist groups. More research and experimentation may produce a significant movement in this land towards a stronger and better moral future with promise.

Another possibility for receptivity occurs where existing urban people are moving into new surroundings and fresh situations such as into new housing. For example, where the government builds new housing blocks or high-risers for urbanites of the lower classes to move into, the changes and the new conditions are often favorable to receptivity, as the people are more open to try new things. In the early 1980s the housing authorities opened a score or more high-rise apartments for occupation at Bangkapi in east Bangkok. Many low income urban families applied to enter them. Some missionaries were assigned to that area to begin a new kind of evangelism and church planting. Much effort in visiting each family in the high rise apartments produced responses that helped start a new church, as well as several home groups. Within this small movement was an army major with his family. He became a key leader in the local congregation.

Earlier in 1973 James Wong proposed a similar strategy for urban church planting in high rise housing estate units in Singapore. Some 220,000 of these units were built between1960 and 1975. Only 33,000 similar units had been built in the previous thirty-three years (1973:129). This explosion of units indicated a major change for the mobile masses of Singapore. This social mobility from the residential upheaval of a quarter of a century was exacerbated by increased mobility through modernization and industrialization in this island state (Hinton 1985:83). The goal of Wong's proposed strategy was to establish one active evangelical congregation, cell group, or evangelistic-community center in every block of these apartment house units (1973:129,133). Unfortunately new government rules and regulations, and the reaction from some sectors of the public frustrated the full accomplishment of this plan (Wong 197:134; Hinton 1985:195-198).

During my ministry in the Uthai Thani Province of Central Thailand, the mobility of rural Christians to other rural regions and to urban areas caused me much concern. In order to track this mobility of church members, particularly in and out of the province, I revamped our statistical form to include keeping record of new categories in the church statistics such as "Transfers out – external" (to areas beyond our local territory) and "Transfers out – internal" (for mobility within the local region). This was necessary because so many rural families frequently, even annually, moved locations. By tracking their mobility we were able to follow up and conserve believers, integrating them into our local congregations or starting new ones as they moved. Likewise our statistics similarly recorded "Transfers in – external" and

"Transfers in – internal". The goal was to advise other churches near to where our members moved so they could be incorporated into those churches rather than be lost (Smith 1977:153-154, 184-185, 216-217, 252-253)

The Vital Loyalty Factor

Another accompanying dynamic of this mobility is the loyalty factor. In many Asian cultures especially, there is a deep sense of loyalty that tends to persist even when people move into the large cities. When rural Christians migrate to urban zones or even to different rural regions, they tend to look for churches of their own denomination or mission group where they can feel comfortably at home. Overseas Missionary Fellowship (OMF) faced this problem in northern Japan. When members from OMF related churches moved to Tokyo they were often lost to the Church, because OMF's earlier policy was to work only in the unreached areas of Japan. However, wise leaders saw the difficulty that this loyalty factor caused and began to do church planting in the big cities, including Tokyo. Rural transfer members responded and maintained fellowship with their familiar kind of churches in the Capital.

The author understands that this is also the case in the Philippines. Also this form of loyalty was another factor for the widespread multiplication of many churches of different Presbyterian denominations across the face of Korea. So the proliferation of churches in large cities by both denominations and mission agencies became a way to conserve the rural migrant populations as they moved into the urban communities from their upcountry churches. Thus it is a wise strategy for both denominational church associations and for mission agencies to be involved in urban church planting. Where a cultural loyalty factor is high, this strategy is not an "either/or" issue, but a "both/and" one.

The loyalty factor also has deep reference and resonance among Asian families, particularly those with an emphasis on ancestral veneration or worship. Strong family ties affect the loyal responsibility the worker has to his nuclear and extended family network. Often the family's wishes, demands and controls limit the kind of work the migrant to the city is able to find. Pecuniary duties out of this loyalty demand sharing the income with the rural family or other relatives. This ameliorates and curtails or controls the individual's independent expenditure. This chain of loyalty opens doors to a double-poled church multiplying strategy through following up the family networks from urban to rural and vice versa.

Strategic Approaches:
Parish, Relational, Structural Foci

To become most effective in meeting the needs of urban multitudes, local churches must return to more of a parish mentality in their strategies for reaching their communities. Only through living in its community will the Christians become truly credible and effective. What we are speaks louder than what we say. Only through utilizing the church facilities (where they exist) as genuine community centers will the Church meet the deep felt needs of urban peoples. Certainly in this way believers can build vital relationships with those in the communities in which they live, learn, work, play and serve. Through parish churches they will then have contact with and truly serve their surrounding communities. This may be easier to do among the defined, concentrated slums than among some of the different urban sociological and ethnic groups. But this challenge must be met with tenacious determination.

Besides witnessing to the family network of relatives and close friends within the urban areas, believers and their churches also need to maintain their rural family connections while they work in the big cities or in overseas employment. These rural networks provide a possible reverse church planting strategy. This can simultaneously arise where intentional effort is expended in planting churches among the urbanites and also consciously following up their members' rural connections. This kind of dual-poled church planting strategy should be implemented both among a select people group in the city and also with their relatives back in the rural regions from which they came.

Christians have at least four crucial arenas in which they will be able to build effective relationships over time in urban contexts:

First is their own neighborhood in which they live and relate to neighbors in mutual, sharing, human fellowship. Being dependent on one another in the community, sharing and borrowing from each other, and showing sincere interest in the needs of the families of that community are some essential ways of building genuine relationships with those living near the members.

Second is building significant relationships with several families in one's community. This goes deeper than the first general arena does, and with fewer people. This process will demand more time and command more sacrifice in developing genuine closer friendships. Unfortunately, believers frequently focus only on other Christian families in their locales, and fail to emphasize building close relationships with other families not related to the Church. These new networks have many needy families. Befriending them may expose deep spiritual and social needs. This provides plentiful opportunities for service by the believers in those communities.

Third is the arena where one works. This may be a different circle of associates than where one lives, though if it is within the same community, all the better. We are thrown together with those among whom we are employed, usually on a daily basis. Each Christian's workplace then becomes a sanctuary for ministry through developing similar relationships as in the first and second, only in a different circle of influence.

Fourth is encouraging the development of relationships during one's leisure pursuits. The circle of those with whom we play and recreate may be different from the contacts in our own neighborhood and workplace. These provide another arena for influence and witness as we cultivate closer relationships with those who are acquaintances in leisure, exercise, sports and recreation.

To enhance the believers' influence to become more efficient and to involve local members in more effective ministry in their immediate communities, specific training of lay families and single adherents is urgently required in the following five crucial areas:

1) Outreach and practical service as loving links from their churches into the local parish community, through building lasting relationships.

2) Evangelism of their own relatives and close friends, whose natural relationships already exist. McGavran called these the "bridges of God."

3) Prayer and prayer cell evangelism, particularly in circles of relatives, associates and friends whose families are outside the churches.

4) Multiplication of house churches in every community and among various people groups.

5) The immediate training of new lay leaders to serve these new house churches.

Conclusion for Application and Implementation

In most nations, the cities on the globe continue to be engorged daily with new influxes of multitudes of humanity. These seekers of fortunes recognize that urban life has its advantages: the convenience of good infrastructure, the abundance of opportunities for work (albeit complicated by qualifications to access certain jobs), the excitement and glamour of the city, and the offer of a variety of experiences in all departments of life. Dangers and disadvantages also threaten city living: the newcomers' struggle for initial survival, the loneliness and isolation in the city through anonymity and anomie, and the gnawing feeling of insignificance in the midst of the concentrated masses. One can feel extremely alone surrounded by masses of humanity. Furthermore, a multitude of uncertainties and myriads of unknown factors increase the level of fear and insecurity. Like gold diggers, comparatively few make it significantly or successfully. Many succumb to the rat-race of the constant struggle for existence. Those who are Buddhist have the answer to both of these conditions for good or bad, namely the effects of *karma* from one's previous lives. Naïve Christians sometimes oversimplify the work ethic as the primary means for success in urban environments.

Other poignant issues in the boiling pot of the city include: 1) the disintegration of the family, often accompanied by a high level of domestic violence, 2) the constant menaces of crime, multiple gangs, and physical bullying with threats of increased robbery, rape and murder, 3) the economic challenge of high prices for housing, rent, food and taxes, and 4) the consequent emotional strain of living on the edge of meager sustenance which, through desperation, sometimes drives some into prostitution or crime in order to survive. In urban zones, the pursuit of happiness and affluence frequently has a high price tag on the psyche. Nevertheless, increased millions of new migrants to the urban centers opt to try the fast life of the city as a quick gamble for possible advancement and speedy prosperity, or to seek relief and survival from worse conditions from which they are fleeing.

Probably four major categories of humanity can be found in most cities: *first* those who were born and raised under urban conditions, *second* temporary or transitory people, like students from up country or refugees from outside, *third* rural migrants who leave the country areas to make their home in the city, and *fourth* some of the local city populations who, over time, changed or compromised their local cultures to put on western appearances. Through the influence of western programs via media such as radio, television, movies, education, music DVDs and such like, this segment of the population has largely assimilated foreign practices. They appear to become Western, at least in outward looks and in certain patterns of thought and tastes. This may be somewhat deceiving for, in reality, they may have adopted some western influences but indigenized them into their native forms. In some cases they may look Western, but at heart are still quite indigenous. At most they are a mixture, though they may have the semblance of global internationals.

The 21st Century's modern media affects the interdependent relationships between urban and rural values and religious culture, as already mentioned. Before, the rural people came to the cities.

Now, the city influence comes to the villages through mass media via satellite communications, cell phones, text messaging, internet cafes, and the worldwide web. Global tourism and the international sex trade exacerbate this problem not only in urban areas but also in rural regions. This urban influence is growingly universal in the global village.

Christian influence in cities appears to be waning, especially in the inner city. Therefore the Church can no longer conduct business as usual or continue using the same patterns and methods of the past. If urban church planting movements are to increase, church leaders must evaluate and research the current dynamics of their cities and make concerted efforts to change strategies, where necessary. They must experiment and adapt their methods to the challenging conditions in modern cities. Here are some suggested practical applications that may help to focus on urban outreach so that it produces more effective movements for the kingdom of Christ.

First, mobilize prayer, the essential base for advance. How can churches and their leaders stimulate, as E. M. Bounds' booklet suggests, a renewal of "Power through Prayer"? Prayer should not be an addendum to the local church's agenda and program. It is the fundamental priority of Christ's mission to the ethne, both in rural and urban settings (Math 9:35-38). Many churches today no longer conduct prayer meetings, organize home prayer groups or give much attention to corporate prayer in the services, except for the pastor's prayer. The early Church was founded in prayer, made decisions in prayer, multiplied and grew through prayer, faced threats with prayer and solved problems by prayer (Acts 1:14, 2:42, 3:1, 4:24-31, 6:4, 12:5). Blessed are those groups where dedicated consistent prayer bathes the churches' activities before, during and after all of their ministries. Prayer is to be the heartbeat of lay-persons, evangelists, pastors, church planters, missionaries and the whole congregation of believers. It focuses our true dependence on God for guidance, action and outcomes. Prayer is the fundamental work of the churches. Andrew Murray once said, "He who prays most, helps most."

Mobilizing prayer groups for the urban complexes in every block of the churches' defined parishes might be a good start.

Training members in setting up simple prayer cells for evangelism to concentrate their intercession for close relatives, friends and associates in the city would enhance and broaden their outreach. Like Gideon's band, truly great intercessors may be few, but their effective service is inestimable. Nevertheless, when all members participate in private or small group prayer, it expands their vision, gets them thinking of others and provides new incentive for outreach to those for whom they are praying. Intercession for families and friends is the first step towards building bridges to others.

Second, building relationships is of paramount importance, especially among urbanites who tend to be isolated, lonely, suspicious of strangers, and distant from their close family networks. They often lack close knit friendships, particularly in the early stages of the arrival of new migrants. Despite their large populations, cities lack a strong sense of community or intimate closeness among their mixed multitudes. Emphasizing building relationships with families and the nearby community is a vital precursor to gaining credibility, entrance, acceptance and effective response from those the church hopes to serve and influence. At least four spheres of influence are available to members of churches: familial, communal, occupational and recreational. Family and relatives are among the most natural, as relationships are already in place through biological and wedded networks. Friends, neighbors and acquaintances in the community are also easily approached. The workplace is another fertile avenue for building relationships with fellow employees and even administrative staff. Times for relaxation give opportunity to galvanize relationships with those one recreates with in play, exercise, sports or leisure. All four of these natural influential spheres can be utilized to good effect for building relationships.

Third, concentrate primarily on whole families, rather than just on individuals. This is a key approach that is crucial if people movements, insider movements or similar dynamics are to be anticipated. This also re-emphasizes the need for cultivating genuine relationships with families. Most communities are comprised of families and their contacts. Where individuals are the initial contact, ways and means to reach their whole families need to be explored and implemented. This is especially true in ministries with children, youth and students, all of whom rarely have the power to make important decisions in Asia without their families' input and consent. Since the disintegration of the family and increasing domestic violence are major urban social problems, the church must focus on the whole family for ministry rather than only the individual. It is better to net the whole school of fish than to catch just one fish on a line. Churches should bring healing and strength to urban families, not increased tension, disruption, or division, as individualized ministry often does. So a family approach is required. At a previous SEANET gathering the author presented a paper along this line entitled "Family Networks: the Context for Communication" due for publication in a year or so. Rather than gaining "one by one against the tide," laypeople and church workers need to spend more time in building lasting relationships with whole familial units and their extended networks. This requires going slowly in that genuine process, and in turn helping whole families embrace the faith. A long time motto is "the family that prays together stays together."

Fourth, focus on a parish style approach, where the local church serves the people directly surrounding it. This changes tactics to stronger relational models, where churches in urban situations adjust their goals onto their immediate communities. However, one must live in the community to be part of the community. Many current city churches draw their memberships from all over the urban sprawl. Many members travel long distances from all points of the compass. They take considerable time in travel to attend worship at their churches. In doing so they travel past dozen of churches, many of them good ones, some of them near their own areas of residence. Despite the factors of personal choice, denominational preference, or loyalty to their churches, sadly they usually lack significant ministry to those in their own local communities where they reside. In a few cases I have known rural Christians who have traveled for hours by train each Sunday to attend the big city church. Generally Buddhist communities give back to their local temples, sending their sons in as novices or monks and giving food offerings to the monks on their daily rounds. *Wats* are central to their communities, providing services to their immediate residents. Should not contextual churches do similarly? Some already do, particularly house churches, but the majority of city churches are gathered congregations from all over the sprawling city. Is it not time for urban Christians to humbly join the local churches near their residences, in order to serve the peoples contiguous to homes and surrounding the local church? They often have good training from their churches that they can use to good effect in their communities. This requires tough changes, but what an impact it might have on establishing relationships in the members' own backyards.

Another model that certain mega churches use is to encourage members to have cell groups in their resident communities during the week. Often these are members' discipleship growth groups or evangelistic Bible studies, not social service ministries or integrated outreaches to the unchurched. Sometimes these are wrongly called cell churches. The members usually attend the large mother city church, wherever that might be located, while at the same time they may serve their communities in certain ways. This local witness and loving holistic service to the felt needs of one's community is essential for Christian credibility, both for the parish church and for its members. The four spheres of opportunities to develop deep relationships mentioned above should be explored to advantage.

Fifth, emphasize house church multiplication in the beginnings of new extensions into sections of urban communities, rather than buildings or new structures for worship. In highly dense populations like high rise complexes, slums, or connected row houses, explore planting family churches or house churches first. In some situations like Singapore and elsewhere, the potential for having house churches within these structures became difficult to establish due to government regulations, local opposition and sometime unwise overzealous Christians (Wong 1973, Hinton 1985). One major problem churches face in their priority to build new worship centers is the current price of land in many major cities. Costs are astronomical and the number of believers often quite small, as in Japan. The house church is one practical answer to this costly investment. Other options include renting shop fronts, hotel meeting rooms, theaters, business facilities (usually closed on Sundays) or even abandoned buildings in the local community. However, that requires a lot of effort, set up time each week, and often leaves the members with a transient feeling, while the house church often does not. Making provision for renting a suitable sizable facility several times a year for broader cooperative worship brings all the scattered churches together for fellowship, prayer, encouragement and praise. This reinforces a sense of unity and of growing strength so that small groups do not feel so isolated and insignificant.

Sixth, stimulate churches to serve the communities in which they are located. The service and ministry of urban churches of all kinds need to be tailored to the resources and the number of members that they have in their fellowships. For example, out of principle one small church south of Seattle requires all new members joining it, along with existing members, to serve each year in at least one community service project in the church's community. House churches can do this in a more intimate though sometimes restricted way. Existing congregations with large church facilities have certain advantages in this realm. With larger memberships, they have much volunteer manpower available to help, more resources, and significant facilities that are generally under utilized, except on Sunday. Churches need to balance what they can do, with their available resources. Some ways churches can serve the urban populations include:

- Welcoming new migrants just arriving in the city. Give them orientation to the city and its challenges. Help them in practical ways to get a good start. Show them where the post office and various kinds of shops are. Assist them in finding their way around.
- Providing some kind of employment information to help them find jobs speedily. Give training on how to prepare for an interview, and write resumes, if needed.
- Arranging transit accommodations for limited times. Help them find permanent living facilities and jobs. Be a resource for locating housing for families.
- Providing supervised day care for their infants and young

ones while the parents work.

- ◻ Integrating children into existing church schools for education and moral instruction.
- ◻ Setting up some exercise or recreation programs for the parents in the church gym or elsewhere.
- ◻ Providing for counseling in view of the high emotional stresses, trauma, and struggles families and individuals face in the city.
- ◻ Making an emergency life line or crisis line available to give advice and comfort to spouses, families or troubled teens.
- ◻ Establish financial training and counseling using business people in the congregation. One serious problem in cities is the loan shark who charges exorbitant interest, sometimes up to seventy percent or more per month in parts of Asia.
- ◻ Using member medical staff to run low cost clinics, immunizations, physical treatments, even drug rehabilitation (like a church in Russia and one in Japan already does.)
- ◻ Developing cooperation with government and Christian adoption agencies, as many orphans and abandoned children exist in some areas of Asia and elsewhere.

Some of these projects require specialized staff, which may already be available in larger congregations and sometimes smaller ones too. Service programs and evangelistic ministries should be integrated and balanced to serve the greater felt needs of the communities. No church could likely implement all of the above suggestions, but each urban church, no matter how small or large, should start with at least one key project that fits the desperate needs of the local immediate community. Given time they may be able to implement several but not likely all of the above suggestions.

Seventh, train many lay leaders for community service and witness. This must include how to reach out to whole family networks and how to start new house churches. Mobilizing and training members is a high priority. Local indigenous servants of the cross, especially if they come directly from the local community, are the best. Multiply them. Women should be included as much as men. Wise men have observed that the more trouble a community is in, the more women are needed. Their sensitive hearts and vulnerability often help diffuse escalating problems or increasing difficulties. Remember Mother Theresa serving in the cities of India, Catherine Booth in England, and the Marachelle in France. The more indigenous local churches are, the more likely they will depend on indigenous support for their work. When they fit comfortably in the community and include local church leaders from it, the faster they are likely to grow and multiply.

Eighth, develop different kinds of churches that fit the varieties of the cultures, social strata, and needs in urban areas. Multiply house churches suitable for each tribe, caste, class and language in the communal district in which the church serves. Insider movements are more likely to be started when believing relatives and friends are sharing their faith vibrantly, sensitively and even intensely. Years ago in Tokyo, Japan a church among the horse racing workers and racetrack community was planted. This racing group was a close and isolated society within the larger community. In Seoul, Koreans organized a church exclusively for the acting guilds in their capital. Elsewhere in Asia churches for recovering prostitutes are functioning. In a major city of India, eunuchs comprise the majority membership of one church. The needs of each of these groups were very different, and it was suitable and wise to plant churches of their kind of people meeting their kind of dynamics and needs. From relatives in urban churches, outreach to members' families back in the rural areas can also be done effectively. The relationships and values earlier discussed, and primarily the family networks and bonding that exists, will in time make for open doors and often open hearts, generating family web movements.

Ninth, provide a theological base for an egalitarian society in urban situations as McGavran advises (1980:330-332). Churches and insider movements multiply best within their own kind of people, usually the homogeneous unit. But it is also essential to pass on the broader truth that the kingdom of Christ comprises a great variety of churches around the globe—a veritable kaleidoscope of all kinds of peoples, classes, castes, tribes, races, nations and languages. This unbiased awareness builds towards a greater unity in the churches. Not only must this perspective of the God of all nations be passed on, but practical ways to overcome potential racism can also be implemented. For example, hold citywide or regional celebrations occasionally to endorse and reaffirm the Church's diversity and its unity in diversity. In this way all churches of different people groups irrespective of economic class, social caste or tribal affiliation are recognized as equal representatives of His Church in the city. Having the mixed kaleidoscope of different ethnic congregations sing common hymns and songs in unison, using their own respective languages simultaneously, would portray a positive expression of that unity of diversity.

By prayerfully planning and determinedly applying these nine strategies to urban situations throughout Asia, healthy new urban movements are likely to arise. This will take much concentrated effort, discerning research, and spiritual analysis. Practicing these principles prayerfully and carefully, one is likely to see a greater increase in urban church extension than in the past. Every family in each segment of population in cities deserves to be reached with the Gospel, as much as the last frontier tribe or an isolated rural group. The good news of a loving Creator God who cares about the world, including its cities and their peoples, demands that His Church focus their energies in serving the multitudes of diverse families in their communities through the deep compassion of Christ, whose sacrifice ransomed them from the clutches of death, pain, sin and suffering.

CHAPTER TWO

Media's Role in (Re)Shaping the Values of Today's Urban Buddhist and Its Impact on Gospel Proclamation

A. STEVEN EVANS

The rose is gone from the garden,
What shall we do with the thorns?
Hakim Jami (Ellis & Niemi 2001:131)

The idea of looking at media's role in (re)shaping the values of today's urban Buddhist and its impact on gospel proclamation is a complex one. Many concepts must be defined, multiple factors must be considered and synthesized and concrete conclusions must be drawn. Perhaps first, though, it would be beneficial to consider the implications of the title. Media comes to us in many forms and packages—from the obvious to the subtle. There are the mass media, traditional media and even interpersonal media. There are electronic and print, verbal and non-verbal. There are the visual media and audio media; the digital and analog media. Then, there is song, dance, art, music, film, television, e-mail, the internet, SMS and instant messaging. The list could go on and on. Added to these are the elements of entertainment, education, information, promotion and advertising. All are influential, all are making their impact and all are to be considered.

What this article proposes is that media in all of its shapes and sizes and with all of its signals and messages, have a tremendous impact on a disenfranchised urban culture bombarded by the effects of globalization but inwardly yearning for identity and community. This began in earnest the 1980s with the emergence of the information age and continues to today. Media forms are reshaping traditional Buddhist values and cultures in the cities and media of various kinds can have influential roles in reshaping the reshaped worldviews of those in urban environments. This has vital implications for gospel proclamation.

It will be important to look at the concept of cities and consider what the word "city" actually means. To be explored is how media in general and globalization more specifically are dramatically and perhaps irreversibly affecting the very heart and soul of today's urban Buddhist, rendering his religion irrelevant and catapulting him into an identity and community that is global in scope. Where is this happening and how? Also, close look will be given at globalization and its contributing factors of entertainment, consumerism and information technology. Is it just selfish materialism and consumerism, or does it go deeper than that? It must be asked: What will it take to connect with the urban Buddhist? How can one touch him or her at the heart level where life transformation takes place?

The vital role of stories and storytelling will be looked at and how they relate to life transformation, relationship building, identity and community. Also to be considered is the inter-relationship among stories and storytelling, Buddhist culture, interpersonal relationships, identity and community building and gospel proclamation.

Defining the Cities

"With the majority of the world's population now living in cities, the 21st century is undoubtedly an urban century," concluded participants of a conference on Youth, Poverty and Conflict in Southeast Asian Cities, held in Bangkok, Thailand in 2003. "Mega-cities add millions of new residents each year and many small- and medium-sized cities are growing at unprecedented rates." Participants said that such rapid urbanization poses serious challenges to local governments and urban managers in the developing world, as they confront crowded slums, congested streets, poor environmental conditions and stark social inequalities (2003:1).

> That urban conditions are harsh in the developing world is not a new phenomenon, but some have suggested that a new urgency exists," the conference summary said. "As many of these countries go through demographic transitions, the potential for increasing youth cohorts to create conflict in cities seems...to be reaching acute proportions (2001:1).

At the conference, Dr. Peter Xenos of the East-West Center noted that the number of youth in the urban areas was on the rise. "Youth increasingly make up a larger share of the national population," he said, "and growth rates for youth populations seem to be significantly higher than growth rates for populations as a whole." Xenos urged that the situation concerning youth must be addressed when considering urbanization, citing as reasons: the "urbanward" movement of youth, later marriage, rising school enrolment and declining proportions of youth in the workforce. The conference report concluded that it is vital to link urban youth to local community (1).

But what is a city? Urban archeologists in Southeast Asia contend that defining the city tends to be problematic. "Until recently, archeologists assumed the city was a cultureless, universal phenomenon, with standard features regardless of time and place," said John Miksic of the Asia Research Institute, Singapore. "It is now acknowledged, however, that the agglomeration of buildings and people was not an evolutionary inevitability. Physical and spatial expressions of social structure, population, political power, economic activity and religion are determined by local factors that vary across space and time," he said. "Different cultures produced cities similar in form, but bearing the stamp of their unique origins. Cities on Java, for example, function differently than cities in Thailand, the Philippines, Myanmar, China and India" (Miksic 2005:30).

British social anthropologist Denise Carter said, "During my ethnographic fieldwork [on cities] I have come to understand that the physical reality of the environment is often less important than the social interactions between the individuals who live within it." She said that ethnographic fieldwork tends to occur in cities, rather than being of cities, explaining that anthropologists have been more concerned with everyday urban processes than with the position of the city in anthropology (Carter 2004:1).

What all this means is that cities are no longer seen as one homogenous unit, but a myriad of cultures and peoples. Attempts to address all cities as the same, as well as all peoples within a city as the same, are a mistake. Instead of a city being a single socio-geographical unit, a city is actually many cities in one. It consists of multiple communities and ethnicities, each with its own customs, cultures and worldview. No single strategy to reach a city will work; its various communities must be taken into consideration, considering the meaning of the root word for community—that of having things in common or relationship. These communities, however, have undergone cataclysmic changes since the 1980s. This is due to globalization and an understanding of this too must be taken into consideration when planning to reach the cities.

Globalization's Expansive Effects

Thomas Friedman in his best-selling book *The Lexus and the Olive Tree* traces the beginnings of globalization back to the 1980s. "When the Information Revolution flowered in the 1980s—and made it possible for so many more people to act globally, communicate globally, travel globally, and sell globally—it flowered into a global structure that encouraged and enhanced all these trends." It is a new system, he said, one that creates drama and tension between what it is and who we are (Friedman 1999:77).

A close study reveals that there are three basic themes which evolved over the last century that set the present course of globalization:

entertainment, consumerism and information technology. These are the drivers of globalization, pushing its effects into the far corners of the world (Evans 2001:3-6).

Entertainment, versus the high-class notion of art, is directed at the largest possible number of the people—the masses, said author Neal Gabler in his book *Life the Movie: How Entertainment Conquered Reality*. American pop culture became synonymous with having fun, he said. To the fun loving masses having fun was a higher priority than having culture, or at least the kind of culture that high society enjoyed. "Entertainment was less about morality or aesthetics than about power—the power to replace the old cultural order with a new one," he said, "the power to replace the sublime with fun." Popular entertainment is primarily about fun, he said. "It [is] about gratification rather than edification, indulgence rather than transcendence, reaction rather than contemplation, escape from moral instruction rather than submission to it" (Gabler 1999:55).

America exported its pop culture around the world, quickly to be adopted and adapted by the common people seeking to have an identity often refused to them by their elite, said Friedman, a journalist and author of numerous best-selling books on globalization. American pop culture and the hybrid versions of it gave recognition to a people starving to be noticed, he said (Friedman 1999: 1-512). It is this pop culture, maybe dominated by the West but surely flavored with international ingredients, that is now a major driving factor of today's globalization.

A manufacturer of soap once said, "Any fool can make soap. It takes a clever man to sell it." Bars of soap, a product of the mechanized industrial age, became one of the first ever branded products and opened the floodgates for the onslaught of commercial advertising. This man's soap, unique because it was clear, was to appeal to Britain's class conscious society and not the average laborer. It was called Pear's Soap. Across the ocean, an employee of a soap factory mistakenly made a batch of soap with too many air bubbles in it and the bars of soap floated. In promoting this mistake, the manufacturer of this Ivory brand soap claimed it floated because it was pure soap, 99 and 44/100 percent pure (Wolkomir 2000:102-109).

Until the push to sell soap by brand became vogue (using paintings and artwork to promote or advertise it), selling soap was just selling soap. "[The] hijacking of art to sell soap blurred for the first time and forever more, the bright line between art and advertising, between high culture and the vulgar, between pristine and corrupt," said the writers of the *Smithsonian* magazine in an article titled "You Are What You Buy" (102-109). Who would have thought that the mere selling of soap would have been a major contributor to the globalization we have today?

James Twitchell, author of *Lead Us Into Temptation: The Triumph of American Materialism*, said

> humans love things, and we've always been materialistic, but until the Industrial Revolution only the wealthy had things— now the rest of us are having a go at arranging our lives around things." During the past twenty years young people have had lots more money to spend, he said. "Now they're driving the market for mass-produced objects. Ask 18-year-olds what freedom means, and they'll tell you, 'It means being able to buy what you want!'" (Twitchel 1999 :1-352).

Twitchell said that with the oncoming of machines churning out cheap goods in mass quantities, consumerism spread rapidly. So did advertising, and branding made advertising possible. Eventually, society moved from mere consumption to conspicuous consumption— displaying possessions to impress others. Today, Twitchell asserts that many buy the brand and not just the product (1-352).

For some examples of how advertising, branding, and consumerism drive culture, consider these:

◻ Christmas was low-key until the 1800s when stores reinvented the holiday to sell their surpluses. On December 24, 1867, R. H. Macy kept his New York store open until midnight, setting a one-day sales record.

◻ Santa as he is known today originated in the 1930s when sales of Coca-Cola went down in the winter months and newspaper ads showed Santa resting and drinking a Coke after delivering toys.

◻ Rudolph the Red-Nosed Reindeer was the 1930s creation of a mail-order company.

◻ Blowing out birthday candles was universalized after Kodak had ads showing what could be done with film, a flash and a Kodak camera.

◻ Mother's Day began when a manufacturer ran full page ads in a city newspaper highlighting a local woman mourning her mother. Soon, very few failed to buy a gift for mother on this newly special day (1-352).

Technology, coupled with an appeal to the masses (whether it be consumerism or entertainment or a combination of the two), created globalization as convergent information technology spreads it around the world at an alarming rate and with a high degree of success. Today—because of communication satellites, the telephone, cells phones and internet phones; television, cable TV and satellite television; e-mail, You Tube, Flickr, MySpace and Facebook; MTV, HBO and global news networks; world trade and global marketing; and long-distance travel made easy—cultural influences can spread across the planet as fast as a click of the computer mouse.

What is seen on the global scale today is intense interaction and high drama among peoples and cultures, both clashes and homogenization. There are sickening ecological disasters and amazing environmental successes. There is the triumph of various political and religious ideologies and backlashes against them. There are super-nations, super-markets and super-heroes, each coming to the forefront and dictating terms to others. There is the rise of super information technologies, thanks to super-conductors, microchips, satellites and the Internet. All of these are weaving the world tighter and tighter together and at faster and faster speeds (speed of travel, commerce, communication and innovation . Marshall McLuhan, author of *The*

Gutenberg Galaxy and "guru" of technophiles today, aptly phrased it "the global village " (1962:31)

So, what does all this mean? It means that most of the world doesn't have a chance against the onslaught of globalization, with its emphasis on a global culture fed by the fuels of selfish and conspicuous materialism. Those with higher and easier access to the media are more susceptible to its effects—primarily those in the cities. As the authors of *Entertainment-Education: A Communication Strategy for Social Change* said, "Entertainment, whether via a nation's airwaves, popular magazines, or newspapers, [or broadband services, could be added] is the most pervasive mass media genre; it tells us how to dress, speak, think, and behave ." Thus folks are "educated" by the entertainment media, even if unintended by the source and unnoticed by the audience. "Often such entertainment can have negative influence on people's lives" (Rogers & Singhal 1999:8).

A Brief Status of Buddhism in Southeast Asia

"In the eyes of scholars and social critics…Buddhism has experienced chaos and crisis since the 1980s," said Pattana Kitiarsa of the Asia Research Institute . He claimed that its institutional and moral foundations have been considerably weakened by eroding penetrations of modern consumerism and materialism. "Buddhism has by and large lost its moral authority, spiritual leadership, and cultural significance in [Southeast Asia], because its leaders and institutions lost their battlegrounds to the aggressive and complex forces of modernization and globalization from outside" (Kitiarsa 2004:1-2). Kitiarsa concluded that the significance of the religious festivals is waning, the monastic body is shrinking and Buddhism is simply a superstition for the elderly. "Buddhism has been undergoing postmodernization, characterized by 'boom-time religions of prosperity' commercialized Buddhism and other phenomena of commercially oriented religiosity" (2004:2).

A somewhat closer look at the status of Buddhism in Southeast Asia will be given—briefly considering Thailand, Cambodia and Sri

Lanka, with a more in-depth study of Bhutan. The picture, however, appears to be the same across the region, especially in the urban areas: an eroding values system and an increasing globalization spurred on by the convergence of its three principle elements of entertainment, consumerism and information technology. While from a cultural and even a Buddhist perspective one may (and perhaps should) lament the destructive and ever-worsening situation, at the same time it must be asked, "What are the implications for gospel proclamation?"

Synthesizing the Three

What is happening now is a collision of multiple cultures, beginning in the 1980s and continuing until today. There is an increasing youth population disenfranchised with society's elite, thrust into the boiling cauldrons of the city (consisting not of one homogenous unit, but a myriad of peoples, cultures, classes, ethnicities, social strata, affinity groups, etc.) and bombarded with messages that empower them and provide them with an identity in a community of a global scale. The gap between the global and the local widens while the traditional elements of culture and society begin to seem irrelevant to them. All of this results in what could be termed "the worst of times and the best of times"—bad because of all the negative influences; good because in times of turmoil and change people are open to new ideas and influences; a plus for gospel proclamation.

According to author and cross-cultural communications expert Gailyn Van Rheenan,"Change occurs during times of tension, stress, and anomaly"(Van Rheenen 1991:80) "Tension or anomaly arises out of the inadequacy of paradigms to depict reality." He said that significant cultural change takes place not when the paradigms of culture adequately express a worldview but when old paradigms are being called into question. "Societies become receptive to change when basic assumptions appear inadequate to explain reality," he said (Van Rheenen 1991:80).

Michael Taber, in his book *Globalization, Mass Media, and Indian Culture*, suggests that no culture can remain totally static and unchanging, because humans have the capacity to cumulate knowledge and alter their external surroundings and internal thought processes. "We are also highly prone to be influenced by external forces and ideas… There is a contagious quality about culture because direct borrowing of cultural traits is extremely common. The more opportunity a society gets to know another society, the more it undergoes transformation. Once an individual or institution in a society accepts something new, it gets diffused…" (Taber 2003:88).

Looking Closer at Urban Southeast Asia Buddhism

A brief look at three situations in Southeast Asia will provide a representation of the eroding effects of globalization on Buddhists and Buddhism in the region. This is followed by an in-depth look at "globalization erosion" in process. First are three "snapshots"—a teacher in Bangkok, Thailand, asking about declining morals and discipline of students at an international school there; an adherent of Buddhism in Cambodia wondering why those in a Buddhist society and culture no longer live and act like "true" Buddhists; and a newspaper columnist in Colombo, Sri Lanka, lamenting the negative effects television advertising is having on the nation's youth. Finally, a close-up look is given to the nation of Bhutan, a nation that opened its borders to the outside world only a few decades ago and didn't even have television until 1999. It is now facing a severe crisis as the effects of globalization in general and powerful media forces in particular are rapidly destroying its culture.

Thailand, Cambodia and Sri Lanka: Three Brief Scenarios

The *Online NewsHour* program of the popular *Public Broadcasting Service* (PBS) in the U.S. addressed the issue of promoting morality in students and children, with a focus on Bangkok, Thailand. The program asked: "Can 'goodness' really be taught? Does moral life begin in infancy, even before language? What should you do when a child cheats? How do children begin to interpret abstract religious and ethical philosophies, and how do they apply them to everyday life?" (1997:1). A teacher in Bangkok pursued these questions with some of her own, along with her concerns:

> When does a child internalize lessons taught or modeled? We live in a multicultural educational community of an international school. We are trying to teach global humanist values and yet 'cool American' kids seem to be the role models that are still most desirable. Can we link the self-centered attitude of a 10-year-old who forgets rules and limits when around friends to breaching more important internal values when she gets older? People say that it is impossible to raise a moral adolescent in Bangkok. We are worried about how far will be too far. Aids is rampant as well as alcohol and drug abuse (1997:1).

"How do we promote morality in our students, in our children and in ourselves?" the program's host asked in response, "...by living it out." He continued:

> A child starts absorbing lessons even in the first year of life, and continues to do so thereafter. You can, indeed, challenge self-centeredness - by making the very connections between small moments of self-absorption and larger ones, and by letting the child know that it matters to you as a teacher to care for others.

> I'm trying to insist as a parent and a teacher and for all of us, that we remember that any lesson offered a child in the abstract is not going to work very well. We live out what we presumably want taught to our children. And our children are taking constant notice, and they're measuring us not by what we say but what we do (1997:1).

A Buddhist adherent in Cambodia commented: "Buddhism has played a significant role in Khmers' lives, both rural and urban.... In Buddhism, the essential teaching rests upon good deeds, accumulation of merits and peace-making. At least 95% of the total population is Buddhist, but the real practices for their daily lives' happiness and peace are very poor" (2008:1) He said that politicians, "powerful" men and businessmen, always take advantage of and exploit the people.

> This questions what the Buddha taught... What some people have done and are doing is not Buddhist at all, because the Buddha taught no killing, no stealing, no sexual misconduct, no telling lies and no drinking alcohol or intoxicants, but loving-kindness, compassion and doing good deeds (2008:1).

He continued by saying that religion and the arts have had a great impact in the shaping of Khmer culture. "The Khmer Buddhist religion has strengthened common beliefs—building solidarity of the people and nation, teaching values, self-esteem, pride and emphasis upon the mental over the physical and the spiritual over the materialistic." Buddhism for Cambodians is at the heart of their tradition, culture and identity, he said. "To many Khmer people, the absence of Buddhism is the absence of Khmer identity." He pondered the recent past and wondered how it is that more than two million people died of starvation, torture, overwork and murder. Today, efforts are being made to restore, revive and preserve Buddhism in Cambodia, he said. "The traditional arts are also increasingly being viewed as valuable resources for community development and urban revitalization... The challenge ahead is not to break away from tradition, but to find a contemporary way of expressing it. Only within the continuity of the past, can Khmer cultural identity be preserved and reaffirmed for its future generations," he said (1).

A newspaper editorialist in Colombo, Sri Lanka, recently reflected on the corroding influence television advertising has on Sri Lankan Buddhist culture.

They [the television ads] show children who lick their fingers after eating, wipe all the slush after walloping on a crunchy chocolate or cone of ice cream or some such stuff. Then, they tell the gaping audience in whose tummies sometimes worms cry due to hunger, that unless you feed the child on a particular kind of cheese that he or she can never grow up properly or attend to studies. For balanced growth and sound education a certain kind of butter or margarine is essential, the children are told (Edirisinghe 2007:18).

The editorialist continued:

I read the other day that the education Ministry on the initiative of the new and enterprising Commissioner of Examinations is planning a symposium to find out causes for poor exam results. Let the advertisers too participate for they contribute enough for the devastation. What easy excuses the TV supplies the children to discourage them from studying but encourage them to fritter away their time before the great liar arisen out of modern technology.

A certain publishing house of long standing has now begun a campaign that unless exercise books with their brand name are used that the children can never go ahead. This is open lying. "Thou shalt not lie." It can also lead to domestic squabbles when children begin demanding from parents the purchase of this particular brand of exercise book or a writing pen, if they are to go ahead.

There was once a TV ad where both father and son steal from a bottle of jam. They get into corners of the house away from the prying eyes of the overbearing female of the house and finish the stuff in stealth. Greed and unhealthy overeating are directly encouraged. ...

How nauseating is the ad where mother boasts how with the aid of her children a fowl was powdered to make sausages at home. What a *Pinkama* where the whole family partakes! Compare this with a piece in Readers Digest magazine where children of a family in England cry on bed the whole of the Christmas night at the memory of the goose they had been playing with, roasted and made center-piece of the dining table! Where are the true Buddhists? Here in the repository of Theravada Buddhism or in Christian Europe? (2007:18).

The writer concluded with the question: "Are we to allow the uninhibited use of evilly designed TV ads to hasten the disappearance of our great religion?" (2007:18).

Bhutan: A Case in Point

"The...media are changing the way we work, live, do business and even our view of life," said Siok Pek-Dorji in his paper *Opening the Gates in Bhutan—Media Gatekeepers and the Agenda of Change* (Pek-Dorji 2007). "Bhutan's younger generation is now being weaned on a new set of values and beliefs perpetuated through the media and the experience of a country opening up to travel, trading and globalization," he said (Pek-Dorji 2007:2). Pek-Dorji continued:

In this atmosphere of change the traditional gatekeepers of family and community value systems are slowly losing their impact. The oral tradition of storytelling, with families sitting around the hearth sharing their beliefs, values, and societal norms, is disappearing. It is evident that this oral tradition was much stronger in the relatively "pristine" state that Bhutan was prior to modernization and the advent of mass media and education. Until the early 1980s, Bhutan was largely a traditional society untouched by the world. The family and community had a more dominant role as gatekeeper of our value system.

Today, with traditional storytelling on the wane and urbanization on the rise, the traditional role of family and community elders in sharing values and societal norms through direct communications with the younger generation is weakening (2007:3).

Kinley Dorji, chief editor of Bhutan's Kuensel News Corp, painted an even grimmer picture, calling on the government to introduce appropriate media regulations—"not necessarily to control, but to prevent a complete destruction of the values systems of Bhutanese society" (Dorji 2007:12). His creative non-fiction short story *Pretty Woman* portrays how the introduction of television and all of its accompaniments (advertising, globalization, a consumer driven market, etc.) to Bhutan in 1999 thrust the country into dramatic and painful change. The story tells how, over a period of seven years, a young boy and a young woman collide with forces much greater than themselves, their community and even their country. She was the prettiest girl around—strong, sun-darkened and hard working, with a face as round as the moon and a singing voice that enchanted all the men. He was a young boy, growing up in a volatile climate of change (still continuing today), confused by what he observes.

Dorji explains, "The story invites important questions. Are the side effects of development taking a toll that is more powerful than the effects of mainstream development? This is symbolized by the immediate excitement over television that far exceeds the advantages of electricity as a source of power for utilities". (Electricity comes to the story's setting in 2003.) "In a country where there are now an estimated 50,000 television sets compared with 14,000 computers, television becomes a major status symbol and dominates the altar in the altar room" (as it does in the story), he said (2007:11).

Over a period of seven short years, the country's hero is no longer the king, but athletic superstars and Bollywood film actors and the beautiful image of the hard working village girl is replaced by singing and dancing Bollywood stars and bikini-clad Pepsi models. The end of *Pretty Woman* is poignant and bittersweet:

Aum Thrimi looks into the distance. "They are so pretty, the girls. They are so thin. They are so fair. They smell so nice." She looks at Kuenley, a gangly five-foot nine-inch boy, standing with his hands in his pockets. She turns and looks out the window again. "Better study hard, Kuenley. Otherwise you'll have to live in the village. You have to work all day in the sun. You have to walk everywhere with no shoes. You have to carry manure on your back and smell of cow dung. In the village you will quickly become ugly. We have no choice because we are already old and ugly." Kuenley says nothing. He does not know what to say. Thrimi is 27 years old. She has not changed. But the world had changed" (2007:8).

Dorji explains that "This is not a happy story. As Bhutan goes through a dramatic period of history, the [story] looks at the excitement and, more important, the pains of change. The rural setting in the story, the people, and their lives are real. Their experiences are very real ." He said that as an effort in creative non-fiction, the story is a journalistic perspective presented with the color that creative narration permits. "It is a memoir that looks at a community's experience without carrying the burden of a conclusion. It is an attempt to make sense, find order, in a response to crisis" (2007:8-9).

Dorji continues, "This story is Bhutan's story. The metamorphosis of a rural society is documented through the eyes, and the confusion, of a Bhutanese youth who personifies a generation in transition. There are no subtleties because the experience is not subtle ." The message that comes through as the pair's community feels the impact of globalization is that there is an urgent need to put on the brakes before it is too late to do anything about it (2007:9).

There is another strong and clear message, however, put forth by Pek-Dorji "The minds of our youth have been opened to the world and to new ideas, and there's no turning back ," he said, but emphasizing that the youthfulness of the media can be groomed and guided. "We have to shape the power that shapes community…," he said (Pek-Dorji 2007:15-16).

According to Pek-Dorji, the national television channel reaches almost all of the nation's 20 districts, while "global TV programming reaches people in 46 towns and urban settlements ." Added to this are multiple shortwave and FM radio stations, various newspapers in both English and vernacular languages, cell phone and internet services and a blossoming film industry (in 2006 24 films were produced in Bhutan). "All this is serving a country of 630,000 people, a country that, until 1999, did not have TV or the Internet," Pek-Dorji said (Pek-Dorji 2007: 2).

When Bhutan was introduced to television in 1999, its citizens were immediately bombarded with 40 channels, most of which originated from or were routed through India, including MTV, Bollywood films, Indian music-video channels and increasingly "risqué" and market-driven advertisement campaigns. Six years later, government officials banned MTV due to its eroding effect on Bhutanese culture and values.

While one must be familiar with the burgeoning pop culture of India to fully grasp the influence of Indian TV in Bhutan, the attitude or frame of mind and vocabulary found in the following interview reveal its influence:

> I am a romantic person. For me life is one big party and I am absolutely sure that I am outgoing, fun, gregarious, and spontaneous. Sitting at home and sulking is not my style. I had plenty of friends and believe in living life to the fullest. I believe in unconditional love. Actually love to me is like in the movies—"falling in love, being together in good and bad times and living happily ever after." My man must have a mind of his own. Only then we can grow together after marriage (T. Dema - 21 year old female) (Lham-Dorji 2007).

This is not to say that the values reflected here are bad or wrong. They do, however, reveal a vastly different value system from one that existed prior to 1999.

The Sweet Strawberry and the Tiger of Urbanization

A popular Zen Buddhist folktale called "The Wild Strawberry" goes like this:

> A man was running, stumbling, and gasping for breath as a ferocious tiger chased him. Dashing for the edge of a cliff, he saw a vine. He desperately reached for the vine and in one last, bold leap swung himself over the cliff's edge. As he hung dangling down, he looked up and saw the growling tiger on the ledge above him. He felt a moment of relief as the tiger clawed the air but was unable to reach him. Then the man looked down. At the bottom of the cliff far below where he hung was *another* tiger. Tightening his hold on the vine, the man wondered what to do. To his further dismay, he noticed two mice, one dark as night, one light as day, nibbling at the vine. He knew that it was only a matter of time before he would fall to the jaws of the tiger below. Just then, he noticed a wild strawberry growing on the face of the cliff. Gripping the vine with one hand, he reached out with the other, plucked the strawberry from the cliff wall, and put it in his mouth. Never before had he realized how sweet a strawberry could taste (Forest 1996: 40).

In the concrete jungles of the cities evangelical Christians must be willing to offer the sweet taste of the gospel to those being chased by the tigers of urbanization. While various media forms may be used to do this, it is suggested that story and storytelling may be the most effective.

The Power of Story

Every people, nation and community have stories and myths that preserve and prolong the traditions that give them their identity.

William Bausch said in his book *Storytelling: Imagination and Faith,* "When a nation is in trouble, if often returns to its traditional stories to look for direction and healing, to regain a sense of what made it great in the past and what will nurture it into the future". Individuals, families and communities also have their identifying stories that link them to who they are, to their culture, Bausch said. "A region or a nation has its story concretized in a shrine, statue, museum," he said. "A person without a story is a person with amnesia. A country without its story has ceased to exist. A humanity without its story has lost its soul" (Bausch 1999:33).

"The influence that cultural narratives bear on our lives makes them the media of ethical inquiry, particularly as it pertains to managing cultural change, which we do according to the values of some narrative," said Bruce Bradshaw in his book *Change Across Cultures: A Narrative Approach to Social Transformation* . "The central issue…is discerning what that narrative is." Bradshaw explains that all cultural change has a moral aspect and is intimately related to cultural narratives, which contain the values that shape human character and govern ethical action. Ethics, often defined as theories or morality, seeks to maintain the integrity of the narratives through which people live (Bradshaw 2002:16-17).

> Narratives are both the templates through which we interpret reality and the means through which we seek continuity in our lives. They emerge from our history, and we could not tolerate life without them. They empower us to organize our perceptions of reality and to locate place within it; they help us to see things not as they are, "but as *we* are." They assist us in discerning the things that are important by communicating the truths about life's mysteries through metaphor and symbol. Because they influence who we are and how we perceive God, they serve as the primary media of engaging ethical inquiry (2002:21).

For Bradshaw, narratives influence the ethics of managing change, whether within or across cultures. "They reveal how values and virtues are developed and shaped over time as well as the nature of truth that governs them" (2002:21). "Cultural narratives explain why people behave as they do, and they can provide social justification for any behavior. This social justification is the starting point to discern how behavior can be redeemed" (2002:24). Bradshaw said that cultures reveal a people's interpretation of reality as well as their values, primarily what they deem to be important in both the temporal and eternal realms (2002:71). He emphasized that meaning gives culture authority because people create it according to the way they construct and perceive reality. "To focus on meaning in the study of cultures challenges the popular notion that cultures should be viewed apart from values, but values establish standards for action ," he said. "No cultural form or function can be value-free or morally neutral. All basic human functions, such as eating, drinking, or working, have values because they have meaning" (2002:72-73).

Carol Birch, in her book *The Whole Story Handbook: Using Imagery to Complete the Story Experience*, said that stories usually address what it means to be a human being within a specific cultural context—from the highest spiritual aspirations of a people to their most basic injunctions for daily living. "Stories resonate by juxtaposing universal experiences with unique ones," she said. "If the universality of a tale is its broth, then ethnic, religious, geographical, cultural and historical details season the broth to flavor the stewpot of story" (Birch 2000: 77).

"Culture grows from community and community from culture," said Joseph Sobol, author of *The Storytellers' Journey*. He said that culture and community are intimately linked, reciprocal terms. "They are also terms—like nation, family, religion, home, tradition and ritual—that have particular empirical applications but in generic usage quickly slip into a mythic dimension." According to Sobol, community is a term of virtually unchallenged good. With story, it is a key element in which "an imagined past is invoked to summon images of a restored future in order to bring hope and fervor to a troubled present" (Sobol 1999:154).

"We live in a world impoverished of story," said Eugene Peterson, author of *The Message,* a contemporary language version of the Bible .

He said that words in our culture are a form of currency used mostly to provide information (Peterson 1999:8).

> Contemporary schooling is primarily an exercise in piling up information. By the time we have completed our assigned years in the classroom, we have far more information than we will ever be able to put to use. Motivational speech runs a close second to the information kind—words used to persuade us to buy something, achieve something, vote for someone, become someone. As important, even essential, as informational and motivational words may be, they are conspicuously impersonal. There is no discovery, no relationship, no personal attentiveness in them. For that we need story and storytellers (1999:8).

For Peterson, "Stories don't tell us something new. They involve us in what has been sitting right in front of us for years but we hadn't noticed, hadn't thought was important, hadn't considered to be connected to us and our lives ." Suddenly we do notice, he said and the story wakes us up to what is there and has always been there. "Without leaving the world we work and sleep and play in daily, we find ourselves in a far larger world. We embrace connections and meanings and significance in our lives far beyond what our employers and teachers, our parents and children, our friends and neighbors, and all the so-called experts and celebrities have told us for so long" (1999:9).

Annette Simmons in her book *The Story Factor* said that providing stories that add new viewpoints to listeners' internal perspectives helps them think about their choices within a novel context. "In the case where choices are unconscious a story can provide a new viewpoint that is more conscious, more objective," she said. "Often self-awareness is enough to change behavior" (Simmons 2001:47). Just as knowledge can become wisdom, Simmons said, facts become story. "A subtle yet powerful shift occurs when you seek to influence people to make wise decisions rather than 'right' decisions. When you decide to awaken sleeping wisdom rather than to convince others you are right, you will produce a much more powerful experience for both of you." (2001:50-51).

Simmons said it is safe to assume that any individual or group one wishes to influence has access to more wisdom than he or she currently uses . It is safe to assume that they also have considerably more facts than they can process effectively, she said. "Giving them even more facts adds to the wrong pile," Simmons said.

> They don't need more facts. They need help finding their wisdom. Contrary to popular belief, bad decisions are rarely made because people don't have all the facts. Bad decisions are made because people ignore the facts, do not understand the facts, or do not give the facts enough importance (:51) .

This is true, Simmons said, because basic human emotions like anxiety, greed, exasperation, intolerance, apathy, or fear have hijacked people's brains and directed them to the easy way out, the path of least resistance, the safe route, or the taking-care-of-number-one option. "More facts will not help them regain perspective. A story will. A story will help the figure out what all these facts *mean*," she said (2001:51).

"A good story helps you influence the interpretation people give to facts ," said Simmons. "Facts aren't influential until they *mean* something to someone. A story delivers a context so that your facts slide into new slots in your listeners' brains. If you don't give them a new story, they will simply slide new facts into old slots ." She said that people already have many stories they tell themselves to interpret their experiences. "No matter what your message, they will search their memory banks until they find a story that fits for them ." Simmons said that inevitably the story they pull up will support their current action or inaction—whatever it is you hope to change (2001:51).

> You can rant and rave all you want over people who won't face the facts or who ignore the facts or who don't live in the real world, but your facts won't reach them until you give them a

new story. If you let the facts speak for themselves, you risk an interpretation that does not fit your intentions (2001:52).

Facts are neutral until human beings add their own meaning to those facts, Simmons contended. "People make their decisions based on what the facts mean to them, not on the facts themselves. The meaning they add to facts depends on their current story ." She said that people stick with their story even when presented with facts that don't fit. "They simply interpret or discount the facts to fit their own story. This is why facts are not terribly useful in influencing others. People don't need new facts—they need a new *story*" (2001:54).

Simmons said that giving people facts as a method of influence can be a waste of time. "When you give a story first and then add facts, you stand a better chance of influencing others to share your interpretation, to see that the evidence means what you propose it means rather than whatever their original story will distort it to mean," she said. "If you give facts first you risk an interpretation that bends your facts to support their existing view or that discounts and discredits your facts in a way that may permanently cripple these facts as tools of influence." Simmons emphasized that sequence is important. "Save your facts until after you are reasonably sure the interpretation is going to support your cause," she said (2001:54).

In his book, *Culture Jam* , Kalle Lasn says, "The most powerful narcotic in the world is the promise of belonging." To that I would add, the promise of being "known"—not understood, not necessarily even valued—but simply to be acknowledged and seen. In our technological economy, human attention is the emerging scarce resource. People need it, crave it, and will pay for it with their cooperation. In today's world almost everyone you want to influence is operating under s deficit of human attention. They are not getting enough time or attention from the people that they love. They *have* enough information. They have all the facts and statistics they could ever want. In fact, they are drowning in information. Desperation is at epidemic levels because all of this information simply leaves us feeling incompetent and lost. We don't need more information. We need to know what it means. We need a story that explains what it means and make us feel like we fit in there somewhere (2000:111).

"When you tell a story that touches me, you give me the gift of human attention—the kind that connects me to you, that touches my heart and makes me feel more alive," Simmons said. She contends that the revival of storytelling over the last few years is no fad. It is a demonstrable artifact of a profound cultural shift in society.

> Becoming a better storyteller is not hopping on some psycho-babble bandwagon. To find your story is to join in a worldwide search for authenticity and those things that are truly important—a search for meaning. The more influential your stories become, the deeper they tap into that which is meaningful" (Simmons 2001:111-112).

Implications for Gospel Proclamation

Stephen Bailey, in his article *World Christianity and Buddhist Societies*, said that what is needed today is not so much the contextualization of the informational content of the gospel but the careful contextualization of relationships.

> The slow response to the gospel has more to do with the failure to shape communication along the lines of the social structure than it does with spiritual hardness. Social allegiance to the group and the rules of social engagement within the group are issues that must be accounted for if the gospel is going to be communicated with impact in this context" (Bailey 2006:107).

"In focusing on worldview transformation, Christian mission is concerned with neither conversion nor the formation of indigenous Christian communities in Buddhist lands but rather that the gospel truly transform society through new ways of being human," said Kang-San Tan in an article on how the gospel can transform Buddhist worldviews (Tan 2006 :25-26). Worldview, he said, is a set of the shared framework of ideas of a particular society concerning how they perceive the world (Tan 2006:26).

Tan said, "From a variety of perspectives then, wherever the gospel is preached, there is a need for deeper encounter with traditional Buddhist worldviews. The purpose is not to compromise the gospel but to confront underlying belief systems at their deepest levels" (Tan 2005:12). He said that God's reign is not an abstract notion but a situation in which he is acknowledged as king. For Tan:

> Within a kingdom perspective of an interfaith encounter is an encounter between *people* rather than between religious ideas, where the focus is on lived issues. By emphasizing God's kingship rather than abstract ideas, the interfaith encounter is prevented from becoming mere religious chatter (2005:26).

In other words, he said, the kingdom-oriented interfaith encounter is about encounters between people within the context of an actual community.

David Lim, in his article *Towards a Radical Contextualization Paradigm in Evangelizing Buddhists*, said, "As we bear witness to Christ amidst the post-modern challenges of the multiplicity of choices between various pluralisms (including religious choices with Buddhists concepts and values), it is not more important to draw out the *sine qua non* essentials of our message ." He continued, "With information and communication overload, people need to hear more accurately what are the central points of our faith. Perhaps the fewer essentials we have, the better access we will have to the busy and confused minds of our complex societies, including Buddhist ones. ...and there seems to be a simple message (thank God !)." The message is this: People need to have a personal relationship with Jesus Christ as the Lord over their lives. "One has just to share about Jesus of Nazareth, and how wonderful he *was* and *is*, and once a Buddhist decides to follow the Jesus being presented, she/he joins the family of God, regenerated and indwelt by the Holy Spirit," he said (Lim 2005:78-79).

The evangelistic message is that Jesus Christ is indeed the Creator God and Redeemer of the world. … Thus we consistently seek to invite people to submit to his lordship and adopt a Christ-centered worldview from whichever cultures and religions they come. Evangelism is the offer of a personal *relationship* with God through Christ, not of a *religion*, not even of Christianity. It is not Christianity that saves but Christ. Hence every religious and cultural artifact, belief, or value (even in Christian traditions) must be evaluated in the light of the biblical revelation about the historical Jesus (2005:79).

…most people, even in the West, and including Buddhists, do not only reason, think, and analyze facts and ideas (or do biblical hermeneutics) rationally, linearly, or logically. We need to develop a more functional concept of truth, beyond just the conceptual and propositional. In Asia, the way one communicates truth cannot be divorced form the truth one communicates. … If Christianity's truth claims are to be taken seriously by other religions, then Christians in Asia need to master social graces not only in behavioral patterns but also in communicational styles and attitudinal changes (2005.80).

Alex Smith, in his article *Missiological Implication of Key Contrasts Between Buddhism and Christianity*, asks, "Can the church effectively communicate with Buddhists? This is a real challenge, particularly for the Asian church, which is usually a tiny Christian pool in a huge majority Buddhist pond ." Smith said that more attention should be given to developing indigenous drama and music appropriate to those cultures, both for evangelism and for worship. Significant symbols and cultural festivals need to be analyzed and addressed and, where appropriate, adequate functional substitutes should be developed. "Above all, in Buddhist Asia, the mode of teaching, preaching, and communicating should focus much more on the use of storytelling, parables, and riddles. Local drama and music are also valuable tools" (Smith 2003:34-35).

A potent illustration of the power of this occurred two year ago when the Muang Thai Church did an indigenous musical presentation adapted from Thai culture for a group of overseas people. Afterwards one of the Thai Buddhist waiters who served our tables expressed his feelings: "As I listened the hairs on my arms stood up. I felt that music very deep down inside of me" (2003:35).

"There is a fairly widespread belief that indigenous media of communication are relics of the past," said Viggo Søgaard in his book *Media and Church in Mission: Communicating the Gospel* . "Those who live and work in the Third World realize how unfounded this belief is. For the Christian mission, traditional or indigenous media and communication systems provide exciting possibilities ". Søgaard believes that the indigenous communications system is consistent with the oral traditions in many countries, where audience participation is not only common but important. "The credibility of the information or messages is transmitted through the channels of the traditional media, which are most effective in promoting changes in beliefs and attitudes," he said (Søgaard 1993:197).

Nantachai Mejudhon, in his article *Meekness: A New Approach to Christian Witness to Thai People*, suggests that indigenous strategies for cross cultural communication of the gospel mean that missionaries and local Christians should know how Buddhists use meaningful indigenous media to convey their ideas, how missionaries and Christians can improve their credibility as gospel communicators, how missionaries and Christians can be family-focused in their Christian witness, how demonstrating God's care and concern through social concern, and how to find suitable roles and status for missionaries and Thai Christians to develop genuine relationships with Buddhists in local society (Mejudhon 2005:181-182).

Mejudhon said that in local Buddhist culture, oral communication tends to predominate while printed media have low impact. "[This] culture has its own primary communication systems, such as indigenous song, dance, drama, music, story telling, illustrations, and other arts. The best media for each culture should be used in evangelization." He emphasized that use and adaptation of local media should be encouraged in all levels of evangelism. "Indigenous illustrations, key historical illustrations, parables, symbols, and analogies are encouraged for use in Christian witness," he said. "In both urban areas and rural areas, Western forms of media such as film and songs have been used indigenously," Mejudhon contends. "Christian communicators should carefully study the principles and process of indigenization behind the acceptance of such media and not follow Western modes" (2005:182).

Conclusion

For Pek-Dorji, "There's no turning back" (Pek-Dorji 2007:15-16). The situation, however, appears reminiscent of the proverb by Sufi master Hakim Jami, "The rose is gone from the garden, what shall we do with the thorns" (Ellis & Niemei 2001:131). It seems obvious that somehow there must be a solution that is amicable to both sides, while at the same time providing for an appropriate and effective platform for gospel proclamation. But what is it?

First, it seems that there must be a marriage between the global and the local—"glocal," so to speak, at least Friedman thinks so. Glocalization, a hybrid of globalization and localization, is the answer.

> I define healthy glocalization as the ability of a culture, when it encounters other strong cultures, to absorb influences that naturally fit into and can enrich that culture, to resist those things that are truly alien and to compartmentalize those things that, while different, can nevertheless be enjoyed and celebrated as different. The whole process of glocalization is to be able to assimilate aspects of globalization into your country and culture in a way that adds to your growth and diversity, without overwhelming it (Friedman 1999: 1 -512).

Marwan Kraidy, an internationally recognized scholar in intercultural and international media, communication and research, said in his article *The Global, the Local and the Hybrid* that we should all expect glocalization—the hybrid—as the norm, the rule rather than the exception, understanding that glocalization is not the summation of differences between the global and the local, but it is the creation of something new, the reformulation of intercultural and international communications in a local setting (Kraidy 1999:456-476).

Second, it seems that there must not be tech without touch. John Naisbitt, with collaborators Nana Naisbitt and Douglas Phillips, present a story in their book *High Tech High Touch* where on one side is globalization with all of its high tech features and on the other side is high touch—all the "touchy-feely" things of life that make life worth living. High tech - high touch is the showdown between the global and home—the local and all that it stands for. We live in a technology intoxicated society, Naisbitt said, creating tension and polarization—paradox—within us. We must learn to deal with this in order to survive globalization and understand the role of technology in our lives. Combining the two, he said, is embracing technology that preserves our humanness and rejecting technology that intrudes upon it (Naisbitt 1999:1 -274).

> It is recognizing that at its best, technology supports and improves human life; at its worst, it alienates, isolates, distorts, and destroys. It is questioning what place technology should have in our lives and what place it should have in society. It is consciously choosing to employ technology when it adds value to human lives. It is learning how to live as human beings in a technologically dominated time. It is knowing when simulated experiences add value to human life. It is recognizing when to avoid the layers of distraction and distance technology affords us. It is recognizing when technology is not neutral. It is knowing when to unplug and when to plug in (1999:1-274).

Third, relationship must be a high priority. While it is easy to get enamored with print and electronic media, don't forget the personal. In a globalized world, all three are imperative for effective communication. When it comes to sharing the gospel, however, personal relationship must be priority. Remember, those within the urban centers, bombarded by the effects of globalization, are seeking relationship. They are seeking identity and community.

This brings us to the fourth point: identity and community are imperative. The appeal of globalization to the urbanite is that it offers an identity and community different from which they seek escape. Those sharing the good news of the gospel must offer a third alternative—identity and community inherent in relationship with Jesus Christ and with his followers.

Stephen Bailey in his article *Communication Strategies for Christian Witness Among the Lao* said, "I believe the key to the communication of the gospel…is communication that engages [people] in terms of the structure of…relationships. This kind of communication taps into the issue of identity" (Bailey 2003:155).

> When Christ died on our behalf, he not only offered us freedom from the sin and a means to be in relationship with the Creator but he also established a new way for us to relate to one another. From that point on the kingdom ethic declared that disciples of Jesus were to live on behalf of others. The missionary task is to bring people into relationship with the Creator through a relationship with Jesus. This is a social message and can only be communicated in the midst of social relations. (2003:160)

Finally, tell them the story and let the facts come later. As the authors of the bestselling book *The Sacred Romance* said, "Life is not a list of propositions, it is a series of dramatic scenes" (Curtis & Eldrege 1997 :2) Eugene Peterson continued, 'We live in narrative, we live in story. Existence has a story shape to it. We have a beginning and an end, we have a plot, we have characters .'" Story is the language of the heart.

CHAPTER TWO

Our souls speak not in the naked facts of mathematics or the abstract proportions of systematic theology; they speak the images and emotions of story. Contrast your enthusiasm for studying a textbook with the offer to go to a movie, read a novel, or listen to the story of someone else's life (Curtis & Eldredge 1997:39-40).

SECTION TWO

CONTEXTUAL ISSUES

CHAPTER THREE

Ethnic Crisis and Christianity in Buddhist Cities

M.S.VASANTHAKUMAR

Ethnic crisis is not a modern dilemma. The enormity of its devastating and awful consequences has plagued human societies ever since people divided themselves by linguistic categories. Hence, ethnic crisis is not an uncommon feature in our histories and contemporary societies. It is inevitable that each community assumes that it has the pure culture and language and consequently other groups are condemned as inferior and even sub-human or non-human entities. Since the entrance of sin into the world human beings are accustomed to dislike and even detest other persons and groups. In the extreme form of ethnic crisis one group goes to the extent of eradicating the group it dislikes.

In the context of ethnic crisis, Christian mission struggles to maintain Christ's concepts of love and forgiveness. Some assume that McGavran's homogeneous church growth methodology (i.e. having exclusive churches for each ethnic or caste group Cf. McGavran 1970) is the best way to deal with this crisis. But such an approach favours the ethos of racism and distorts the basic tenets of Christianity. This paper makes an attempt to establish some missiological guidelines when ethnic crisis becomes a hindrance to the progress and expansion of Christianity, with special reference to the Buddhist cities in Sri Lanka.

Even though ethnic crisis is not confined to cities, its presence in urban societies is much more intense and palpable than in rural areas where only one community lives or dominates. But in cities, more than one community lives and the tendency for an ethnic crisis is always present. In Sri Lanka, the ongoing ethnic crisis has become one of the major hindrances to communicating the Christian message to Buddhists. The present paper does not involve itself in great detail in depicting the nature or investigating the causes of ethnic crises in Sri Lanka, which are obviously beyond the scope and intent of this forum (For details see Bartholomeusz & de Silva 1988; de Silva 1998; Wickremeratne 1995; Wilson 1988), but it correctly understands that the current situation of the country is plagued with racial prejudices and problems, which has created an unwelcome atmosphere for the progress of Christianity. Nevertheless, this paper highlights some historical and traditional realities, which will enable the reader to comprehend the difficulties involved in communicating the Christian message to the contemporary Buddhist mind in Sri Lanka.

In Sri Lanka, Buddhism has been identified with the Sinhalese (majority ethnic group) and Hinduism with Tamils (one of the minority groups). At present there is no Tamil Buddhist or Sinhalese Hindu in Sri Lanka. Hence these religions are categorized on an ethnic basis contrary to their multi-ethnic adherence in other parts of the world. Further, Christianity has been viewed by the Sri Lankan Buddhists as intimately interwoven with Tamils and western powers. In the eyes of the Buddhists, western powers favour Tamils and are in the process of eradicating Buddhism and the Sinhalese language. The fact that the Christian community in Sri Lanka is largely comprised of Tamils, that the majority of the leaders in Churches, Christian institutions, and even non-governmental organizations are Tamils, as well as the fact that most of these groups had links with western countries, has created an image in the minds of the Buddhists that Christianity is waging war against Buddhism. The situation is perceived as though the country is once again under the attack of colonial military and missionary powers. To the Buddhist mind, Tamils and Christians have become a real threat to Buddhism and the Sinhalese language in contemporary Sri Lanka.

Some Historical Realities

The perception that Tamils and Christians are a threat to Buddhism is not a recent development. Even though the present ethnic crisis has its origins in the events of the recent past, "the intensity with which the Sinhalese (as well as Buddhist) identity is expressed in modern time appears to be the outcome of over two millennia of mainly conflictual contact with Dravidian neighbours, particularly the Tamils" (Dharmadasa 1992:2). Some trace the roots of the current ethnic conflict only back to the nineteenth century (Harris 1999:174). It is true that both communities were organized themselves with nationalistic fervour against the British rule and Christianity only in the nineteenth century. But the roots of these ethnic and religious assertions and antagonism go beyond that century (Singer 1992:711-722). The South Indian invasions of Sri Lanka go back as far as the third century BC (de Silva 1981:12-16), and continued even up to the fifteenth century AD. The very frequency of such invasions "refurbished the Sinhalese image of the Tamil both as an invader and a wanton destroyer of life, property, religious edifices, and the great reservoirs of the north central plain" (Wickremratne 1995:23). Hence, "a strong tradition of mutual antagonism between the Sinhalese and the Tamils had sprung up and taken deep root" in Sri Lanka (Wickremratne 1995:22). Therefore, it is not surprising to note that even non-Tamil incursions were depicted as done by the "devastating Tamils" in the Sinhalese historical documents (Cf. *Culavamsa*, Ch.1. vv. 58-73; *Pujavaliaya*, p.690). In fact, such a stereotyped negative descriptions "indiscriminately generalized to all South Indian elements, singled out as inimical to Sinhala Buddhist interests" (Dharmadasa 1992:15).

The south Indian invasions were not only devastating, they had actually pushed the Sinhalese Kingdom from North and North central plain (the classic centre of ancient Sinhalese Kingdoms), to the south-east and then to the south-west eventually to form a separate Tamil kingdom in the North. The Tamils argue that their race had lived in Sri Lanka even before the spread of Buddhism and they were the original inhabitants of the island (Swamy 2007:29). Unlike the Sinhalese historical records which go back to third century BC, the early history of the Tamils in Sri Lanka were not written until the thirteenth century AD (Gunasingam 2005:17). Nevertheless, there is evidence even in the Sinhalese historical records that Tamils had lived in Sri Lanka as early as the third century BC. The question as to who were the original inhabitants of Sri Lanka or who came first to the island has become a hot controversial issue in contemporary ethnically strained Sri Lanka. Though both ethnic groups have lived in Sri Lanka for two millennia, as Dharmadasa has correctly observed, "while there were periods of peace characterized by cultural and religious assimilation, inevitably, during periods of conflict and stress, there was an upsurge of historical antagonism between the two communities" (1992:14).

Prior to the formation of the Northern Tamil Kingdom, there were some Tamils who had ruled the Sinhalese populace in Anuradhapura. Of the twenty-nine rulers of Anuradhapura from 250 BC to the beginning of the first century AD, nine were Tamils. But all were overthrown by subsequent Sinhalese Kings. In the seventh century AD the Sinhalese kings sought the assistance of the South Indian Pandyan kings to retain their position on the throne. But when the Pandyan power was eclipsed by the rise of the Chola Empire in South India, Sinhalese kings encountered the wrath of the Chola Kings because of the connections they had with the Pandyans. The Cholas invaded Sri Lanka in 993 AD, and made Polonnaruwa their capital. Consequently Sri Lanka became an appendage of the Chola Empire. Nevertheless, the Chola rule was toppled by Vijayabahu (1055-1110), who restored the Sinhalese dynasty onto the throne of Sri Lanka in 1070 (de Silva 1981:24-26). It should be observed that under the Chola rule Buddhism "suffered a severe setback" (de Silva 1981:61) in Sri Lanka, which obviously created an image in the minds of the Buddhists, that a Tamil regime is typically detrimental to their religion, even though some Tamil Kings who had ruled Sri Lanka had actually supported and promoted Buddhism. Concerning the Cholas, the *Culavamsa* (second part of *Mahavamsa*) states that the Tamils "plundered the whole country like devils" (Geiger 2003:64-66). In fact, the way Tamil Kings were depicted in Sri Lankan chronicles gives the impression that they were perceived as invading enemies, whose rule should be overthrown in order to restore Sinhala rule and Buddhism in Sri Lanka. In fact, according to *Mahavamsa*, the Sinhalese were "protectors of Buddhism and saviors of the Sinhalese language" and the Tamils were "invaders, vandals, marauders and heathens" for it has been "written unabashedly from the Buddhist stand point, lauding the victories of the Sinhala kings over the Tamil kings" (Swamy 2007:21).

Even though the kings of the South Indian *Nayakar* dynasty were absorbed into Sinhalese royalty and ruled the central Kandyan Kingdom from 1739 to 1815, whenever they found themselves in unfavourable situations with the Sinhalese nobility, they were vehemently criticised as "heretical Tamils." Thus in the Sinhalese literary works of the early nineteenth century it is stated that "heretical and thieving Tamil hordes were destroying the most immaculate *sasana* (religion)." The Kings of *Nayakar* dynasty, who had established marriage ties with the Sinhalese kings, were accepted as rulers of the Sinhalese Kingdom only because there was no Sinhalese royal heir in 1739 that could fulfil the traditional requirements of a ruler (i.e. having both father and mother belonging to *Ksatriya* caste). Even though the kings from the *Nayakar* dynasty ruled the Sinhalese kingdom until 1815, when it became the possession of the British, from time to time, local uprisings against the *Nayakar* kings erupted in an ethnically prejudiced manner. And the tradition of viewing the South Indians, under the blanket term Tamils, as enemies of the Sinhalese people and religion has continued down the ages (Dharmadasa 1992:15; Bechert 1974:48-72; Roberts 1979:2-39).

Like the South Indian invasions, the western colonial expansion, from the sixteenth century onwards, became a real threat to Buddhism and Sinhalese language. The Portuguese in the sixteenth century captured the Maritime Provinces of Sri Lanka. They were perceived by the Buddhists as "cruel, inhuman, rapacious, bigoted and savage persecutors of Buddhism in their endeavour to impose their faith… on the people of Sri Lanka" (Perera 1988:60). In fact, the Portuguese had persecuted the Buddhists and destroyed their temples and sacred objects in order to eradicate Buddhism and establish Christianity. Since

Buddhism came to Sri Lanka in a peaceful manner in the third century BC, it is unbearable for the Buddhists to observe that Christianity, as a religion, had come to Sri Lanka as a dreadful conquering western force when the Portuguese arrived in the country in 1505. Even today the Buddhists allege that Christianity was introduced to the country by the power of the sword. The subsequent colonial government of the Dutch also "looked upon Buddhism as a form of paganism, something that the Protestant Christians could not allow to exist or prosper" (Karunaratna 2000:145). During the Dutch rule, various laws were passed which brought pressure on non-Christians to accept baptism . Even though in 1815 the British promised to protect and provide state patronage for Buddhism under the famous Kandyan Convention, the colonial government had to give up connections with Buddhism as a result of the missionaries, who castigated Buddhism as well the British government's dealings with the Buddhists in their ardent efforts to evangelise the Sri Lankans .

During the time of English missionary activities, Buddhism experienced a remarkable revival with nationalistic overtones in Sri Lanka. This revival was counterproductive to the Christian missionary enterprise, because the nineteenth century Buddhist revival was nothing else than "Buddhist reaction to the missionary onslaught" (de Silva 1997:198). The negative attitudes formed in the minds of the Buddhists concerning Christianity during the time of Buddhist revival continue to the present day. The activists of the Buddhist revival vehemently condemn Christianity and the conduct of the colonial missionaries. For instance, one of the major figures in the nineteenth century Buddhist revival, Anagarika Dharmapala, was convinced that the main objectives of the Christian missionaries were the defeat of Buddhism and destruction of the local culture .

Dharmapals's concepts did not die with him. He is one of the national heroes of contemporary Sri Lanka, and his views are shared by the Buddhists even to the present day. Hence they assert, "the Buddhists do not want to exchange gold for lead, or bread for filth; they want to hold fast to their compassionate, refined and reasonable view of life, and their noble culture, which is founded, on the *Dhamma*.

CHAPTER THREE

Some Traditional Realities

In the history of Sri Lanka, South Indian and European invasions have created negative images about Tamils and Christians in the minds of the Buddhists. In fact, such negative images were formed, not only due to the military activities of the invading political powers, but also due to the perceived threat to some treasured beliefs of the Buddhists. Today, Buddhists are worried that their treasured traditional beliefs will be nullified by the activities of the Tamils and Christians. Hence, in order to understand contemporary Buddhists, it is necessary to know their traditional beliefs, which were cherished for more than two thousand years in Sri Lanka. These traditional realities prevent the Buddhist minds appreciating the message of Jesus Christ.

Sri Lankan Buddhists believe that they were specially chosen and appointed, by the Buddha, to be the guardians of his teachings and their country was specially chosen by the Buddha to be the sacred land in which Buddhism would flourish and spread to the rest of the world. Hence, they consider themselves as the sole and rightful heirs to the island . They believe that the Buddha visited Sri Lanka three times, arriving by air, to consecrate the chosen Buddhist land. According to the *Mahavamsa*, the Buddha's first visit was to Mahiyangana, at the eastern foot of the central massif. The second time he visited Nagadipa, an island near Jaffna peninsula. On his third visit he went to Kalaniya, on the west coast near Colombo, and on his way back planted his footprint on Sripada (known in English as Adam's Peak), in the southwest part of the hill country. He had also meditated in a cave at the foot of Sripada, at Dighavapi on the east coast, and four or five spots in Anuradhapura .

Even though there are no historical records in the contemporary Buddhists texts to verify the visits of the Buddha to Sri Lanka, and Buddhists in other countries have their own records of Buddha's visits to their respective nations, according to the Sri Lankan Buddhists, the *Mahavamsa* is an "irreplaceable source for the reconstruction of the early history of the Sri Lanka" (de Silva 1981:3). This being the work of the Buddhist monks, was obviously "permeated by a strong religious basis and encrusted with miracle and invention" (de Silva 1981:3). Nevertheless, "the central theme was the historic role of the island as a bulwark of Buddhist civilization" (de Silva 1981:3). Hence, for the Sri Lankan Buddhists, *Mahavamsa* is a reliable record of the ancient history of their country. Further, the concepts of *Mahavamsa*, which have been "repeated time and again in the course of history in various contexts, literary, ritual and historical, crystallize the situation of the Sinhalese identity" (Obeyesekere 1997:358). In fact, "the Mahavamsa's charter for the Sinhalese, Buddhism and its relationship to Sri Lanka echoes in the post-independence constitutions of the country as well (Harris 1999:174).

Not only had the Buddha visited Sri Lanka and consecrated the land also for the growth and spread of Buddhism, according to the *Mahavamsa*, the Buddha also on his death bed admonished Sakka, the ruler of the gods, to protect Vijaya, the first outside settler of Sri Lanka and the founder of the Sinhalese race. Sakka in turn handed over the guardianship of Sri Lanka to the god Vishnu. Hence, the god Vishnu went to Sri Lanka prior to the arrival of Vijaya, assumed the guise of an ascetic, and blessed Vijaya and his followers when they came to Sri Lanka on the day the Buddha passed away (*Mahavamsa* Ch. VI). Even though the *Mahavamsa* "contrives to synchronize the advent of Vijaya with the passing away of the Buddha" (de Silva 1981:3-4) this has become "the most powerful historical myth of the Sinhalese and the basis of their conception of themselves as the chosen guardians of Buddhism, and of Sri Lanka itself as a place of special sanctity for the Buddhist religion" (de Silva 1981:4). Therefore, invasions of Sri Lanka by other ethnic or religious powers are seen by the Buddhists as a threat to their race, religion, and land. Hence, defending their religion and country becomes the paramount and natural reaction of the Buddhists to foreign invasions.

Some Contemporary Realities

Christian churches in Sri Lankan cities comprise both Sinhalese and Tamils, except in areas where only one ethnic community lives. The majority of Sri Lankan cities have churches with either bilingual services, or separate services in the same building at different times for each ethnic group. In fact, almost all the churches, in most of the cities, do have ministries in both languages. Hence, mission among the Buddhists in Sri Lankan cities cannot exclude either the direct or indirect presence or involvement of Tamils from its scope. Churches which do evangelism among Buddhists have Tamil members as well. Therefore, the Churches in Sri Lankan cities are not in a position to exhibit themselves exclusively in Sinhalese terms, like Buddhism in Sri Lanka. Since there is antagonism between Sinhalese and Tamils in Sri Lanka, Christianity, having more Tamil associations, finds it very difficult to reach the Sinhalese Buddhists in a meaningful way.

Not only in the historical past, but even in contemporary Sri Lanka a segment of Tamils have become a real threat to Buddhism and Sinhalese language. A Tamil group called LTTE (Liberation Tigers of Tamil Elam) has been waging war against the government troops, for more than twenty years, in order to establish a separate Tamil state in the Northern and Eastern provinces of the country. Significantly, two important Buddhist sites are located in these two provinces. According to the traditional belief, these two sites were visited by the Buddha and are sacred to the Buddhists. One is Nagadipa, an island near Jaffna peninsula, and the other is Dighavapi in the eastern province. For the Buddhists it is unbearable to lose these two sacred sites. Their fear is that if Tamils have sole authority over the Northern and Eastern Provinces, the sacred Buddhists sites will be destroyed, and such a situation would become the beginning of the extinction of Buddhism in Sri Lanka. The Buddhist rationale behind such fear is the decline and disappearance of Buddhism in its original country due to the activities of Hindu kings. Apart from a few kings, under whose state patronage Buddhism flourished in India, most of the Hindu rulers of

India were indifferent, and some even intolerant, towards Buddhism. Hence Buddhism virtually disappeared in its motherland. Therefore, it is not strange that Buddhists in Sri Lanka fear that if Tamil power is consolidated in certain provinces, it will eventually eradicate their language and religion from the whole island.

According to the Buddhists, the Christians and LTTE have mutual understandings and help each other to achieve the same objectives. Hence, they say that the LTTE has destroyed Buddhists temples in the North and allowed Christians to build churches (*Divayina* 7 Sep. 2003). The Buddhists assert that they have ample evidence to confirm that some Tamil Christian leaders have provided money and even materials to the LTTE for manufacturing arms (Wijayathunga 2003:64). For them, almost all non-governmental organizations which do social work in Northern and Eastern provinces fund LTTE and function as spies for terrorists (Wijayathunga 2003:51). Therefore, Christians' attempts to bring peace in Sri Lanka have been often interpreted by the Buddhists as a conspiracy to divide the country and give support to the LTTE. They vehemently condemn Christians for depicting the leader of LTTE as a kind person, and for describing him as the Savior of the Tamil people by comparing him with Moses (*Divayina*, 7 Sep. 2003). Further, they say that Tamil Christians are refusing to pray for the government soldiers (*The Island*, 28 Jan. 1993; *Divayina*, 31 Jan. 1993), but go to the extent of fasting for the release of people who have been arrested by the government as terrorist suspects (*Divayina*, 7 Sep. 2003). According to the Buddhists, the LTTE had peace talks with the government in the past due to the pressure of Christians, and the intention of Christians is to establish a Tamil Kingdom in the North. They say that the Norwegian government has bribed the Sri Lankan government to settle the ethnic conflict via peaceful negotiations. Therefore, Christian activities such as praying for peace in Sri Lanka, having peace conferences and peace walks have been seen by the Buddhists as a means to create a Tamil kingdom in Sri Lanka, and destroy Buddhism (*Divayina*, 7 Sep. 2003; Wijayathunga 2003:52).

Some Biblical Realities

Human beings, due to their different cultural, national and linguistic differences find it difficult to live with mutual understanding and peaceful cohabitation. As Jesus clearly pointed out, in the last days, due to the increase of wickedness "the love of most will grow cold" (Matt.24:12). Indeed, we live in such a loveless, pathetic, era. There are people who do not love even their own kith and kin in contemporary societies. Hence, it is not surprising that people who belong to different ethnic groups have conflicts with one another. Jesus also foretold that "nation will rise against nation and kingdom against kingdom" (Matt.24:7). We witness this in our very own societies. Nevertheless, despite this ruthless and loveless world, Christians are expected to exhibit the true love, which embraces even our enemies. Therefore, Christians need to comprehend certain biblical truths, which will enable them to communicate the gospel message to others more effectively and meaningfully.

All have Come from One Person

According to the Bible, all people, despite their different ethnicity, have come from one single person, namely Adam. He is the first human being. He and his wife Eve were the original parents of all the diverse linguistic groups of people who have ever lived and are living in this world. Hence, Eve has been depicted as "the mother of all the living" (Gen.3:20) because "all human life has its source in her body" (Mathews, 2001:254). In fact, the name Eve (*hawwah*) is a word play on the Hebrew word for life (*hay* Sailhamer, 1990:58). As Paul has explicitly stated, "from one man he (God) made every nation of men that they should inhabit the whole earth; and he determined the times set for them and the exact places where they should live" (Acts.17:26). According to Paul, *from one man* clearly refers to Adam, who is the first man God created to live in this world, and all human beings are his descendants, which the rest of the Bible clearly shows. Since all

85

can trace their pedigrees back to Adam, there is no room for ideas of racial superiority. All are on an equal status, because all have come from a single person, and therefore, all are humans and absolutely nothing else. A common feature of ethnic crisis is viewing the opposite group as nonhuman, but the Bible is opposed to such opinions, and Christians need to have an estimation of other people as humans on an equal status.

It is interesting to note, that Sinhalese and Tamils who are divided on the basis of language in Sri Lanka are related to one another. According to *Mahavamsa*, the forefather of the Sinhalese race Vijaya had come from India. The Sinhalese insist that he came from North India, in order to separate themselves from Tamils who had migrated from South India. Vijaya married a local princess, and their offspring became the aborigines of Sri Lanka. Subsequently they were separated. In the meantime Vijaya and his 700 friends who came with him from India, married South Indian women and their descendants were the modern Sinhalese race. Some doubt the historicity of Vijaya's episode, and suggest that "it symbolizes the successful migration of a group of North Indians to Sri Lanka" (de Silva 1997:20). Many contemporary Sinhalese are reluctant to accept *Mahavamsa's* depiction of Vijaya and his descendants. They assume that their forefathers were original inhabitants of Sri Lanka, and the Tamils were alien intruders from South India. However, historical as well as contemporary DNA tests has confirmed that both Sinhalese and Tamils had come to Sri Lanka from South India (Kink 1976:91-100), and due to the influence of Buddhism, and the Pali language, the Sinhalese language and race has developed as a separate entity (Papina, Mostara & Jeyasekara 1996:707-737). Vijaya and his companions may have come from North India, but their wives came from South India. Between the fourteenth and eighteenth centuries, large numbers of people, from the South Indian state of Kerala, settled in Sri Lanka and assimilated as Sinhalese. The Sinhalese cuisine (and costume) even today reflects this connection (Swamy 2007:26).

CHAPTER THREE

All Languages are Derived from One Dialect

According to the Bible, divisions among human beings, on the basis of different languages, occurred when God confused the one common language people had from the beginning, when people deliberately determined to go against the divine intention for the world. When God created Adam, He intended that people should inhabit the whole world, instead of confining their habitation to one particular place. God's command to Adam, Noah and Noah's sons, "be fruitful and increase in number; fill the earth and subdue it" (Gen.1:28,9:1,9:7) clearly indicates such divine intention. As Paul has put it, "from one man he (God) made every nation of men that they should inhabit the whole earth" (Acts.17:26). But contrary to this, people organized themselves to build a city, with a tower reaching to heaven, which could become the sole territory for human habitation and prevent them moving to other areas of the world. Genesis 11:4 explicitly states that the people built a tower to "make a name for themselves, and not to scatter over the face of the whole earth." They wanted to live in one particular place. Therefore, in order to send people all over the world, God confused their language. Concerning this Genesis 11:6-9 says, "the LORD said, 'If as one people speaking the same language they have begun to do this, then nothing they plan to do will be impossible for them. Come, let us go down and confuse their language so they will not understand each other.' So the LORD scattered them from there over all the earth, and they stopped building the city. That is why it was called Babel—because there the LORD confused the language of the whole world. From there the LORD scattered them over the face of the whole earth."

Genesis 11:6-9 is the divine portrayal of the origin of different human languages. It is one language (Gen.11:1) being confused into several languages. The statement "now the whole world had one language and a common speech" in verse 1 means that originally "all spoke the same language and apparently even the same dialect (Leupold 1942:388). Since all the people of that time were descendants of Noah, it is beyond any doubt that they all spoke the same language. And this one language, when confused by God, became many languages. That is why research in comparative linguistic grammar has demonstrated that known languages are related and could have descended from one language (Free 1950:46-47). Therefore, having conflicts on the basis of ethnic differences is utterly meaningless.

All Are One in Christ

Though our contemporary world is filled with people with different ethnic groups, which find it difficult to live with harmony and peace, they can become one family in Christ. The Bible explicitly states that in Christ there is neither Jew nor Greek, slave nor free, male nor female, for all are one in Christ Jesus (Gal.3:28). Of course Paul does not mean that in Christ people will lose their ethnicity, economic capacity, and sexuality. Nor are these social categories removed if a person is in Christ, as Paul has clearly explained in 1 Corinthians 7:18-19, 21-23. His point in saying that *all are one in Christ Jesus* is that divisions among people, based on social categories, are decisively demolished by Christ. Christ has indeed destroyed the dividing wall between people, when he died on the cross (Eph.2:14-15). Therefore people from different ethnic groups can become one in Him. Indeed in Christ they have become the descendants of Abraham, as Paul explains in Galatians 3:29. Hence they are related to one another. Hence the Bible says, "consequently, you are no longer foreigners and aliens, but fellow citizens with God's people and members of God's household" (Ep.2:19).

Paul's threefold affirmation in Galatians 3:28 corresponds to a number of Jewish formulas, in which the threefold distinction is maintained (Bruce 1988:187), as in the Morning Prayer in which the male Jew thanks God that he was not made a Gentile, a slave or a woman (Singer 1939:5-6). Jewish men thought that they are superior to Gentiles and women. But in Christ all human beings are equal despite their unequal social status. The distinctions in societies are done away with by Christ, and people who are in Him are united in

Him as people who belong to a single family. "If Christ has saved a person he is a Christian therefore, whether he or she is Jew or Greek (Sinhalese or Tamil) is irrelevant" (Morris 1996:121). We need to accept Christians of other ethnic groups as our own brothers and sisters, for the New Testament term for addressing other Christians as "brothers" (which at that time included females as well) literally means "born from the same womb" (Brown 1976:254). Since all Christians are in Christ, they are one in Christ. They are related to one another as brothers and sisters of one family. Therefore they cannot be divided on the basis of ethnicity.

Conclusion

As the Bible clearly reveals that all human beings have come from one person, and all languages originated from one dialect, and all human beings can be united as one family in Christ, Christians need to give up their ethnically harmful identities and become active peacemakers.

Giving Up Harmful Ethnic Identities

People naturally like to be identified with their ethnicity. And there is nothing wrong in loving or highly valuing one's own country and language. But as Christians, we have to remember that we are not of this world, and our ethnic identity is only a temporary label attached to our earthly existence. Further, Christianity is not confined to one particular nation or language. Therefore, when we live in a multi-ethnic society, we need to give up our ethnic identity if it is harmful to others, for the sake of our Lord Jesus Christ, who has given up his heavenly position, and humbled himself to the lowest state of this world for us (Phil.2:6-7). In this respect, the apostle Paul serves as an excellent model for us to follow. Even though he was a racist and an extremist religious fanatic prior to his conversion, he gave up all his racist feelings and identity to reach out the Gentiles, whom his native Jewish community vehemently detested.

According to the Jewish belief of Paul's time, the Gentiles were merely created to be the fuel for the fire in hell. Jewish men in their daily prayers made it a habit to thank God for not being born into a Gentile family. The Jewish community eagerly anticipated the day in which God would save them and cast all the Gentiles into the ever burning hell. Paul was such a chauvinistic person from his birth. Nevertheless, when he met Jesus Christ, he was transformed to the opposite extreme. Therefore, instead of having feelings of hatred, his heart was filled with unconditional and unlimited love which enabled him to sacrifice his life for the salvation of the Gentiles. Such a kind of sacrificial love should compel and motivate the Christians when they are confronted with any ethnic crisis.

It is vital to observe how Paul gave up his Jewish identity. First, he gave up his Jewish nationalistic name, Saul, and used his Gentile name, Paul, after his conversion, or most probably from his first missionary journey onwards. He was called Paul for the first time in Acts 13:9, but prior to this the author of the Acts calls him Saul. In fact, Acts 13:9 indicates that "Paul was his second name (Saul Paul), for Paul was a Roman surname which does not occur as a first name in the writings of that time" (Dunn 2002:24). Or most probably, Paul was "not even the name used by his enfranchised family, but chosen by him because of its assonance with his Jewish name Saul" (Cole 1991:64). Paul never used the name Saul for himself, which "indicates a shift in the familiar name Paul wished to be known by" (Dunn 2002:24). In fact, the decision to be known as Paul rather than Saul "reflects a new sense of status on Paul's part" which is nothing else than a shift of identity "from Jewish to Greco-Roman identity" (Dunn 2002:24). Paul did take pride in calling himself Saul prior to his conversion, but his Gentile mission "demanded the renunciation of his Jewish past" (Cole 1991:65). And he willingly gave up the Jewish name which he cherished from his birth. Like Paul, we too need to relinquish our ethnic identity, if we are to become better witnesses to our Lord Jesus Christ.

Paul not only gave up his Jewish name, he also gave up his Jewish way of life while he was ministering among the Gentiles. He explains this in his letter to the Corinthian believers as, "Though I am free and belong to no man, I make myself a slave to everyone, to win as many as possible. To the Jews I became like a Jew, to win the Jews. To those under the law I became like one under the law (though I myself am not under the law), so as to win those under the law. To those not having the law I became like one not having the law (though I am not free from God's law but am under Christ's law), so as to win those not having the law. To the weak I became weak, to win the weak. I have become all things to all men so that by all possible means I might save some. I do all this for the sake of the gospel that I may share in its blessings" (1Cor.9:19-23). Like the apostle Paul, Christians need to renounce their ethnic identity in their name and conduct, if they really want to communicate the message of Jesus Christ to others.

Giving up ethnic identity does not mean that Christians are expected to become non-ethnic beings. In this world we will be known by our ethnicity, but our ethnic identity should not become a hindrance to relating ourselves to the people of other ethnic groups. Christians are expected to give up the elements in their ethnic identity which could become harmful when relating to people of other ethnic groups. For this reason, the Jewish Christians were vehemently criticized by Paul when they wished to be known by their native Jewish identity. Jews of that time considered the Mosaic Law more than mere religious regulations. It had become their national and racial code. Hence the Jewish Christians expected Christian converts to adopt their lifestyle by following the rules and regulations of the law. But Paul vehemently opposed this Jewish nationalistic whim and practice because such kind of conduct would produce an ethnically oriented Christianity. The Jews were expected to give up ethnically identifiable practices (such as observing special days, food laws even circumcision) when relating themselves to the Gentile Christians. Likewise, the Gentile Christians were expected to give up certain practices which could prevent them having fellowship with the Jews. At the Jerusalem council, prohibitions were directed against the Gentiles, with the objective of making Jewish Gentile fellowship possible. Therefore the Jewish Christians were told "they must recognize and embrace Gentile believers as brothers and sisters in Christ, and not burden them by asking them to add to their faith in Jesus either circumcision or the whole code of Jewish practices... (And the Gentile Christians were requested)... to respect the consciences of their Jewish fellow-believers by abstaining from a few practices which might offend them" (Stott 1990:248).

Becoming Peacemakers

Christians must become peacemakers and contribute substantially to solve the ethnic crisis. Christians generally pray for peace. Indeed prayer changes things. But Christians are expected to do more than merely praying. Many Christians think that praying is the only thing that we should do. But Jesus says that we should become peacemakers. According to him, peacemaking is a basic characteristic of a true child of God. Hence one of his beatitudes says that "blessed are the peacemakers, for they will be called sons of God" (Mat.5:9). Christians should make an active and ardent attempt to bring peace between two people or two communities which are hostile to one another. Some try to limit the scope of Jesus' saying to personal quarrels only, but it "includes bringing peace between two communities or countries that are engaged in war as well" (Morris 1992:100). In fact, "peacemaking is a means of involvement in the human predicament of warlike conditions" which "implies assuming responsibilities against all odds, risking peacemaking out of a situation of powerlessness, and demonstrating the conviction that in the end God's kingdom will prevail" (Betz 1985:140).

Even though the Christian community in Sri Lanka is a powerless tiny entity, this is not an excuse for not getting involved in bringing peace to the country. Instead of withdrawing from society to personal prayer mountains and towers, or enjoying prayer walks and tours, Christians need to be actively and directly involved in convincing the government, militant groups, and the international community to bring peace to Sri Lanka. Christians need to use their God-given brain and come out with practical activities which would enable them to be the peacemakers between Sinhalese and Tamils, which could eventually enable them to reach the Buddhists and Hindus for Christ.

In the light of the whole Bible, peacemaking includes all kinds of combinations of reconciliation; this includes peace between individuals, groups, communities, countries and so on. In the context of the beatitudes, "the peacemaking is directed against the Zealots, who wish to bring the Kingdom of God by violent activities... the Zealots by their militarism hoped furthermore to demonstrate that they were the loyal sons of God. But Jesus announces the kingdom, entirely apart from human effort and indicates that the status of children of God belongs on the contrary to those who live peaceably" (Hagner 1993:94). While recognizing the fact that the government has the duty to defend the country against terrorist attacks and suicide bombers, Christians must take an active stand against all forms of violence, in a non-violent and peaceful manner. For Christians are expected to be peacemakers and not warmongers.

Since Christians are peacemakers, it is important to comprehend the biblical concept of peace. Peace in the biblical sense is more than absence of strife or war. In the Old Testament, approximately fifty or sixty times *shalom* means absence of strife. About twenty five times it is used as a greeting or farewell. But, out of its more than 250 occurrences, in nearly two thirds of times, it describes the state of fulfilment which is the result of God's presence. There is also a strong eschatological element present in the meaning of *shalom* in the Old Testament (Harris, Archer & Waltke 1980:931). In fact, during Jesus' time peace was interpreted messianically (Carson, 1984:135). In the Old Testament the promised Messiah is called the Prince of Peace (Isa.9:6-7), and all the themes of peace in the Old Testament are linked with him (Harris, Archer & Waltke 1980:931). Since according to the New Testament, Jesus Christ is the Messiah, he is our peace (Eph.2:14), and his method of peacemaking is crucial to our understanding of true Christian peace. Jesus Christ not only made peace between God and people by his sacrificial death on the cross, he has also made peace between people (Eph.2:13-16). That is why loving God as well as loving our neighbor becomes the essence of Christianity according to Jesus. Hence making peace in contemporary Sri Lanka involves not only making peace between Sinhalese and Tamils, it necessitates making peace between God and people as well.

Peace making is an essential part of contemporary Christianity. Christian evangelism in the midst of ethnically divided communities needs to take this as its paramount duty, for peace is the essence of Christianity. Jesus made peace not only with God and human kind; he made peace between individual people as well. In evangelism we are not only reconciling people with God, we are expected to bring reconciliation between individual people, too. Today, much time is spent on prayer for evangelism and peace among Sinhalese and Tamil Christians throughout the world. This is indeed a good thing. But the answer to many decades of Christian prayer has not yet materialized. One of the major reasons for this pathetic situation is that many Christians pray for their own ethnic community's peace only. Even in united prayer gatherings, Sinhalese and Tamil Christians are not united in their minds concerning the nature and scope of the peace for which they are praying. For many Tamils, peace means normalcy in areas where predominantly Tamils live in Sri Lanka. For Sinhalese, it is eradication of LTTE. Christians need to come out from their racial prejudices, and pray with one heart and mind, for the peace of the whole country and for the people of all communities. Praying for other ethnic communities should enable the Christians to show love and concern for the people of other ethnic groups, not in mere words but in real deeds. Such unconditional love is the key to peace and evangelism not only in Sri Lanka, but throughout the world.

CHAPTER FOUR

Understanding Sri Lankan Urban Buddhists

SANTHA LAL DE ALWIS

Sri Lanka is at the tip of Southern end of the Indian Subcontinent and considered as the pearl of the Indian Ocean. It is a beautiful country blessed with serenity and a people of high literacy, who are friendly and are very hospitable. Sri Lanka has a Sinhala Buddhist majority and civilization dating back to the sixth century B.C. Prince Vijaya, an exile from the Northern part of India, arrived in the Island with a band of his seven hundred followers. The Aryan immigrants from North India in the sixth century B.C. brought their own religious practices and beliefs influenced by the Vedic religion; Brahmic rituals and Jainism were among these cults. All of them believed in karma, rebirth, magic and astrology.

Buddhism was introduced to Sri Lanka during the reign of King Devanampiyatissa (250-210 B.C) in 237 B.C. Buddhism began to spread in Sri Lanka after its introduction by Bhikku Mahinda, and in that era the people were practicing the worship of *yakka*, *deva*, Na and Nuga Trees and rocks. They believed that the *devas* (gods or spirits) were dwelling in these rocks. Bhikku Mahinda introduced the Bo-Tree in place of the Na and Nuga trees in order to divert their attention towards the enlightenment of the Lord Buddha under the Bo-tree. However, we still notice some rural folks adhere to the practice of worshiping the Na and Nuga trees due to the influence of these past practices.

As the people were in the practice of worshipping the Yakkas and Nagas, Mahinda changed their Concept, and instead advised them to worship the Buddhist priests and the Buddha statues. In place of the rocks, he introduced the shrine which is known as Chaitya. It was through his contextualising vision, that he was able to propagate Buddhism in Sri Lanka without encountering any objection or opposition from the people.

Since the sixteenth century, the Island has been ruled by three colonial powers in succession. The Portuguese first arrived in 1505 and ruled for over 150 years. Following the Portuguese, the Dutch ruled for nearly 140 years. The final colonial ruler was the British who held control for over150 years. These three powers had a great influence on the people of Sri Lanka with regard to education, culture, and religion.

When we look at the heritage of Buddhism prevalent all over the world, we come across a varying and manifold difference of the adherents in the belief of their religion. Once Buddhism is established in a territory, the prevailing culture of the inhabitants tends to experience a radical change and the infrastructure of their religion undergoes transformation. We could also observe a number of changes taking place in Buddhism itself in the course of history.

In addition, there are differences between the urban and rural adherents. One could see a vast difference between the two sectors over their pattern of belief and conduct towards their religion. It is necessary to understand the worldview of the people before we can approach the individual to introduce the Gospel. We need to make an effort to acquaint ourselves with individuals to study their attitudes and concepts. Then, we can engage in a close relationship to find out their needs in life, present predicaments, thoughts and so on. From there, we can surmise their position as to whether they are in a position to accept the Gospel.

According to the Pali Chronicles, Buddhism was introduced to Sri Lanka by Bhikku Mahinda, the son of the emperor Dharmashoka (269-232 B.C) in the year 237 BC. He made a valiant effort to consolidate Buddhism within the cultural trend prevailing at that time in Sri Lanka. He was able to understand the people's culture and beliefs and was able to introduce Buddhism accordingly, without causing any rift or dissention in the society. As a result of his ability to contextualize Buddhism he never encountered any objection, threat, or persecution in his endeavour in spreading Buddhism.

The prevalence of the three denominations in the Buddhist religion categorized under Hinayana (Lesser Vehicle), Mahayana (Greater Vehicle) and Vajrayana (Diamond Vehicle) has to be understood thoroughly according to the cultural differences in each country. Similarly there is a difference between rural and urban Buddhist practices. Though it is difficult to see a difference between urban and rural Buddhism in Sri Lanka, one can notice distinctions in their patterns of conduct and belief.

Educational and Social Standing

When we consider the arrival of the Portuguese in Sri Lanka during the year 1505 A.D., the educational system of the Sri Lankans at that time was solely handled by the Buddhist clergy and the children were taught under them in the respective Buddhist Temples. It is also well documented that all Buddhist priests are mandated to work for learning or teaching purposes. This was also a customary practice carried out from the inception by the Buddhist priests. The temple was considered the learning institution for the Buddhist priests and layman. Though the laymen were traditionally engaged in paddy cultivation or farming, they were not interested in any higher education as they never anticipated any state sector employment. As such, it was evident that the temple was the main educational centre during the period prior to the arrival of the Portuguese.

The women of that era devoted much of their time to childrearing. When they conceived a child, they went to the Buddhist Temple to listen to the *Angulimala Pirith* chanting by the Buddhist Priest and to make a vow that, once the child is born safely, they will dedicate the child to the Buddhist way of life. When the child is born, the child is first taken out to the temple to fulfil the rituals of the vow. Once the child is weaned, it is again taken to the temple for the symbolic "first meal" and receives another blessing from the Buddhist priest.

The child is taught its first letters by the Buddhist priest either at the child's home or at the temple. The social status of the individual does not have any bearing on such practices. This is considered to be the cultural heritage of the Buddhists. However, in the present era there is always a close link between the local school and the Buddhist Temple of the area. Therefore, these rituals are incorporated in to the pattern of village living.

This trend differs vastly when we look at the urban child in an urban school. During the colonial era, a child of the urban area commenced his education in a Christian school affiliated to a Christian church. The education imparted in these Christian schools was of a higher standard because of motivation and discipline in every area of their education. This caused a real challenge and paved the way for the urban Buddhists to approach to Christian churches with the aim of giving their offspring a sound and better education in an entirely disciplined environment.

The Catholic churches maintain a family history book for each of their adherents. It became mandatory to submit the relevant baptism, or dedication certificates of the child as a prerequisite for the admission of children to any Catholic or Christian school. This position has caused a tremendous effort to acquire the necessary documentation on the part of Buddhist families who wanted their children to attend Catholic schools. Those who were without these documents were compelled to renounce their Buddhist religion and accept Catholicism, receive baptism, and become members of Catholic Churches so their children could gain admittance into the Catholic schools.

Though there are many leading Buddhist schools and Colleges in the urban areas, the bulk of the people strive to find admission in a Catholic or Christian School for their children due to the high standard of education and the discipline which the child undergoes in a conducive and Christian environment. The Buddhist parents go out of their way to find finance as well as use influence in order to prepare the relevant documents with a view to obtaining admission to a Catholic school. However, we could observe there are a few who oppose Christianity and are bent on persecuting the churches, causing harm to Christian priests. The have somehow managed to enrol their children to the Catholic and Christian schools, using their social status and political influence.

Some of the renowned longstanding Catholic and Christian schools and colleges have set a trend in the sphere of education and discipline. As a result of their standing as leading institutions of learning they have been able to instil a great reputation and respect among the urban population. Therefore they have been able to attract attention, interest, and admiration. It has now been an accepted fact among the city dwellers that these Catholic and Christian schools have far excelled in the sphere of quality education. They are credited for instilling love, care, respect, and discipline to each child from the basic education starting from the Montessori schools.

Sri Lankan Urban Life Style

The lifestyle of an urbanite as compared to a villager has its own set advantages and disadvantages. The lifestyle in the urban area is comprised of a busy schedule, as most of them are employed. It is almost a daily routine that those reporting to their work places must either leave their home early in the morning in the midst of heavy traffic either by their own mode of transport, public transport, or by foot. In the evening, they return home tired after a day's work and hassling with traffic delays. This group of people struggles due to a lack of leisure time and financial constraints. Urban people do not have much time for social activities, relaxation, or for any active religious participation. Though a fair number attend church services as a ritual, they really do not have time to mingle with other church believers or take part in church activities or programmes, unlike those in the villages.

For the Buddhist, the *Poya* is a day of religious observance. However, in the urban areas, most people do not participate in these observations at the temple, but spend the time on their personal needs. In the past, Buddhist adherents had a code of dress while they observed religious activities in the Temples but this trend has drastically changed with the modern world. The urbanite is not particular about his neighbour's social strata or position, freely socializing with the people around them.

It is the opposite with Buddhist villagers who treat neighbours according to their caste, creed, and social standing. The people in the urban area are from all walks of life and various places in the country. They belong to different social levels, races, and religions. They have migrated to cities to settle down permanently. Many do not know their neighbour, except a selected few with whom they associate.

The race and the caste system prevalent in India are still prevalent in Sri Lanka, too, specifically in the rural areas but it has a minimal effect in the urban areas. In the rural area caste rules are strictly followed; a low caste person is not entertained with others or allowed to mingle with the upper caste people in any ceremonies or festivities. They are segregated from the others and treated as second class citizens.

However, the urban Buddhist does not follow these formalities but freely mingles across caste lines. They may attend a function, child dedication, wedding or any special event organized by Christian Churches. It is also a practice of the Buddhist to gather with their kith and kin and the neighbours in organizing pilgrimages to distant ancient religious sites once or twice a year. Although this is still prevalent in villages, it has been dwindling in the urban areas. The villagers on such pilgrimages abstain from eating fish, meat, and consuming liquor but the urbanites, specifically the younger generation, are totally different. They organize such pilgrimages as pleasure excursions with fun and frolic combined with entertainment and consumption of liquor. Such young urbanites do not have the basic respect for the elders, are not religiously inclined, and do not follow any Buddhist precepts.

Caste System In Urban and Rural Areas

There are almost thirty-five categories of castes prevalent in Sri Lanka. These are clearly recognized by their names or surnames which distinctly reveal one's caste status. Though a small minority of people observe the caste system in the urban area, the majority are not concerned about the caste prejudices. In the rural areas, the caste differentiation is evident. The rural low castes are not treated in the same manner as the urban low castes. The rural low castes are treated in a very downtrodden way. In some cases, these people are offered a small bench rather than a chair for sitting. They are debarred from partaking in meals on the main table where the high castes sit. Instead, they are made to sit on spread out mats and are served meals using different utensils. However, in the urban area, as people are engaged in their various activities, such as business engagements and employment, they disregard such discriminatory practices. The urbanite is focused mainly on their welfare, status quo, luxuries, entertainments and extravagant lifestyle.

The rural villager now has a tendency to come out from the shackles of village life and enter the urban lifestyle to escape from the downtrodden treatment meted out to them, preferring the urban area that gives respect according to their skills.

In Sri Lanka the caste system is prevalent in all sections of the society.

Rank	Name of Caste	Traditional Functions
HIGH CASTE	Govigama Radala Mudali Patti Kattupella Nilamakkara	Agriculture Holders of Royal appointments Popular Leadter Cowherds men to the king Royal Clerk Temple servant
SUB CASTE	Poravakkara Vehal Gettara Karawa Salagama Hewapanne Durawa	Wood Choppers Domestic servant for the Radala Govingama outcaste Fisherman Cinnamon peelers Soldiers Toddy Tappers

Rank	Name of Caste	Traditional Functions
SUB CASTE (cont.)	Navandama	Craftsman including smith
	Hannali	Consumers of time
	Hene	Laundry man for high caste
	Hinna	Laundry man for Salagama
	(Hakuru) Rahumpara	Jiggery maker
	Bedhal	potters (Pottery)
	Paniku	Barbers
	Panna Durayi	Probably grass cutters
	Berawa	Tom Tom beaters
	Oli	Dancers
	Pali	Laundry man for low caste
	Kinnara	Mat weavers
	Gahala Berawa	Beggars
	Kavikara	Temple Dancers / Singers

(De Silva, 1978:15-16)

The above is the caste system generally prevalent in Sri Lanka. The nominal Buddhist urbanite does not bother much or take notice of this system. However, the three denominations of Buddhism namely, Siyam, Amarapura, and Ramanna are based on caste affiliations. The Siyam Nikaya ordains only the high caste personnel, which is known as Goyigama. The Amarapura Nikaya ordains members of the non-Goyigama-castes; and Ramanaya Nikaya enrols the low castes as well. Though these are the three main denominations, they are subject to subdivisions.

In the village setting, temples are mainly established according to the denomination relevant to the particular caste living in that village. The Buddhist priests who are the leaders of such temples strictly adhere to the clan of their denomination. However, the ordinary Buddhist adherent is ignorant of these caste prejudices. They may observe the religious rituals in any Buddhist temple. Nevertheless, the urban Buddhist is even less concerned about these denominational differences than is the village Buddhist.

Urban and Village Lifestyle

The temple is the main focal point of village life. However, in the city, temples are often overlooked. In urban development projects (highway construction, buildings, or infrastructure work), the project is always headed by a state minister or parliamentarian of that particular district, religious dignitaries, or people of high standing. However, in a rural area, prominence is always given to the high priest of the local village temple.

It is also a general practice that generations of village folks live closely knitted to each other living on their own land in a cluster and there is always unity prevalent among their clan. However, when an outsider settles down among them they are treated as aliens. If he belongs to a different clan, caste, creed, or religion from the village, he would be subjected to humiliation and ridicule. This also happens when anyone from the family group or a relative chooses to follow a different religious faith. He or she is immediately ostracized from and condemned by their society. They are debarred from partaking in any of their festivities and functions such as weddings or funerals. But in the urban area, such attitudes are negligible as people and religious leaders live independently and follow their religious faith according to their beliefs in a spirit of mutual respect.

Marriage Rituals and Ceremonies

A village's caste, creed, and ethnic differences are seriously considered in marriage. Auspicious times and formalities follow the traditional customs. In the case of a wedding ritual in the urban area, the couple may organize their wedding in a church or hotel, which would be followed by a reception with a meal. The celebrations end on the day of the wedding itself, but it is different in the case of the village folk. The concerned parties of the bride and bridegroom prepare their marriage ceremony days ahead, arranging and decorating the venue. The preparation of sweet meats and arrangements done for cooking of meals for the invitees and participants are done at the venue itself. The wedding rituals are performed according to their tradition and they can continue for days, starting from the day of preparation until all the rituals of the wedding ceremony have been completed.

Funerals and Last Rites

An individual at his deathbed in a village is subject to chanting of *pirith* and preaching of the *Dhamma* by a Buddhist priest of the local temple. When he performs these rituals, surrounded by the householders, kith and kin, it is believed that merit is bestowed upon the dying person. Once the person dies after all these rituals, the family, neighbours, and relatives are bound to stay over in this house day and night for seven consecutive days. The corpse is in the house for two or three days before the burial or cremation. Meanwhile, the *Jataka* stories are recited for the others to hear at the funeral house. During the seven day period, the neighbours supply the meals for each day to those who are at the funeral house. Such customs are not followed in the urban area as these practices become obsolete.

The urbanite values an expensive coffin for the deceased, either for burial or cremation. They invite a high priest of the main temple along with the other Buddhist priests to recite the rituals connected with last rites. They place a condolence book for the participants' record of their condolences. Elaborate flower arrangements are made to be borne by people of stature and good standing in the society. All these things are done in order to exhibit their financial and social standings. Rituals surrounding the burial or cremation last only one day. Due to the difficulty of performing all these rituals by the urban elite at their residence, it has now become a practice for the urban Buddhists to hand over the body to the funeral undertakers. After embalming, dressing etc, they place the body in an expensive coffin as directed by the family members. Then, the body is laid in a funeral parlour for the family, relatives, neighbours, and friends to pay their last respect before the cortege is taken in a procession for either burial or cremation. During the days that the body is kept at the funeral parlour, the family members only receive visitors during the open hours of the funeral parlour. The last rights are performed by the Buddhist priests before the cortege leaves the funeral parlour for burial or cremation.

Almsgiving and *Poya*

Alms giving is an essential principle in the Buddhist culture. The rituals vary from urban to rural context. It is a custom of every Buddhist home to offer flowers, burn incense and joss sticks, light oil lamps, and spread varieties of food items to the Buddhist shrines in their homes. This is done each morning and noon. At dusk, an offering of a drink or tea at the shrine would be made. This custom is still prevalent in the rural areas. However, this trend has dwindled in the urbanite Buddhist homes except for a few elders who are old and feeble.

Buddhist Education at Temples

It is mandatory for every young Buddhist child to attend the *Daham Pasala* (Sunday school) at their respective Buddhist temples. These children are taught all about the teaching of the Buddha either by the chief incumbent Buddhist priest or by an appointed layman for this purpose; this is very evident among the rural children. But in the urban area, most of the children do not follow this practice; instead these children are busy following private tuition classes to better their educational studies. To arrest the preference among urban children for private tuition classes over the *Daham Pasala* at the Temples, the state is contemplating and is in the process of eradicating private tutorials which conduct tuition classes on Sundays.

Bodhi Pooja and Pirith Ceremony

It has been a traditional practice for both the rural and urban Buddhists to conduct these rituals. The word *Pirith* is *piritta* in the Pali language.

In Sanskrit *Parittra* or *Parittrana* derives the meaning protection or safety. *Pirith* or *parittrana* is a collection of certain Buddhist texts which are recited on special occasions to ward off any evil effect, illness, or danger. It is, therefore, one of the foremost ceremonies of great significance in the domestic and social life of the urban people. It is also a traditional custom among the Sinhala Buddhists that no house warming and other ceremonies, social functions, and religious festivities are held without chanting *pirith*. It is also a belief among the Buddhists that chanting of *Pirith* would certainly ward off any evil spells or terminal illnesses encountered by Buddhists. It is a custom that *seth pirith* is chanted before embarking on any new projects, employment, or business etc. to confer merit for the success of those ventures. Further, *Seth Pirith* is organized and chanted to confer merits on the heads of the state: the President, the Prime Minister, Ministers and Parliamentarians and also on heads of state institutions and organizations. The chanting of the *seth pirith* on all such instances are organized in an elaborate and grand way by specially invited recognized Buddhist Priests from Buddhist temples.

In contemporary society, *seth pirith* is given high prominence and popularity among the Sinhala Buddhist citizens of this country. When our national cricket team embarks on a foreign tour for playing a game against another country outside Sri Lanka, the players and team members are gathered in a special enclosure at the airport. The Buddhist priests then chant *seth pirith* and tie the *pirith* thread on each one's wrist before they emplane for their destination.

Almost all Sinhala Buddhists of the older generation believe in the safety that is supposed to lie in chanting *seth pirith* which are in the Pali language. They impart these teachings to their offspring and make them recite these stanzas in the morning and at night before they go to bed. It is also a customary procedure that the *seth pirith* is aired and broadcasted each morning before the commencement of the day's programmes by the Broadcasting stations and again at the close of transmission in the evening.

The Bo-Tree is very sacred to the Buddhist. It is venerated by the Buddhists in every part of the Sri Lanka. A Bo-tree is planted and nurtured in every Buddhist temple. There is always a four tiered half-built wall around the Bo-tree. There is a pedestal at the top to facilitate the offering of flowers, burning of incense, joss sticks, and oil lamps and to set out varieties of fruits and also to hoist relevant flags. The adherents gather around this Bo-tree for worship, recite the Pali stanzas, *Bodhi Puja kavi, seth kavi* and *seth geethika* to ward off any malefic influence of the evil spirits and astrological influences.

Though the *Bodhi Puja* was a religious ritual given much veneration by the rural Buddhists, it is now less evident in the lives of urban dwellers. Today, it is considered as a business concern and given much publicity with the aim of material gain in order to draw a crowd. Prominent Buddhist priests from recognized temples are brought to boost the image of the *Bodhi Puja*. The elite urban Buddhists in such instances contribute large sums of money to the organizers to conduct the *Bodhi Puja* on an elaborate scale to bestow merit on the donor, without being physically present. These *Bodhi Pujas* are conducted to bestow merit on the nominee in evening meetings that run for a period of three days, seven days or twenty-one days. The purpose of conducting *Bodhi Puja* has many significant features, such as healing of the sick and infirm, freedom from evil spirits, success in exams, interviews for employment, marriages, in legal litigations, for peace in the family and so on. Politicians also chant *seth pirith* to gain entry to the legislature. In the conduct of *Bodhi Pujas* the urban Buddhist focuses the chanting on personal needs which vary according to their circumstances.

Superstition Among the Urban Buddhist

The beliefs and the customs of the Buddhist religion prevailing today among the Sinhala Buddhists in the 21st century is certainly not derived from the ancient concept of Buddhist principles, but has changed following societal changes and current trends in the lifestyle of the present day Sinhala Buddhist society. However superstition still prevails among urban Buddhists as they classify reasons for each category of illness, sufferings, misfortunes, disease, and evil spells according to their beliefs. The superstitious beliefs in demonic possession, the perception of evil spirit manifestations in the day to day life of these people, can easily be observed in their behavioural patterns. The exorcism of demons is a part of their daily lifestyle, not only among the rural folk, but also among the urban Buddhists living in the southern and western coastal areas of Sri Lanka.

The rituals are specifically directed at the removal and destruction of illness-causing demons and ghosts. These rituals are a combination of Hindu and Buddhist beliefs and practices. The Sinhala Buddhist has a strong belief in the maleficent affects of someone with an "evil eye" and curses by word or thought. They also believe that one's evil thoughts against someone can cause marital breakdown, general family discord, failure of business, loss of property, and wealth. This is common belief among the Sinhala Buddhists in Sri Lanka.

Conclusion

Asians have a strong belief that Sri Lanka is predominantly a Sinhala Buddhist Nation, practicing pure Buddhism. But folk Buddhism, not doctrinal Buddhism, is how Buddhism is practiced in Sri Lanka. Urban Sinhala Buddhists are totally independent; they enjoy freedom in every aspect of their lives and are prosperous in all their endeavours in the sphere of education, employment, business, and social activities. They are open to beliefs of others, giving due respect and reverence to the religious faith of their neighbours. Urban Buddhists live in a society made up of various castes, creeds, religions, and social strata. Therefore, they seldom observe any kind of extremism towards other religious faiths due to their openness in living among a mixed society.

There has been a vast development in understanding between the various religious leaders today. The Buddhist prelate, Catholic and Christian clergy, Hindu priest and the imam of the Muslim faith, may gather together on the same platform on ceremonial and social events, illustrating a new willingness to co-exist together as religious faiths.

Further there is harmony prevailing today among the various religions in urban areas. The Buddhist temples, Catholic and Christian churches, Hindu Kovils, and the Muslim mosques are all located in close proximity to each other. The adherents of each faith go about with their religious activities without any hindrance, objection, or persecution. This shows how, in urban areas, there is a peaceful co-existence with other religions that is not prevalent among the rural Buddhists. In the rural village only the Buddhist Temple is given prominence and the other religious faiths face persecution or are not welcome among their midst.

1) How should the Gospel sound in the ear of the Buddhist?
2) How should the church be seen by the Buddhist?

It is the main intention of the Christian to know the worldview of the neighbour in order to communicate the Gospel effectively. It is essential to understand the beliefs, practices, and life style of the people around the church. Therefore, a familiarity with Buddhist social practices in the urban environment would enhance the capacity of evangelism among them.

The present day believer and the new converts, instead of winning others to Christ, tend to utilize their belief and knowledge gained in the Buddhist culture to ridicule Buddhists instead of drawing them to the Gospel. Believers should show the love of God and witness through their life to others, so that they can see Christ and find transformation. It has already been proven that a Buddhist cannot be won to Christ through debates, arguments, or contests. Today, the Buddhist is rejected by Christian who state that Buddhists belong to the devil.

Once a person in the Buddhist culture is saved and accepts the Lord as their personal Savior, there is always a rejection of that person by their family members and relatives. Also, when unwarranted statements are made that the family members who are not saved are demon possessed and living in total darkness, it distances them from their relatives and causes pain of heart. Such a situation not only creates dissension, it also keeps them from accepting the gospel. Some believers are under the impression that reading other religious books and materials is sinful. This is a wrong impression. Actually, reading and gathering knowledge about other religions enhances the believer's ability to talk with them and share the Gospel.

Believers in Christ should have a change of attitude in dealing with the Buddhist adherents. They should not confront them, but rather make the Gospel accessible. We should avoid saying our religion is better, that we are in light and they are in darkness or that they are practicing devil worship. This creates barriers rather than bridges of relationship. Our life and conduct should be like that of the Lord, who loved you and me, and the Gospel should be the message of everlasting life in God's presence to the unsaved Buddhist.

Though Buddhist adherents draw inner strength from belief in their precepts, they also are inclined to various deities. They look to these deities for their protection, progress, and success in all their endeavours. One must really know and understand their beliefs to avoid any religious controversy or confrontations, and the believer must be prepared and ready to proclaim the true, one and only living God.

CHAPTER FIVE

Addressing the Challenge of Reaching the Neo-Buddhists in Urban India

J.N. MANOKARAN

Reaching Neo-Buddhists in urban India is a complex of several interwoven issues. Social factors in villages provide impetus for migration from villages to cities. Urbanization brings its own set of additional problems. The caste system brings a set of social problems which will be explained further in this paper. Economic empowerment through education and employment in the cities bring in other challenges to understanding Neo-Buddhists.

It is also important to understand that there are at least two major groups of Neo-Buddhists in Indian cities. The first is the poor urban migrant and the second is the urban elite. Even among the poorest urban migrants, the second generation is better educated and economically well off than those in the rural areas. Reaching all of them with the gospel and making them disciples of the Lord Jesus Christ is a real challenge.

In spite of these many challenges reaching urban Neo-Buddhists is excitingly fruitful in many cities in India. This is especially true in the state of Maharashtra, as well as some cities in Gujarat. The reasons for this positive response relate to the social, political, and economic aspirations of the people. Economic empowerment provides deliverance from the shackles of the caste system especially in the cities. As migrants minds are opened, people are willing to move from one faith to another.

Understanding Neo-Buddhism is not possible without grasping the context of Indian society. Unlike western society where social equality is at least a value if not a total reality, in India the caste classification plays a very key role. Understanding the caste system, as sanctioned in the scriptures of Hinduism, will help in understanding the context of Indian Neo-Buddhism.

Understanding the Caste System

Indian society is riddled with the caste system. Kanch Illiah writes how the Hindu scriptures describe the layers of hierarchy of the caste system:

> Krishna in the Bhagwat Gita elaborates that Brahmins must stand for serenity, self control, austerity, purity, forbearance, righteousness, faith, knowledge and realization. The Kshatriyas must stand for heroism, boldness, firmness, bravery, steadfastness on the battlefield, generosity and lordliness. The Vaishyas must do the duty of agriculture, cattle rearing and trade. Work in the nature of service (to the above three castes) is the duty of "others"—that is, the modern Dalit-Bahujans (2004:7).

These layers are merely broad classifications and each has within it several sub-castes or clans. Ambedkar described the caste system as, "an ascending scale of hatred and a descending scale of contempt" (Luce 2006:14). Nobel Prize winner Amartya Sen writes, "India has a terrible record in social asymmetry of which the caste system is only one reflection" (2005:34). Discrimination, oppression, and exploitation are results of the rigid caste system.

New Mass Movements Towards Buddhism

Quite unexpectedly from the middle of the present century large numbers of untouchable Hindus, mostly Mahars and Jatavs (or Chamars), started converting to Buddhism. Their numbers grew rapidly in the decade from 1951 to 1961 when the number of Indian Buddhists increased by 1,670 percent. By 1991, India had about six million Buddhists, the great majority of these being Neo-Buddhists living in or near Maharashtra. In that state, Neo-Buddhists are now more numerous than Muslims or Christian converts (everyculture.com/South-Asia/Neo-Buddhist.html. Accessed 1 July 2007). This shows the higher aspirations of Dalits. They opt for Neo-Buddhism since social and political workers communicate that it is a native religion that has "messianic" hope. Dalits also continue to receive government-sponsored affirmative action benefits such as a quota of faculty seats in educational institutions, scholarships in schools, and quotas in government employment if they convert to Buddhism. If a Dalit chooses to follow Christianity or Islam however, all these benefits are lost. It may be not legal to deny the positive affirmation or reservation for the Dalit Christians as they are also socially oppressed and economically poor. The representation in the Courts has not been fruitful to get justice for the new Christians from Dalit background. The argument provided by the opponents is that religions like Islam and Christianity do not believe in caste system, so after conversion a Dalit does not remain Dalit but just a Christian and there is no Dalit Christian.

According to the 2001 census, there are currently 7.95 million Buddhists in India, of which at least 5.83 million are in Maharashtra. This makes Buddhism the fifth-largest religion in India and six percent of the population of Maharashtra, but less than one percent of the overall population (answers.com/topic/dalit-buddhist-movement. Accessed 1 July 2007).

Who Are the Neo-Buddhists?

Though the Indian sub-continent is the home of Buddhism, today Buddhists are a small minority. In ancient days, Buddhism dominated the region from Afghanistan to many countries in East Asia. In India, Hinduism fought against the domination of Buddhism and gradually defeated it. Hinduism fought Buddhism at different levels. First, the Brahmins adopted vegetarianism to take moral high ground over Buddhism that taught *ahimsa,* non-violence. Second, Buddha was declared as one of the several Hindu *avatars* (incarnations) of God.

Dr. B.R. Ambedkar was born in a family belonging to the Mahar caste, which occupies the lower rung of social hierarchy in Hinduism. He was trained as a lawyer and wanted to uplift his people from the oppression and exploitation of higher caste people. As a social reformer, thinker, and political activist, he discovered that the empowerment of the oppressed classes was impossible within Hinduism. Though he was born a Hindu, he declared that he would not die a Hindu, and sought various options out of Hinduism. After considering many religious faiths as well as communist ideology, he decided to convert to Buddhism. He viewed Buddhism as a more appropriate avenue for social empowerment of the downtrodden masses. He himself converted to Buddhism on 14 October 1956 along with his followers, estimated at 380,000. After his death, the movement was hindered but continued in many villages. Among many Dalits his ideology is still revered. Many Dalit activists favor conversion to Buddhism while others favor conversion to any religion including Christianity and Islam.

Hindutva is a fundamentalist right wing political Hindu ideology against this. It worships motherland as sacred and brands all who follow "foreign" faiths like Islam and Christianity as "traitors" and objects of hate. This ideology is spreading in several places. Though it professes to treat all Hindus including Dalits as equals, for all practical purposes it actually perpetuates discrimination. Even backward caste leaders within the Hindutva bandwagon are marginalized as happened to Uma Bharati and Kalyan Singh, former Chief Ministers of Madhya Pradesh and Uttar Pradesh respectively.

Dalits influenced by Ambedkar ideology in Uttar Pradesh, Haryana, Gujarat, and other places are turning to Buddhism. In dozens of villages across Uttar Pradesh, Dalits have stopped depending on Brahmin priests for weddings, funerals, and other ceremonies. Instead, they have turned to a Buddhism-inspired book which has rituals that can be performed by any literate person. In contrast, Christian priesthood has strict prohibitions against laity. Due to education, only the elite can attain that status. The wide use of the Neo-Buddhism's *Bhim Putra*, named after Bhimrao Ambedkar, is part of a quiet rebellion against upper caste domination. Weddings are performed before the statue of Ambedkar. The ceremony is inexpensive and takes only a couple of hours. The bride and the groom light candles, take wedding vows, and garland each other. Hindu priests are feeling the effects as many Dalits have stopped coming to them (Misra 2006:1). As any religion has classical, popular, and folk versions; this is considered the lowest or folk version in the hierarchy of Buddhism.

"In this modern democratic phase of Indian society two things become central for the exercise of the right to religion. One, the right to priesthood and second, the right to communicate with the divine in one's own mother tongue" (Illiah 2004:103). The right to priesthood or spiritual democracy comes into operation in Buddhism. Educated Dalits are thrilled to use this privilege and consider their whole community deserving of dignity. While most of the puja or worship is done in Sanskrit language (considered sacred), in Buddhism common languages like Hindi are used for worship. I refer to this as "Democratization" of worship language, a great attraction for Dalits. What I mean by this is that anyone can now pray and worship in their own heart language.

Recent Example of Mass Movements Towards Buddhism

The impact of Ambedkar's bold decision to quit Hinduism and embrace Buddhism became a watermark in the history of the Dalits. They consider this as a heroic act and wish to follow the same path. Since then, many leaders have lead people to convert to Buddhism.

Upara, a book originally written by Laxman Mane in Marathi, has influenced Dalits and other oppressed castes in Maharastra. Many of them converted to Buddhism. This book received the prestigious Sahitya Academy Award for literature. Mane was just thirty-one years old when he was recognized, one of the youngest authors to receive this coveted award.

Born in a poor, low caste family, Mane used to travel with his parents to several villages to find work as laborers, sometimes begging for food. Since they were landless, they had to be nomadic in order to survive. During his childhood, he suffered humiliation at the hands of upper caste people. His parents wanted to make him a "master"—meaning a teacher and sent him to school. He did well and found favor in the eyes of his teachers and friends and was able to graduate. He got married to a high caste girl and both sets of parents boycotted him for doing so. He again went through harassment along with his wife. Later, with education, economic mobility, and wider recognition he has been accepted not only by his family but by all oppressed classes.

In October 2006, Mane took the "Deeksha," the official ceremony of initiation to Buddhism. On that day an estimated 100,000, most of whom were tribals and followers of Mane, converted to Buddhism in the city of Mumbai (Prachi Pinglay, *One Lakh People Convert to Buddhism.* hindu. com/2007/05/28/stories/2007052806851200.htm. Accessed 28 May 2007). About 400,000 people attended the function. Newspapers reported it as a revolution in the lives of many tribals and Dalits. Mane said, "Thousands of people from forty-two different nomadic tribes have embraced Buddhism." He said tribals did not follow Hinduism and so the event could not be termed a move away from Hinduism. Tribals claim that they are animists or nature worshippers and cannot be described as Hindus.

Why Do They Move to Buddhism?

It is essential to understand the many reasons for the move of people from one religion to other especially from Hinduism to Buddhism. Not only have they moved from one religion to the other, they have moves from villages to cities. "Migration and Urbanization like proverbial Siamese twins cannot be separated. Migration is an important feature in the process of urbanization" (Manokaran 2005:167).

There are various "push" factors and "pull" factors that determine the migration of people. Push factors are unfavorable circumstances in the village, that push people out of rural environments into urban centers. They could be social, economic, political and even displacement due to development (like mega dam projects) and natural disasters. The attractiveness of the city, with glamorous lifestyle promoted by media, aspirations, hopes and economic prosperity are pull factors towards the city.

Oppression

The caste system is very rigid. It denies a person any upward social mobility. There is no possibility of horizontal mobility either as people from a particular caste are allowed only one particular job. For example, if one is born in a family of barbers (*nai* is the caste name), then they can only be a barber. A young boy born in this family cannot become a potter or a fisherman. As long as a person accepts his caste, there is no possibility of any mobility. "In Hindu civil society, the full range of options in choosing a direction in life (spiritual, secular or political), is closed to all except Brahmin youth. For all others, the right to choose a spiritual profession is closed" (Illiah 2004:109). To get away from caste oppression, people have to get away from the religious system that sanctions caste social order.

Exploitation

More than fifteen million rural households in India are landless. Another forty-five million rural families own some and, less than 0.10 acre each ("Landlessness True Index for Poverty." hindu.com/2007/12/09/stories/2007120953911200.htm. Accessed 9 December 2007). These people have no other option but to work in the fields of the rich who generally belong to upper castes. According to village caste tradition, these people are expected to provide free service and be satisfied with some grains given "generously" by the landlords. If they demand more, they are thrown out of their jobs. Without any leave or benefits, they are bonded to this kind of service throughout their lives.

"In class societies, the hope of moving from ownership of skills to ownership of products to ownership of the history of production—

the material wealth of that history, or in other words, capital—is an attainable reality for the oppressed. In a caste society that hopes remains a mirage" (Illiah 2004:70).

In addition, the women in the low-caste communities are violated with impunity by upper caste men. Although they are "untouchables" and even their presence would pollute them ceremonially, they are frequently raped when alone in the fields not just out of lust but out of a desire to enforce subordination and servitude. Social stigma prevents rural women from reporting this to local authorities. Even when they report, there is not much action as the police force is generally dominated by non-Dalits. To protect themselves people migrate to urban areas where political activism and non-government organizations gives them hope, although never completely eliminate, such abuses.

Aspiration Mirage

Dr. M.N. Srinvas is an insightful anthropologist who introduced the concept of "Sanskritization." "Sanskritization is the process by which a low Hindu caste, or tribal or other group, changes its customs, ritual, ideology and way of life in the direction of a high, and frequently "twice-born," caste. Generally, such changes are followed by a claim to a higher position in the caste hierarchy than that traditionally conceded to the claimant caste by the local community" (Srinivas 2001:6). If sanskritization provides Dalits with political power, they will adopt it. Often, however, it is merely a cover for a sophisticated form of political oppression, economic exploitation and slavery.

Political Tool and Victimization

In a train accident in the city of Godhra, a few Hindus died. Muslims were blamed and there were riots in which at least two thousand Muslims were killed. The right wing political party of Hindus, used Dalits and Tribals as their foot soldiers to kill the Muslims. A

Dalit who was misdirected by the Hindu fundamentalist said, "When they need us to kill the Muslims, they ask us to shout, '*Garv se kaho hum Hindu hain!*' ['Tell with pride that we are Hindus!'] Once their dubious purpose is served, we are once again reminded that we are Dalits, the untouchables." This former Dalit has decided to convert to Buddhism in the city of Ahmedabad in Gujarat (Darshan Desai, Embracing Buddhism, countercurrents.org/dalit-desai080503.htm. Accessed 6 December 2007). Like Emperor Ashoka, who regretted of his war against Kalinga turned to Buddhism, many Dalits and tribals are turning to Buddhism in Gujarat. It is important to remember Emperor Ashoka sent out missionaries to various parts of the world to spread Buddhism and it is evident in several regions of Asia.

Conversion: The Tool of Deliverance

Historically, it was during the struggle of the Dalit-Bahujans against the Hindu order, the Brahminical system which had captured the state and used it as an instrument to impose caste ideology, that Dalit-Bahujans converted in large numbers to Buddhism, Sikhism, Islam and Christianity. These were social protest movements to gain social rights and self-respect. The whole Buddhist phenomenon in our early history was a story of Dalit-Bahujan protest. The Buddha said, "Just as various different streams flow into a river and become one, so, too, the different castes, when they come into the *sangha* [the community of the Buddhist faithful], they join the sea of colorless water." This stress on social equality is, of course, in marked contrast with Hinduism, which cannot be defined in terms of a universal religion with a universal social rights concept (*Interview with Kancha Illiah*, swaraj. org/shikshantar/resources_ilaiah.htm. Accessed 19 October 2007).

Role of Ambedkar and Laxman Mane

From a missiological perspective it is essential to evaluate the role of Ambedkar and several of his followers including Laxman Mane.

Ambedkar, from the Mahar Dalit caste in Maharashtra, rose up as an intellectual giant and legal expert. The path was not easy. Though Dalits in the early nineteenth century were not ready for a great revolution, Ambedkar wisely put his thoughts and ideas into writing. He contributed to the Indian nation as the chairman of the Drafting Committee of the Constitution. Politically he was not successful as his ideas were far ahead of his time. Though he could not trigger a liberation movement like Moses, he sowed the seeds for liberation of this oppressed caste by his writings. In his lifetime, he decided to convert to Buddhism and called his followers to do likewise. In 1956 at *Diksha Bhoomi* (a ground on which the initiation to Buddhism was held) in Nagpur he lead his followers in a mass conversion.

Did Ambedkar offer a Messianic hope or was he a prophet for his own people? His writings have continued to inspire many. There are several social and political splinter movements around the country that derive inspiration from his writings. Kanshi Ram, one of the most successful followers of Ambedkar, built a strong political party based on his philosophy and principles. He founded the *Bahujan Samaj* Party. His successor Mayawati has become the Chief Minister of Uttar Pradesh the largest state in India and has set her eyes to become Prime Minister of India. She has declared that she would convert to Buddhism when she becomes the Prime Minister. Laxman Mane, on the other hand, did not build a political movement but a socio-economic movement of liberation by using conversion to Buddhism as tool. He has succeeded in convincing over 100,000 people to perform the Buddhist act of conversion. Were these in the mould of John the Baptist preparing a way for the fuller knowledge of the truth to be revealed?

Missiological implications in understanding these (and other) leaders' roles who emerge every decade promising deliverance, upward mobility, power, peace and economic prosperity have proved to be inadequate and a mirage. If that is so, there is one great quest for deliverance in the minds of the Dalit people who represent over twenty-five percent of Indian population. Among them some have been trying to use Buddhism as an opportunity for empowerment since the 1950s. In spite of their conversion, deliverance has not happened as they had expected. They continue to look for the true Messiah. It is reported that there are more than fifty evangelistic books/booklets published in a variety of Indian languages in the last fifty years by Neo-Buddhists appealing for all Dalits to convert to Buddhism.

Neo-Buddhism is producing leaders who have charismatic appeal and gain huge numbers of followers. They are able to communicate apologetically the benefits of converting to Buddhism. With the government of India offering benefits to keep Dalits within the Hindu fold, it also provides the same benefits to those who convert to Buddhism, hence there is nothing to lose in terms of governmental social benefits through conversion. Naturally many Dalits opt for Buddhism instead of Christianity.

Will there be a large scale conversion of Dalits into Buddhism if Mayawati becomes the Prime Minister of India in 2014? Will she be in the mould of Constantine who brought Christendom in the west? This may be a hypothetical question but one that is relevant when seen from the political environment in the country. If that were to be the case, there will be huge number of Neo-Buddhists in India who will need the gospel in the next two decades.

Our Challenge

Neo-Buddhism has implications in urban centres throughout India. Historian Ramachandra Guha writes that Ambedkar was not only a scholar but a shrewd analyst. He considered the village as a sink of localism, a den of ignorance, narrow-mindedness and communalism (2007:107). The Neo-Buddhists, following his advice, migrated away from the social, religious, economic and mental oppression in the villages and moved to the cities. In cities the caste is not the primary identity but the profession so there is less social domination. In busy city life the oppressed Dalits can act as they like in their religious life. Also, they become aware of the democratic political process and the value of their vote. Seeing the positive results of the early pioneers who migrated, many more of them have started migrating into cities where they have obtained better education with a resulting upward movement in the social and economic scales.

Migrants in a new environment are more open to new ideas, including the gospel. God loves migrants and speaks to migrants. There are numerous examples in the Bible. God spoke to Jacob when he was running away from his home. Moses had encounter with God, in the Burning Bush, when he was a migrant. As migrants, Joseph, Daniel and Nehemiah rose to high levels of civil service. Ruth and Esther were also migrants.

Upper Class Neo-Buddhists

On one side poor Neo-Buddhist migrants are coming into cities. On the other hand, urban educated are also getting attracted to Buddhism. Vineetha Mokkil, journalist of Tehelka reported that a large chunk of educated urban India has discovered a lifeline in the Buddhist faith. Is this attraction a passing fad or a more intense, meaningful search? One of the strains of Buddhism, which has become very popular in India since the late 1980s is the Soka Gakkai sect. Soka Gakkai International is a Buddhist organization which has branches in most Indian cities. The Bharat Soka Gakkai has 7000 practicing members in Delhi, 2000 in Mumbai and an all-Indian membership of over 15,000. Tibetan Buddhism attracts a steady stream of followers, too. Many see Buddhist philosophy as empowering, a self-help tool, and many have turned to Buddhism at a moment of personal crisis (Mokkil 2004:30-31). This is typical of the postmodern mindset to experiment, explore, and experience anything new. With more belief in sophisticated superstitions such as Feng Sui, Vastu, charms, tattooing, and other expressions considered as post-modern spirituality, Buddhist rituals are getting wider recognition.

How Do They Come To Christ?

In cities like Nagpur, Aurangabad, Amravati in Maharastra and Surendernagar, Ahmedabad in Gujarat, many from Neo-Buddhist background have come to know Jesus Christ as Lord and Savior.

It is estimated that there are 2,000 Christians from Neo-Buddhist background in the Nagpur, Amravati and Wardha region of Maharastra (Interview with Vijay Mohod, Bharatiya Sevak Sangati, Nagpur, 27 May 2007). Speaking with them and hearing their testimony was a process of learning for me, as was the interaction with pastors in whose flocks these new disciples join to worship the Lord. Here is the list of methods God has used in the recent past to bring Neo-Buddhists into the kingdom of God: miracles, affirmation, attraction to the person of Jesus Christ, deliverance from demonic oppression, friendship evangelism, through relatives, holistic missions, counseling, and camps (Interview with Vijay Mohod, Bharatiya Sevak Sangati, Nagpur, 27 May 2007).

Miracles

Neo-Buddhists who have recently migrated from villages to cities are in a state of turmoil. Getting uprooted from a familiar place to a new overwhelming city is extremely difficult. In the new city, the lifestyle is different. In the village, water and firewood were taken for granted as available free of cost, but in the city it costs money to have water and fuel. Slums in the cities are unsanitary.

Those who live there are exposed to all kinds of diseases, and suffer from malnutrition and anemia. Going to the doctor is expensive. This is the time they turn to other sources for help. Sometimes they use traditional home medicines and look for charity hospitals. Prayer by a Christian pastor is a wonderful resource for them. Hearing through neighbors or friends, they visit churches with the hope of receiving a miracle. Many believers who attend the local churches like New Covenant Church, (Interview with Pastor Ajay Masih, New Covenant Church, Nagpur, 27 May 2007). Bharatiya Sewak Sangati in Nagpur and Indian Friends Fellowship in Aurangabad testified they received miracles of healing, deliverance from demon possession, and miraculously answered prayers (Interview with Pastor Amit Aryan, Indian Friends Fellowship, Aurangabad, 16 May 2007). When they receive the blessing of God through miracles, their faith grows and they become disciples of the Lord Jesus Christ.

Human beings always have needs. Needs are different for different sets of people. For the poor it can be physical need like healing or material need like clothing, while for the economically advantaged it can be emotional needs like a sense of belonging, or social needs for friends, or psychological needs for self-esteem. There are always needs for new poor migrants who enter the city that cannot be met by their own resources. The resources they can tap into are from government social security measures, social welfare organizations, or anyone who serves as a good Samaritan. But new migrants do not have a legal status in the city. To have a legal status, a person must be registered with the government and receive a "ration" or "family" card. With so many hurdles, new migrants are looking for help. Social welfare organizations also have their own set of pre-conditions. Access to good Samaritans is not always predictable. In this context, independent church pastors should be available to pray, counsel, and offer practical help. During counseling sessions, they may offer hope and give testimonies of God's work in the lives of others in similar circumstances. New migrants become new seekers whose faith is aroused. The fervent sincere prayer of faith works miracles. Such miracles help them to take the next step of deciding to follow the Lord Jesus Christ.

Affirmation: A Sense of Respect and Belonging

An auto-rickshaw driver was carrying a southern Indian missionary in Gujarat, west India as a passenger in his vehicle. Unlike most, this particular vehicle did not have pictures of gods or goddesses but just a slogan, *Prabhu Krupa* ("Mercy of Lord" in Hindi). The missionary started a conversation with the driver based on this slogan. Finding the conversation interesting, the driver invited the missionary to his home for further discussion. The missionary and his wife went to the driver's simple home that same evening. The house did not have an extra room or any other special facilities to accommodate the guests. The man, a Neo-Buddhist convert from a Dalit background, served them dinner and requested they stay overnight as his guests, to which the missionary couple readily agreed. The rickshaw driver was so impressed by this unconditional acceptance that he wanted to become a follower of the Lord Jesus Christ. The simple gesture of a missionary of accepting hospitality had great impact upon this man. He said, "Pastors ask us to come to church on Sundays, other times they do not seem to want us. Politicians come to get our votes during elections, other times we are not needed. Hindu priests come to offer puja and take away our money, but I was looking for someone who would really respect us, who would treat us with dignity and seek our welfare."

People in urban contexts lose the human touch. They lose a sense of belonging. The gospel brings back fellowship, intimacy, and a sense of belonging. The principle of incarnation modeled by the Lord Jesus Christ is a relevant missionary method even today. The missionary in this incident, though well-educated, was willing to engage with a less-educated blue collar worker. When invited to his home, he went with his wife showing genuine interest and love. Without hesitation, they ate the food offered by a person from an "untouchable" caste. Inter-dining is anathema in both rural and urban contexts in India. Staying in an "untouchable" home is unthinkable; members of other castes would never do this. Even politicians who ask for votes will never drink water with or enter the homes of the untouchable. Here the love of Christ was practically demonstrated and the auto-ricksaw driver was accepted without any conditions. This open minded missionary opened the mind of the Neo-Buddhist seeker to become a follower of the Lord Jesus Christ. Until people accept the missionary messengers, they will not accept Christ. Today there are about twenty-five families who have come to Christ in this suburban location in the past year because of this.

Attraction to the Person of Jesus Christ

Some Neo-Buddhists are attracted to the person, the life and the ministry of Jesus Christ. Luke's gospel is attractive for them. Christ's ministry to the marginalized, the downtrodden, and to women is attractive to these people. Sharad was a daily wage earner living in the city of Aurangabad in Maharastra. His father was framed and kicked out of his job. The family went through severe hardships. Sharad could not trust anyone and thought that the whole of humanity was not trustworthy. When he heard about the Lord Jesus Christ, his personality attracted him. Now, he is member of the Indian Friends Fellowship church in Aurangabad.

As the personality of Christ is taught to these young people, it becomes a challenge and an attraction. They tend to compare the personality of Jesus with the various personalities they know in their own communities. First, they compare Christ as the self-giving God with other gods and goddesses where expensive rituals are routinely followed. Second, they compare Christ with the priests who do not interact with them but are interested in taking their money by offering so-called spiritual services during special occasions like the birth of a baby or a marriage. Third, they compare Christ with leaders in society who try to keep a distance from them. The Lord Jesus Christ was willing to receive water from the "untouchable" Samaritan woman in John's gospel. He was also known as a "Friend of Sinners," a friend of the downtrodden, the marginalized, the poor, the ostracized like Zacchaeus, sinners such as commercial sex workers, and even the sick such as the lepers.

Deliverance from Demonic Oppression

Witchcraft and demon possession are very common problems among the poor and illiterate communities such as the Neo-Buddhists in India. Since they are poor, they have aspirations to move up the economic ladder. But when one person moves up using the props of education or hard work, he becomes the victim of envy from friends and relatives.

Like proverbial Indian crabs that do not allow any others to scale up and escape, these people try to pull down any others who are trying to move up. To accomplish this proverbial pulling down various methods are used, and one being employing those who practice black magic or witchcraft. People who perceive they are affected by witchcraft try to counter it by going to another more powerful magician, provided they can afford the cost. If not, they look for alternative solutions. In some instances where Christians lived among them, they have suggested a solution through prayer and a visit to the local church. Some have willingly explored this option.

The poor, including Neo-Buddhists, bear many hardships in life. Bitterness through experiences such as the loss of dignity, loss of employment, illness, accidents, internal strife, and the general uprootedness of life in the city all contribute to a sense of hopelessness. They become depressed. Women who face domestic violence along with the brunt of all other hardships also become depressed. This depression can be exploited by evil spirits. It opens them to demonic possession or mental health problems. They may have no discernment to understand or handle this problem. Generally, they visit "gurus" who claim to have power. Most of the time, solutions offered by gurus is expensive and not effective. Some try and come to the church. Some pastors have a gift endowed by the Holy Spirit to deliver such people and there a numerous stories of such deliverances experienced by Neo-Buddhists.

Friendship Evangelism

One church planter goes to the gym to make friends among young people in the city of Aurangabad. Here he met several Neo-Buddhist young people such as Praveen, an M.B.A. student. His genuine friendship and willingness to help has attracted some college youth to Christ, who are now disciples of the Lord Jesus including Praveen (Interview with Parveen, Aurangabad, 16 May 2007).

Young Neo-Buddhists often migrate alone to cities to study, and stay in hostels or with their families living in low income neighborhoods. If they study in government colleges and stay in government-run hostels they can avail themselves of government scholarship funds. Generally, these students are looked down upon by other students as they are considered "untouchable". There is an unwritten law of discrimination in Indian educational institutions. All India Institute of Medical Sciences is one of the premier institutions in India. Namrata Biji Ahuja reports that the Scheduled Caste and Scheduled Tribe (SC/ST) students at the All-India Institute of Medical Sciences (AIIMS) face the worst forms of discrimination. These students allege they are physically tortured, segregated, and subjected to other forms of discrimination in the hostels, and the classrooms of the country's premier medical institute. The SC/ST students claim that they have been "ghettoized" in the hostel where students from the general category refuse to even share a corridor with them. The private mess at the AIIMS hostel has allegedly banned the entry of SC/ST students. According to their claims, discrimination has entered the classroom as well.

They say that AIIMS faculty members insist upon knowing the caste and background of students during the MBBS examinations. Untouchability is a term used to define an ancient practice, now illegal, wherein people refuse to interact with others on the basis of caste (Namrata Biji Ahuja, *AIIMS dalits are treated as 'untouchables'* asianage.com/presentation/leftnavigation/news/top-story/aiims-dalits-are-treated-as-'untouchables'.aspx. Accessed on 11 May 2007). When such young students are discriminated against they look for friendship outside the student body. At times they get into groups of friends who lead them into drug addiction, alcoholism, extremist movements or ultra political movements. When Christians offer the hand of friendship they are willing to listen to them.

The gospel is generally communicated through relationships and genuine friendship is a good channel to do this. Pastor Amit Aryan takes proactive steps to reach out to students who are discriminated against and long for friendship by going to a gym. Some Neo-Buddhist students are there to tone up their bodies in order to take physical revenge against the humiliation and discrimination they have encountered in their educational institutions or hostels.

Through Relatives

Neo-Buddhists who are migrants in the cities are a close-knit community. They maintain good family relationships and interact with one another. Many Neo-Buddhists came to the Lord through the witness of their relatives—brothers, sisters, uncles, and aunts. Neetha is an Engineer who lives in Aurangabad. Her sister was married and lived far away in Uttar Pradesh where she was sick and was healed by the prayer of a pastor. Through her Neetha came to believe in the Lord Jesus Christ and attends the church in Aurangabad.

People live in India as close knit groups. The relationship within family and clan is valued. For example, from the Indian perspective even marriage is not considered as covenant between two individuals (bride and bridegroom), but it is an alliance between two families. There is a practice of marrying within the kith and kin so that inheritance, property, and assets do not get out of family control. Testimonies of Christians to their relatives are powerful to bring people into the kingdom of God. Many Neo-Buddhists observe the transformation of those who have come to Christ and want to know the secret of the change. That means the message does not come from an outsider who could be suspected but by their own flesh and blood who can be trusted. A biblical illustration of this is from John 4 where our Lord did not knock on each door in the Samaritan village to proclaim that he was the Messiah but he let the Samaritan woman, who had the relational and communication channels do the job, which was done remarkably well. The people in that village came to Christ just to verify the facts and accepted the Lord Jesus' claims.

Holistic Missions—Tuition Centers

One young Christian man runs a tuition (for minimal fee and also free instruction) center for those who are preparing for competitive exams to get admissions in the best institutions or jobs in the city of Nagpur. Here many aspiring youngsters who wish to become bureaucrats in the government or management professionals come for coaching. They are trained in personality development, grooming, leadership skills, study skills etc. In this course, the local pastor, Ajay Masih of New Covenant Church in Nagpur, teaches leadership skills. He always shares Christ's model of leadership and presents the gospel. At least three engineers who attended the coaching classes came to the Lord and are part of a local church.

It has become a trend in AIIMS that SC/ST students get lower marks than the general category students because they lack English proficiency (Namrata Biji Ahuja, *AIIMS Dalits are Treated as 'Untouchables.'* asianage.com/presentation/ leftnavigation/news/ top-story/aiims-dalits-are-treated-as-'untouchables'.aspx). Accessed on 11 May 2007. Of the 822 resumes that an IT major received from engineering students, only six were selected. The rest were rejected not because of their lack of technical skills, but because they were found wanting in English (*English Stumps Engineering Students.* timesofindia. indiatimes.com/articleshow/1518501.cms. Accessed 7 May 2006).

English language proficiency is an essential requirement for jobs and higher education in Urban India. Neo-Buddhist youth attain admission to institutions of higher education through hard work and scholarship, but they often do not succeed due to lack of English language proficiency. When the church steps in to provide private tutoring for such students, the students are willing to consider the claims of Christ. Not only college students need this help in English but younger ones also.

In Gujarat, The Transformation Movement (TTM), a Protestant para-church mission agency, runs "Transformation Centers" for children. Here they learn English along with few other subjects like mathematics and science. TTM provides supplemental education for children. Children are not only taught the school lessons, but also English conversation, hygiene, moral stories and Christian songs. These children are open doors into their families. Through this the gospel is reaching Neo-Buddhists in the city of Surendernagar.

Counseling

Neo-Buddhism does not profess a belief in God. Even the educated among them get confused when they see family members influenced by demon possession and other spiritual influences. Since Buddhism denies the existence of spirits, they do not find explanations for issues such as demon possession and witchcraft. When they start asking questions, a local pastor (if he or she is wise and patient), may counsel them through the Bible to help them to know Christ.

Normal questions that educated Neo-Buddhist young people ask are in regards to identity, destiny, and the meaning of life. The issue of identity is paramount in their lives. Change of identity from Dalit to Neo-Buddhist may provide a new perception of the world, but there is no inner transformation. The social status improves a little but inner peace, the confidence that is in Christ, is missing. The question of life after death also bothers these people. Especially when they lose their beloved parents or a brothers or a sister, they ask this question. Changing to a new faith is not our purpose in life, though it might seem that way before conversion to Christ. Neo-Buddhism does not offer them meaning in life.

Apart from this, they have problems coping with the stress and pressures that are part of urban life. With an ingrained inferiority complex and unknown fears, they find it difficult to face the world even though they are educated. Pentecostal pastors affirm that the power of the Holy Spirit could give them the courage and the wisdom to face the world.

Camps

Bharati Sewa Sangati of Nagpur conducts summer camps for youth in the nearby hill station of Chikaldara. Neo-Buddhist youngsters from poor backgrounds do not have the luxury of going on picnics or excursions. When invited by Christian friends to come to a free camp, they willingly attend. The camp is designed so that believers are intentionally grouped with unbelievers to give opportunity for relationship building and sharing the gospel. During the three days of camp programs include personality development, general knowledge quizzes, cultural events, sports, and spiritual components. Each year two bus loads of young people (around 100 youngsters) go to these camps. Approximately sixty percent are Christian and the rest non-Christian. About fifteen to twenty accept the Lord Jesus Christ through these camps each year. (As told by Vijay Mohod, 27 May 2007).

Praful Gaddalwar was one such young man who was attracted to the camp (Interview with Praful Gaddalwar, Aurangabad, 15 November 2007). He went to camp because it was the best picnic he could have in his life. Missing this opportunity means missing a once-in-a-lifetime opportunity. At camp, he committed his life to Christ. Today he is serving as a church planter in Chandrapur district in Maharashtra.

The Unreached Elite Neo-Buddhists

As mentioned earlier there are two types of Neo-Buddhists, those from outcaste background, and those from upper castes who are usually well-educated. Educated people in certain cities are turning to Buddhism in a number of Indian cities. This elite group is attracted to Buddhism through the philosophical discourses promoted by the Dalai Lama, leader of the government of Tibet in exile based in Dharmasala, Himachal Pradesh, India. As far as I am aware, no attempt to reach this people group for Christ has been reported. Perhaps it is because they are not in huge numbers that they are not being targeted but this is an area that needs to be further explored.

Spiritual Or Social Quest?

Neo-Buddhists from oppressed castes have a deep desire for deliverance. For them, this is primarily a social aspiration rather than spiritual. They are seeking a new identity that gives them dignity and honor. This is impossible within the context of Hinduism, where the caste system is upheld and sanctioned by religious texts. They are seeking a Messianic faith to release them from the slavery of the caste system. Historically, they have three options for change: Christianity, Islam, and Buddhism. In most cases they have opted for Buddhism since it is of Indian origin and they do not loose benefits from the government. Islam and Christianity are generally rejected as being foreign religions.

Due to media propaganda by Hindu militant organizations, Christianity is perceived as a western religion and therefore not an attractive option for Neo-Buddhists. Another reason it is not attractive is the widespread denominational divisions found within Christianity. Oppressed people who have experienced discrimination perceive denominations as another form of the caste system which they abhor. Also, the forms, the language, the instruments of Christian worship are sometimes understood as propagating western culture.

On the part of many Neo-Buddhists, there is a great economic quest in their minds. Living without land ownership or any assets, they depended upon the upper castes for subsistence and survival. They desire to break this bondage through living in urban areas. They need new skills to survive in the cash economy that operates in cities. Buddhism fails to offer this. For some, education has helped them to come up in life. Education is from government schools and colleges and not from Buddhist institutions. In this context, the Christians' offer of education through schools and practical help like English language proficiency training attracts them to Christ.

Another aspiration of the Neo-Buddhist is the sense of belonging. Buddhism does not offer this, though it professes to. Congregational worship in Buddhism is attractive because all sit at the same level on the ground. But the interaction between people does not change as dramatically as a Neo-Buddhist would expect. It is not a dynamic relationship but a cold relationship. There is no genuine love, regard, or mutual help. In the local church, it is different. The dynamic relationship within the church as covenant community is transformational power. Group orientation becomes really dynamic within the church and has great potential for mutual growth.

With the electoral win of Mayawati as Chief Minister of Uttar Pradesh, there is growing sense of political aspiration among the Dalits and among Neo-Buddhists. Some Neo-Buddhists dream of the golden age under Ashoka, the first Buddhist Emperor of India who spread Buddhism to several east Asian countries by sending out Buddhist missionaries. With the expectation of Mayawati becoming Prime Minister of India and then converting to Buddhism, the religion has gained a higher political status. She had declared that she would become a Buddhist along with her party followers once she takes charge as Prime Minister and has been following Buddhist customs and rituals even now (*Mayawati to Embrace Buddhism.* hindu.com/2006/10/17/stories/2006101705021200.htm. Accessed 29 December 2007). Will this mean that a majority of Dalits will convert to Buddhism as in the time of Constantine when masses converted to Christianity? Will the 150 million Dalits and 100 million tribals mass migrate to Buddhism? Will it become increasingly difficult to reach Neo-Buddhists in the future?

According to Vijay Mohod, leader of Frontline Pastors Fellowship of Nagpur, there are fifty pastors from Neo-Buddhist background working in the district of Nagpur. This shows that Neo-Buddhists are very responsive to the gospel and they are coming into the Kingdom of God in large numbers. There is a rapid growth of churches among them. It would be wise to accelerate this process as a church planting movement in cities where there is a considerable concentration of Neo-Buddhists in India.

It is high time for the Church in India to strategically focus on reaching Neo-Buddhists living in the cities. They are generally open, willing to listen, and want to change their destiny. Evangelism combined with social and economic empowerment of these people will bring great rewards. There are several models and methods that have proven successful and could be adopted more widely to bring large number of Neo-Buddhists into the kingdom of God.

It is God's time. The people are ready and open to the gospel. There are a number of passionate young people willing to share the gospel to this community, and in the future they are going to be strategic as they are nearer to political power structures in India. As the Spirit of God moves among them, let us be sensitive to his voice and share His love with these people in need.

CHAPTER SIX

The Urbanization of Buddhism in Sri Lanka and its Impact on the Christian Church

G.P.V. SOMARATNA

Our attention in this article will be confined to the nineteenth and twentieth centuries in Sri Lanka as it was the period of Buddhist resurgence. Urbanization and modernization of Buddhism went hand in hand in this period. The facts dealt with in this paper will be on the rise of Buddhist urban culture in that period and its impact on Christianity.

Christianity, Roman Catholic and Protestant, came to the island with the three colonial powers, Portugal, Holland and Great Britain who had control over parts of Sri Lanka. The British gained control over the whole island from 1815. Roman Catholicism with the Portuguese, Calvinism with the Dutch, and Anglicanism under the British were religions of prestige and authority as they were the official brands of the religion of the day.

The Roman Catholics and the Protestants in Sri Lanka composed about a tenth of the population during the period of British rule (1796-1948) and continued so until the early years after independence. This was a very significant proportion of the total population compared to the rest of South Asia. Nine-tenths of the Sri Lankan Christians were Roman Catholics. The Protestant Christians in particular were a privileged group with a larger number of persons of elite status than any other religious group in the country.

Buddhism in Sri Lanka is primarily of the Theravada school, and constitutes the religious faith of about 70% of the population. Sri Lanka has a long and continuous history of Buddhism. The Sangha has existed in a largely unbroken lineage from its introduction in the 3rd century B.C. During the colonial period since the sixteenth century, Buddhism underwent suppression and decline. Under the Portuguese and Dutch, Christians were treated as a privileged group, but severe restrictions and, at times, penalties were imposed on the practice of Buddhism. However, Buddhism did not decline to the point of becoming moribund as the independent Sinhalese Buddhist kingdom in Kandy continued to support Buddhism till its demise in 1815.

Urbanization

Buddhism in Sri Lanka, before the nineteenth century, was rural and feudally organized. Its institutions were medieval. It depended on the king for its upkeep and maintenance. The rural monastic establishments performed daily religious activities in the traditional way. Therefore, the Christian missionaries of the nineteenth century believed that Buddhism would disappear due to the pressure of modern Christian evangelical impact supported by the technological advances of the West.

Urbanization in Sri Lanka has been influenced by historic, economic, social and cultural factors. The modern urbanization of Sri Lanka is of nineteenth and twentieth century origin. It was largely the result of the British administration after the reforms of 1833 introduced by the Colebrooke-Cameron Commission (De Silva, 1973:77-88). During this period Colombo developed to be the administrative capital. Together with its harbour, Colombo became the premier commercial centre in Sri Lanka (De Silva 1973:296). There were 26 urban areas in 1901 and the number had grown to 46 in 1946. The urban population in 2001 was 14.6% of the total population in the country. This census is a partial one as the areas under LTTE domination could not be enumerated by the government enumerators in 2001. 6 districts out of 24 were not enumerated (Census 2001:22).

The development of British administrative machinery and the opening of new agricultural areas also helped the formation of new towns. The administrative decentralization on a district basis also helped the development of educational, civil and cultural centres in these cities and towns. The rehabilitation of the dry zone areas of the island together with the development of roads and railways created new routes and junction settlements of various sizes. The towns which emerged as a result of the development of transportation became centres of trade and communication. It is important to note that a majority of these urban centres, although they emerged in the traditional Buddhist homeland, did not have a Buddhist establishment before the nineteenth century.

The greatest growth in urban population, however, has occurred around a few large centres. During this process, the growth rate of urban areas has doubled the pace of overall population increase. Urbanization has proceeded rapidly in recent decades. In 1981 the urbanized population was 32.2 percent in Trincomalee District and 32.6 percent in Jaffna District, in contrast to the rural Moneragala District where only 2.2 percent of the people lived in towns. Colombo District, with 74.4 percent urban population, underwent the biggest changes.

Heterogeneous City

The modern Sri Lankan city, even in predominantly Buddhist areas, consists of a diversity of ethnic groups, languages, religions and cultures. Government employment since the beginning of the nineteenth century brought various social groups to the city. There were a large number of ethnic Tamils arriving in these cities to take up government employment as station masters, postmasters, public work overseers, bank clerks as well as professionals. The Muslim traders were able to take over a good part of the business activities in Sri Lankan cities. There was a large concentration of Eurasians in many of these cities. The heterogeneity more or less was the norm in these cities. The Christian, Hindu and Muslim worship centres also were there often before the Buddhists were able to purchase land in these modern cities even in traditionally Sinhala Buddhist areas. Population, size, density and space which were basic characteristics of the city influenced social relationships and individual behaviour. This heterogeneity has had a tendency to break the caste lines and to cause the appearance of new and complicating forms of class structures.

The Protestant Christians were the first to enjoy the modern urban facilities. The Roman Catholics, after a lapse of over a century of Dutch persecution, began to move into the cities in the last quarter of the eighteenth century. However, the Indian Oratorian missionaries who looked after the spiritual needs of the Roman Catholics in Sri Lanka were used to a rural rather than urban environment. It was after the arrival of the European missionaries since 1842 that the Roman Catholics were able to begin work in the urban environment.

Christian churches often owned the prime land in the cities before the Buddhists were able to own property in the areas that came under urbanization. Even in the Buddhist centres like Kandy and Anuradhapura, Christians had set up churches and schools within the close vicinity of the traditional Buddhist sanctuaries in the nineteenth century. The conspicuous presence of St. Paul's Anglican Church virtually within the precincts of the Temple of the Tooth Relic in Kandy was perceived by the Buddhists as a glaring example of the aggressive behaviour of the missionaries and Christians.

Buddhism in the City

The Buddhist establishment had to adjust itself to meet the challenges brought about by the new situation in the urban environment. The main threat to Buddhism in this period came from Protestant and Roman Catholic Christianity.

On the other hand the Buddhist establishment in Kandy was conservative and on the decline. Quite unlike the urban Low Country sects, the activities of the Siam *Nikaya* were confined mostly to the rural setting. *Nikaya* is a religious order of the Buddhist sangha (monks).

There are three religious orders in Buddhism, Siam (1742), Amarapura (1803) and Ramanna (1835). The monks of the Siam *nikaya* cover only one shoulder with their robes and carry conventional black umbrellas. Amarapura cover both shoulders and also carry umbrellas. Ramanna monks also cover both shoulders and also carry palm leaf umbrellas. The low country is the western and southern coastal area of Sri Lanka which came under European domination since the second half of the sixteenth century. These traditional Buddhist centres were located in the lands donated by the kings or the nobility. The upkeep of those centres was also done on the *rajakaraya* system (a system of compulsory labour; literal meaning "duty by the king") which was the Sri Lankan form of feudalism. It was the Siam *Nikaya* which emerged in the Kandyan kingdom that continued to have these privileges even in the nineteenth and twentieth centuries long after the termination of the Sinhala Kingdom. The Siam *Nikaya* is a monastic order within Sri Lanka, founded in 1753. It is so named because it originated within Siam (Kingdom of Thailand). The Siam *Nikaya* even today grants Higher ordination only to the Goyigama caste. Restricting higher ordination only to the Govigama caste by the Siam *Nikaya* is attributed to the year 1764 (De Silva 1981:202).

Unlike in the previous colonial regimes, the more liberal British policies permitted the Buddhists to promote their religion. Since the British administration followed a secular policy they were not very enthusiastic about Christian religious activities. Some governors such as William Gregory (1872-1877) and Arthur Gordon (1883-1890) were in fact sympathetic towards the Buddhist cause (Gunasekera 2003:79). In addition to this, the Anglican Church was disestablished by 1880 thereby severing any formal connection between the church and state (De Silva 1981:342-3).

It took a little time for the Buddhists to acclimatise themselves to the new situation which arose as a result of the introduction of a capitalist economy. They had to acquire land to establish temples, sanctuaries and residences for the monks. They had to purchase land in the open market. The land that they could acquire was comparatively small; therefore they could not depend on them for living. They had to adjust their living and monastic practices to suit the new urban environment where cash transaction rather than land produce were necessary for living. As this happened, Buddhist temples, *dagobas,* and *avasas* (residence) began to proliferate.

In this atmosphere, the Buddhist sangha wished to obtain property to rival the Christian establishments which were already there. A good example is the Kotahena temple (1832) which was built within the close proximity to the Roman Catholic headquarters at Kotahena (1762) (Prothero 1996:110; Wickramasinghe 2006:116). Similarly the Buddhists planted sacred trees known as *bodhi* trees near the Anglican churches in some cities and then gradually developed the environment to accommodate a full fledged temple. The best known example of this is the temple associated with the famous Kalutara *bodhi* tree built near the Anglican Church.

Monks of Non-Goyigama Castes

The establishment of the Buddhist sangha underwent radical changes in the nineteenth century. The emergence of new sects in Buddhism early in the British period determined the rise of urban Buddhism. The leaders of these new sects were of low country and non-Goyigama (farmer) caste origin. Goyigama is the largest caste among the Sinhalese population. The traditional occupation of this caste is linked to farming. Its equivalent among the Tamils is Vellala. That means they did not belong to the traditional high caste of the Sinhala society who monopolized the Buddhist priesthood. The majority of the members of these castes belong to the low country area of Sri Lanka. Therefore three castes known as Karawa, Salagama and Durawa with numerical strength were able to challenge the Goyigama domination which persisted in the Kandyan kingdom in the hill country. They had responded positively to Christian evangelism in the Portuguese period (1505-1658). Unlike the Hindu system, the hierarchical status of the Sinhalese Buddhist caste system has depended on demographic factors rather than religious. Therefore, the castes which handle dead matter have come to a high caste status in the Sinhala society while in the Hindu system they remain as dalits.

Some of the Buddhist leaders of the nineteenth century had in fact been baptized Christians in their childhood. For example even prominent Buddhist monks like Ven. Mohottiwatte Gunananda (Miguel Silva, 1827-1891) and Ven. Hikkaduwe Sumangala (Johannes Gunawardene, 1827-1911) were baptized in their childhood (*Colombo Observer* Mar. 27, 1992). The traditional Kandy based Siam *Nikaya* (religious order) was confined to the Goyigama caste and had endowments of land donated by the kings of Kandy which it had held over a long period. The new sects that emerged in the nineteenth century were known as Amarapura *Nikaya* and Ramanna *Nikaya*. They were segmented along caste lines into three main groups (Bechert and Gombrich 1995:219-220) based on the above mentioned three non-Goyigama castes. Therefore the Amarapura *Nikaya* which arose as a rebellion against the restriction of the sangha to the Goyigama caste in the traditional Siam *Nikaya* was a non-Goyigama caste movement. They were funded and supported by the emerging elite of the Southern and Western provinces of Sri Lanka which had come under Christian influence for over three centuries. However, there were no doctrinal differences among them.

The low country monks could not seek the support of the Sinhala king as the Siam *Nikaya* had done in the past. The monks of these new sects did not have royal endowments. They had to obtain the support of the clientele for their subsistence from the immediate area where they lived on a small scale and on day-to-day basis. They had to go on rounds collecting alms in the morning to meet the daily needs (Bechert and Gombrich 1995:144). In doing so they had to make themselves worthy of the sustenance they received from the laity in the urban environment.

The formation of the *dayaka sabha* (committee of devotees) was an early method of successfully raising the support for the temples which came about as a result of the urbanization. The economic changes which took place under the British in the second half of the nineteenth century created a social fabric which could support the new Buddhist establishment. This support came mostly from the new rich laity which benefited from the economic opportunities made available to them under the British colonial rule. Therefore, the conversion of Buddhists to other religious faiths was opposed by the Buddhist establishment as it was detrimental to their income which had to come from their devotees (*dayaka*).

The sangha is a community which received respect and honour from the Buddhist society. However, they did not receive it from the non-Buddhists. When it did not come from Sinhalese people who were converted to Christianity the urban monks were offended.

The so called Protestant Buddhism is an urban movement. It developed as an answer to the new challenges brought about by urban society. It came mainly from these newly formed non-Goyigama Buddhist *Nikaya*s. As we noticed earlier newly emerging castes which were non-farmer castes took the leadership. They were more militant as they had to make their own way in society. The Kandyan Siam *Nikaya* hierarchy, on the other hand, was an elite group even in the British period. They had the land and the traditional Buddhist establishment and they were consequently interested in maintaining the status quo. Therefore, some scholars have stated that the Buddhist revival at the beginning was a Low Country caste revival rather than a national religious revival.

It was at the same time anti-Christian in outlook. They had to make the Buddhist religion comparable with Christianity which had become the lifestyle of the urban elite. The powerful Low Country Buddhist elite needed a respectable religion to enable them to rub shoulders with Christians on an equal basis.

Measures Taken By Low Country Monks

The new *Nikayas* were at an advantage because they had a long experience of association with Christianity in the Low Country. Therefore, they had the ability to deal with the situation better than the conservative Goyigama monks in the former Kandyan kingdom. They made use of several methods to deal with the situation.

They adopted the methods followed by Christian missionaries, wherever suitable, in their endeavour to adjust themselves to the new economic and social environment. They also had to compete with Christian missionaries for devotees who were supporters of the temples. The modern competitive market effected their relationship with the Christian missionaries as the loss of a devotee would mean the diminution of economic support. These new Buddhist sects imitated and adopted Christian missionary methods for their benefit very often using them against the activities of the missionaries.

It is for this reason that the Buddhist revival which began in the second half of the nineteenth century is also referred to as Protestant Buddhism. In the second stage they also became politicized; and the competition became further intensified as the political atmosphere became more liberal towards the last quarter of the British rule. English missionaries who noticed this wrote in 1900 stated, "Finally it is supported by the traditions of the past and the strong feeling of conservatism and attachment to the ancient customs by which the Singhalese (*sic*) are peculiarly animated: they are now from a kind of patriotism setting themselves in many ways against western fashions, and reverting in dress and manners to ancient usage" (SPG 1900:78).

Using Modern Urban Facilities

Organizational changes in Buddhism which appeared with the urban environment were seen in the new associations and societies which arose in the low country from the latter half of the nineteenth century. This was a direct result of the Christian-Buddhist encounter.

The Buddhist Theosophical Society which was formed in 1880 equipped the Buddhists with western institutions and organizational tactics. In this respect the American Theosophist, Henry Steele Olcott (1832-1907), strengthened the burgeoning Buddhist movement. Their schools, printing establishments and preaching halls were mostly urban oriented. Olcott created a network of voluntary associations for Buddhist evangelization, education and social reform. His International

Buddhist League was similar to the Protestant Evangelical Alliance. The Young Men's Buddhist Association created by Olcott was on the model of the YMCA. Olcott made societies and organizations similar to the Christian ones to revive Buddhism. The Buddhist Temperance movement which began in 1904 at Matara was also a replication of the Christian principle (*Ceylon Independent* Sept, 12, 1904).

Role of the Buddhist Monk

Buddhism in the pre-colonial era was liberal, tolerant and pluralist (Seneviratne 2004:20). Lorna Dewaraja has traced the cordial relations between Buddhists and Muslims in the Sinhala society up to the year 1915 (Dewaraja 1994:19). However, Buddhism suffered at the hands of the colonial rulers for over three centuries. In the nineteenth century Protestant missionaries made every attempt to undermine Buddhism in order to convert the local population to Christianity. The Buddhists in the early period politely refused confrontation (Malalgoda 1976:210). However, in the wake of growing missionary onslaught the monks of the newly formed sects took upon themselves the leadership of defending the cause of Buddhism. They were interested in protecting their community and their traditions (Deegalle 2006:136).

In this exercise they used the methods they learned from the westerners as well as other methods they knew to meet the Christian missionary challenge. They used these techniques to convert the rural Buddhists to a more formal urban Buddhism. They tried to make the ritual religion into an ethical one thereby making Buddhism to suit the changing cultural and social environment (Deegalle 2006:145).

Debates

The debate with the Christians provided as opportunity to the Buddhist leaders to make a public display of Buddhism in the urban environment which they did not do in the rural society in the past. It began in the famous debates which lasted from 1865 to 1890. The missionaries had used debates effectively in the past to prove their point. But their real significance is in the fact that the Buddhists were able to face the arguments of the missionaries by using the very practices of the missionaries with a vigour and confidence that had hardly ever been evident before. The debates succeeded in providing Buddhist spokesmen with a platform for an assertion of the virtues of their own belief. George Parson of the CMS station at Baddegama stated "The one aim of the fifty priests and their two thousand followers who assembled here on February 8, 1865 was not to defend Buddhism but to overthrow Christianity" (Balding 1922:120).

Preaching

The Christians were ahead in the use of preaching in their evangelism and the impartation of knowledge of Christian ethics. In this period there was an increasing demand for knowledge of Buddhism among the urban laity. The Buddhist elite were especially interested in the ethical aspect of Buddhism. However, the Buddhist preaching style in the period prior to missionary influence was different, being intended to help the laity to acquire merit. It was not intended to deal with any threat from another religion. The sermons were all night performances. The *bana pinkama* was a recitation of sacred texts. It lasted several days often extending to fifteen days, or even a month (Copleston 1908:257)

The urban monks, having realized the inadequacy of this method acquired the styles of the Christian preachers to meet the new situation. Among the erudite preachers, the best known was Ven. Mohottiwatte Gunananda, who followed a style of preaching which differed from the traditional Buddhist preachers. In contrast to the seated and motionless traditional position he stood up when he spoke and made free and skilful use of gestures. His style was influenced by contemporary Protestant preachers. Thus, a Buddhist sermon suitable for the changing environment was evolved during this period.

The new preaching was confined to a period of one hour, a radical departure from the all night preaching sessions practiced in the period prior to the nineteenth century. The Reformed Buddhist preacher expounded a Pali stanza he chanted. These are similar to the sermons preached by the Protestant missionaries of the nineteenth century.

The religious expectations of the urban society coincided with the spiritual and material aspirations of the newly emerging urban monks. They adapted Buddhist preaching to unconventional methods. In the second quarter of the twentieth century the Vajirarama monks of Amarapura sect in the Colombo city introduced a new style of preaching which made their sermons short, devoid of ritual, well integrated and focused on a theme (Deegalle 2006:133). This type of sermons mainly gave attention to the issues of daily life in order to improve the person and society (Seneviratne 2004:53). This style was appreciated by urban clients and was soon followed by other Low Country monks. The passages they selected extolled the virtues of honesty, hard work, austerity, and saving (Pannasiha 1967:36). These were ethics which suited the national middle class and were encouraged by the Buddhist leader Angariaka Dharmapala (1864-1933). These sermons had application to the day-to-day life of the individual and society. They also condemned the practices such as fireworks, dancing, drumming and other performances which accompanied the traditional sermons. The traditional sermon, on the other hand, was a merit making process, in which weight was given to reading *gathas* (Pali stanzas) from the Buddhist texts.

The introduction of radio preaching (1925) also reduced the time frame of the sermons. The use of radio took the preacher beyond the confines of his monastery to the wider national audience. It also enabled the lay Buddhists to listen to sermons on an every day basis. The prominent monks also made preaching tours with the support of the Buddhist middle class in the cities. However, Buddhist preachers did not deliver sermons in places where there was no public or private invitation (Deegalle 2006:9). Therefore, they did not go to the extent of the evangelical preachers who preached at any place where they could find a crowd. In fact, Buddhist monks of the British era were critical of such practices (Malalgoda 1976:197). But in the 1980s there was an experiment undertaken by some popular monks to preach under the bodhi trees. In 1980s Ven Pandure Ariyadhamma (1940-1986) introduced this style of preaching as *bodhi puja* (offering to the bodhi tree). He used poetic language in preaching which was undertaken in public places often under a bodhi tree. Recently, another Buddhist monk Ven. Gangodawila Soma (1948-2003) used a public platform for preaching making use of modern sciences such as psychology.

The Press

The first newspaper in Sri Lanka was the *Colombo Journal* started in 1832. Thereafter, the British merchants created their own newspaper, the *Observer and Commercial Advertiser* in 1834. The limited freedom of the press allowed by the British government also provided an atmosphere for Buddhist as well as Christian activities in the urban environment. The Christian missionaries used the vernacular press for their evangelical activities.

Printing was another area where the Buddhist urban society could rival the Christians. In the early stages of the nineteenth century the Christians bombarded readers with printed matter that openly or subtly criticised Buddhism. In 1862, the Buddhists were able to purchase a printing press and prepare counter publications against Christianity. At the end of the British period, the Buddhists were firmly in control of the situation where they could express their opinion with a large number of printing presses under Buddhist ownership. Newspapers like *Lakmini pahana* (1862), *Lak Rivi Kiresa* (1863), *Sarasavi Sandaresa* (1880), and *Sinhala Jatiya* (1901) were especially prominent in enhancing Buddhism against Christianity.

Education

Education was important in the growth and development of cities in this period (Newbiggin 1989:186). Missionary schools grew in number in the nineteenth century in Sri Lanka. In 1841, the Protestants had 325 schools of which 21 were English medium schools. In the last quarter of the nineteenth century, the number of English medium schools increased as the Roman Catholic Church also began to open schools. These educational establishments were powerful agencies of modernization and urbanization of Sri Lanka. At the initial stages the Christians opened schools mainly as a tool for converting non-Christians. In the 1880s when the English medium schools prepared candidates for the Cambridge Matriculation Examination the urban elite, mostly Christian, were able to benefit from them.

Like in the other areas the urban Buddhist recognized the value of the field of education. It was the Buddhist clergy who took the lead at the beginning. Ven. Vakaduve Subuthi and Ven. Dodanduwe Piyaratana Tissa were the pioneers of the first Sinhala medium Buddhist schools. The original Buddhist English medium schools were established with the support offered by the American Theosophists in the 1880s. The Theosophists started nine Sunday schools in 1881. In 1886, they opened the first English medium school in Colombo. It was named Ananda College. Next year, Dharmaraja College, Kandy, Maliyadewa College, Kurunegala and Mahinda College, Galle were opened with teachers recruited from England and America. These were boys' schools. The girls' schools came later. The first among them was Mahamaya Ladies' school in Kandy opened in 1928. Nevertheless, the lead of the Christians in the field of education continued well into the time of independence. It is interesting to note that these Buddhist schools were named after Buddhist sages imitating the tradition of the Christians who named their schools after Christian saints.

Sunday school played an important part in the Protestant churches from the early years of the nineteenth century. Towards the second half of the same century the Roman Catholics also introduced Sunday schools. As we noticed earlier Buddhist Sunday schools began in 1881 as a result of the American Colonel Olcott's involvement. They have gradually developed into a system of Sunday schools controlled by the YMBA (1898). Today, all Buddhist temples in the urban areas run Sunday schools. They are known as *daham pasala* (school for religious education) and are supported by the government.

The whole character of Buddhism changed within a short time after the introduction of modern type of schools. The Society for the

Propagation of the Gospel which undertook English education in Sri Lanka since 1848 reported in 1900, "Whereas some time ago the mass of the people knew nothing of Buddhism, and had for their religion little more than devil worship, Buddhism is now a popular force opposed to Christianity. It is taught in schools which vie with our own and are like them supported by Government grants" (Koscherke, Ludwig and Delgado 2007:88). The chanting of *pansil* (five precepts) which was so far the monopoly of the monk became current among the laity after the introduction of Buddhist schools.

Social Work

The Christian missionaries considered social involvement very important. Many prominent Christians were active in the socio-political sphere. They also campaigned vigorously for a wide range of humanitarian causes—the care of orphans and street children, efforts to cease child prostitution, prison reform, and legislation to regulate the conditions under which women and children were employed in factories and so on . The boys' industrial school opened by the Methodists in 1818 and the home for juvenile delinquents by the Roman Catholics in 1892 were some such examples. A large number of converts were attracted by the humanitarian activities of the Christian Church during the period of early urbanization.

The urban Buddhist clergy as well as the laity realized the value of the philanthropic institutions run by the Christian missionaries. The disciplinary codes of Buddhism did not permit their clergy to engage in the activities associated with social services. Further, Buddhists found it difficult to compete with the Christians for reasons of not being able to raise funds and the absence of trained personnel. Nevertheless, criticism was directed against Christian institutions on the ground that they were agencies for conversion (de Votta, 2007:33).

It was long after Sri Lanka's independence that the Buddhists were able to open homes for the aged, orphanages, job training programmes, drug rehabilitation centres, and other philanthropic work. These activities have come up mainly as a response to such institutions of the Christians. A recent tendency has been to designate the Buddhist monk to the role of patron of community development projects.

The role of parish priest is another new area that the urban monk attempted to adapt. Traditionally, the role of the monk is a world-renouncer. Normally the traditional monk used to confine himself to the passive virtues of renunciation and imperturbability (Bechert and Gombrich 1995:58). According to the *vinaya* (disciplinary) rules the monks were prohibited from involvement in life cycle events. The urban Buddhist monks disregarded some of these restrictions as they tried to reproduce the role of the Christian parish priests. New institutions had to be developed to suit the parish role of the monk.

The role of the parish priest in the Catholic environment attracted many converts to that faith. Some Buddhist monks who realised the advantages of that role began to experiment with it in the urban environment. The participation of monks in funeral activities was the only area of life cycle event that was allowed in the Buddhist tradition. Although the monks are unable to solemnize weddings due to the concept of inauspiciousness attached to them as unmarried persons, some have encouraged couples to visit the temples and receive the blessing of monks.

Missionary Monks

The work of Colonel Olcott and later of Angarika Dharmapala brought Buddhism to a missionary stance. Dharmapala preached that the task of the Buddhists was not only to spread Buddhism locally but also to propagate it internationally (Seneviratne 2004:37). The missionary monks began to move out initially to India and eventually to the western countries as well. Since independence, Buddhism has flourished and Sri Lankan monks and expatriate lay people have been prominent in spreading Theravada Buddhism in Asia, the West and even in Africa.

Participation in politics is another area where the urban monk excelled in the British period and after. In the era of Buddhist kings, the sangha could have power only as a handmaid of power. They were used as tools of power. The sangha also had the capacity to be opinion makers.

The political role of monks came about in several stages. The public activities of monks in the debates of the nineteenth century made monks like Ven. Gunananda, a popular figure and opinion maker. Anagarika Dharmapala made a great impression on the Buddhists as a social reformer and an agitator for Sinhala Buddhist rights. The two Buddhist colleges set up in the nineteenth century, Vidyodaya (1872) and Vidyalankara (1875, helped to develop this trend further. It was in the late nineteen thirties that the new phenomenon called "political bhikkhus" appeared in the field of Sri Lankan politics. Prominent among "the political bhikkhus" in early forties were Vens. Walpola Rahula, Udakendawela Sirisarankhara and Narawila Dhammaratana. At present the *Jatika Hela Urumaya* (National Sinhala Heritage) is a political party of the Buddhists which is led by bhikkhus who have contested parliamentary elections and won seats in the parliament.

The present trend is that the Buddhist monk is not only an opinion maker but also in the legislative and executive branches of the state. They are in every field of activity thus becoming *bhumi putra* (sons of the soil) rather than *Buddha putra* (sons of the Buddha). Although, according to the *vinaya* rules the monks are not expected to handle money or be involved in politics, the Sri Lankan Buddhist monk has acquired every benefit of the urban culture.

Urban Buddhist Laity and Modernization

The Sri Lankan economy began to influence the formation of the social hierarchy since the second half of the nineteenth century. Merchants, professionals, bureaucrats, and skilled workers made a great impact on the new city. The new cities provided education, professional and employment opportunities. The social elite in these cities formed a mixed ethnic and religious community. This class was composed of agricultural land owners, coconut and rubber planters, merchants, small industrialists and professional men. "Their high social status depended on leadership, caste, occupation, education or combination of all these" (Jayawardena 1972:70). A good percentage of them were Christian in the nineteenth century and the first half of the twentieth century (Jayawardena 1972:71). The Christian clergy also were in this category on the strength of the fact that they held educational qualifications. The English speaking population in 1911 was about 2.3 percent of the total population (Denham 1991:433). The social breakthrough of the new middle class came from education. The Christians were leading in the sphere of English education at the end of the nineteenth century.

Part of the middle class which served in the British administration converted to Christianity. Protestant Christianity and Roman Catholicism, to some extent, was a middle class urban movement. They were able to rise in the service of colonial rule. The Christian middle class remained a relatively prosperous minority until the time of independence.

Some Buddhists who were able to come to elite status in the society were also living in the cities. However, most of them were either westernized or aspired to become westernized. The traditional Buddhist middle class included landowners, village officials, influential monks, ayurvedic (native) physicians and teachers of vernacular schools (Jayawardena 1972:70). Their roots were Sinhala Buddhist and the majority of them lived in rural areas.

The transformation of Buddhism in the urban environment making accommodation to meet the religious needs of the urban laity was a felt need from the beginning of the nineteenth century. The new urban elite were mostly self-made and were therefore eager to grasp new opportunities open to them (De Silva 1984:328). Secondary education became available to the Buddhists in the late nineteenth century beginning in 1870. This education was supplied by the Christian educational institutions. The missionaries were well ahead of all other religious groups in the field of education. They had their centres of education mostly in the cities of the Southern, Western, North Western, and Northern provinces.

In addition to this the Sinhalese families which made large fortunes from graphite mining and export and arrack production created a new rich class. They sought urban property to consolidate their economic foundation. The editor of the English newspaper *Ceylon Observer* reported in 1883:"There are a considerable number of wealthy native gentlemen enriched by trade and agriculture within British times and nearly all the property in large towns as well as extensive planted areas belonged to them" (Ferguson 1883:64). The numbers of the Sri Lankan urban elite increased with the expansion of the economic base.

Life Cycle Events

The incorporation of Christian symbolism into contemporary Buddhist practices enabled the urban Sinhalese Buddhists to rival the popularity of Christian rites amongst the local population. Christianity was associated with the rising middle class in Sri Lanka, whereas Buddhism at the early stages was associated with the rural unsophisticated people of the country. By imitating celebratory techniques utilized by the missionaries, Buddhists acquired the capacity to compete with Christianity which was the religion of the affluent urban middle class. Thus, it was the Christian missionary activities that helped to form a modern urban identity for the Buddhists.

As the Buddhist monks were not able to participate in family affairs other than funeral ceremonies, it was the Buddhist laity who took the lead in modernizing Buddhist ceremonies associated with family life. The urban Buddhist middle class found several areas in the traditional life cycle events that lacked respectability. Buddhist marriage as practiced was not a formalized union. There was polygamy, polyandry, bigamy, as well as monogamy all accepted and sanctioned by Buddhism . There was no social function to celebrate marriages. Monks did not participate in wedding ceremonies or act in a pastoral capacity (Copleston 1908:260). Therefore, most of the Buddhist middle class in the nineteenth century sought to solemnize their marriages in Christian churches. The introduction of monogamous marriage by law in 1855 made it necessary for the Buddhists to give respectability to their marriages. As a result of this, Buddhists introduced the *poruwa* ceremony to institutionalize marriage and to curb the attraction to the Christian marriage ceremony. The *poruwa* ceremony has now become the symbol of Buddhist marriage and a Sinhala heritage. Even some Christians have been attracted to it in modern times.

The funeral ceremony was another area of adaptation of Christian practices. Prior to the nineteenth century, the traditional Sinhala Buddhist funeral practice was to throw the dead body into the jungle for the vultures to eat. Naturally, this practice did not suit the urban environment. Therefore, Buddhists had to seek the church yards to bury their dead. Buddhist monks, following the tradition of the Roman Catholics, visited the burial ground to chant *gathas* and preach words of comfort to the bereaved family. To these practices numerous other rituals mostly deriving from Christian and western practices have been added together with practices of popular Buddhism.

The Buddhists also introduced a practice known as *rankiri kata gama* (application of milk on the lips of the new born with a golden ring) in place of Christian baptism. The Buddhist leaders who met in Sailabimbaramaya at Dodanduwa in 1860 proposed that the parents should take their babies to the Buddhist temple of the village to get the monks to bless them with *pirit* chanting. However, this practice without a religious tradition did not last long.

Lay Religious Leadership

The missionary schools and the research undertaken by European scholars in the nineteenth century helped the Buddhist laity to learn Buddhism deeply. In the past, deep knowledge of the *dhamma* (doctrine) had been the monopoly of the Buddhist monk. However, the traditional role of Buddhist monk as the most educated person in Sinhala society was no longer valid in the nineteenth century as a result of the breakthrough brought about by the missionary education. Lay Buddhists began to be actively and directly involved in shaping their own religious experience. The Sri Lanka Vinaya Vardana Society which began in the 1930s was an organization which encouraged a Buddhism without bhikkus (Bond 1992:208). They were more concerned about the ethical aspect of the Buddhism than the performance of rituals. The practice of lay *pirit* and other ritual activities became popular in this period. The teaching of Buddhism in schools reduced, to some extent, the monopoly of the *dhamma* by Buddhist monks. Nevertheless, the institution of the sangha was able to withstand these new developments.

Contribution of the Theosophists

As we noticed earlier, the Theosophical Society founded by Colonel Olcott played a key role to urbanize and modernize Buddhism. He made several visits to the island to encourage the Buddhists from 1880 until his death in 1907. The Theosophical Society provided the facilities for opening English medium schools for girls and boys and was instrumental in introducing a system of Sunday Schools for Buddhists.

Theosophists, especially Colonel Olcott, also helped the Buddhists to communicate with the Colonial Office in London to obtain the Wesak *poya* (full moon day) as a public holiday. He worked with the Sinhala Buddhists to create a Buddhist flag. Fund raising, preaching tours, and Wesak carols are among other areas where his assistance was useful.

Buddhist Festivals

The celebration of Wesak was used as a political tool for identity consolidation in this period. The transformation of Wesak from a rural religious ceremony celebrated within the precincts of the temple to a public ceremony was an introduction with the first Wesak public holiday of 1885. It was used as a display of Buddhist power after the relaxation of the prohibition of Buddhist processions placed by the government in the wake of the Kotahena riot of 1883 (Wickramasinghe 2006:115). The Christian influence upon the Wesak festivities is also an example of how incorporation of Christian social practices and festivals was used to create a distinctive Buddhist identity. In order to give Wesak a colourful character Wesak *pandals* (arches), Wesak cards, Wesak carols, and Wesak lanterns were introduced on the very first Wesak public holiday. Even the age old practices of *dansala* (free distribution of food and drinks) was given a new look by making it a public activity. The earlier *dansalas* were given by the kings in the ancient period. Even the Roman Catholic practice of way side drama and *pandals* were also included in the Wesak day celebration. Some of these practices taken from Christian tradition are now proudly looked upon as the Sinhala Buddhist heritage.

Road Side Statues

Early in the Buddhist resurgence the Buddha statue and the bodhi tree were also used as a political tool. The Buddhists began to build statues in the public places such as road junctions. Although Buddha statues are meant for worship, in this context, they were used as public display of Buddhist presence. Similarly, the bodhi tree was also used for the same purpose. Ven. Mohottiwatte Gunananda set up a society known as *Bodhi Raja Samitiya* in 1840 to object to the cutting of bodhi trees by the government to build road ways. They also planted bodhi trees at road junctions and other public places in urban areas. Eventually, some of these bodhi trees paved the way for the construction of temples in their vicinity.

The recent introduction of broadcasting *pirit* over loud speakers in public places is also intended for purposes other than worship. It looks as if it was introduced to counter the Muslim call to prayers broadcast at various intervals during the day from city mosques.

Conclusion

The urbanization process created conditions in which new forms of Buddhism could emerge. The new social and economic conditions formed the seedbed for the rise of urban Buddhism. This process was stimulated by the formation of new Buddhist orders in the British period. These new structures deliberately imitated and borrowed from Christian traditions and brought about a sophistication and confidence to the new urban Buddhism. Buddhist movements appropriated Christian methods in the areas of preaching, the press, printing, education, social work, Sunday schools, and use of ritual and symbolism. This "Protestant Buddhism" formed its urban identity from Christian mission activities.

Contrary to the views expressed by some scholars on the pacifism of Buddhism, our studies show that the urban Buddhism since the nineteenth century was protestant and militant (Premasiri 2006:82). The events surrounding the Kotahena riot of 1883 makes it clear that from the time of Ven Mohottiwatte Gunananda violence and physical force were used whenever they felt necessary.

The legacy of interaction between Buddhism and the intrusive Western culture and civilisation and Christian religion has had a profound influence on the history of Sri Lanka. When the British won control of the country at the beginning of the nineteenth century, Buddhism, after nearly three centuries of suppression, was well into decline. It was weak, vulnerable to missionary onslaught, did not command respect in the urban environment and lacked effective leadership. This situation emboldened the English missionaries to flood the island with anti-Buddhist propaganda and embark on a programme of evangelism. But against all expectations the monastic and lay Buddhists brought about a major revival. From about 1860 onwards the movement went hand in hand with growing nationalism. The Sinhalese Buddhist revolutionary ideology finally raised Buddhism to the level of a privileged religion at the end of the colonial period. As a result of Buddhist resurgence conversion from Buddhism to Christianity during this period was marginal.

On the contrary, judging from the statistics displayed in the population data available in the census from 1871 to 1991, conversion to Buddhism from Christianity was comparatively significant. Mr A. E. Buultjens, a Christian Burgher, embraced Buddhism and became the Principal of Ananda College, Colombo (1890-1898). Ananda

Samarakone, (1911–1962) born to a Christian family as George Wilfred Alwis, embraced Buddhism and changed his name. He was the composer of the Sri Lanka's national anthem. An Anglican Christian S.W.R.D. Bandaranaike, (1900-1959) who embraced Buddhism in 1929, was the prime minister of Sri Lanka from 1956 to 1959. Another former Anglican Christian, J.R. Jayawardene (1906-1996), was the first executive president of the Republic of Sri Lanka from 1977 to 1989. This list can go on.

The depletion of the numerical strength of Christianity is expressed by K.M. de Silva, "A great many of their disappointments sprang from their over-confidence and their underestimation of the strength of ... (Buddhism)....and the extent of their disappointment was in proportion to the immensity of their expectations" (De Silva 1995:20). Patrick Johnstone has stated that Sri Lanka is the only non-Muslim Asian country where the Church has steadily declined (1986:386-387).

Urbanization brought sophistication and confidence to the Buddhists. By the end of the colonial period, the Buddhists had absorbed almost all the external paraphernalia of the Christian mission. In the same period, the task of the Christian church gradually shifted from evangelism to the task of making gentlemen out of the non-Christian. The Buddhists agitated hard to stop the missionary advantages in the field of education when they received political power with the introduction of universal franchise in 1931. The struggle of the Roman Catholics as well as the Protestants to protect their educational establishment was of no avail against the anti-Christian tide, which culminated in 1960 when the government was forced by the majority of the oters to take over the denominational grants-in-aid schools. Thereafter, the Christian church was stripped of most of its power and influence on the urban society.

One would notice that there was a clear interrelationship between the new Buddhist orders which emerged with new expressions of urban Buddhism and the decline of the Christian missionary movement in Sri Lanka. Urbanization in the second half of the nineteenth and the first half of the twentieth centuries has helped the modernization of

Buddhist practices and activities in Sri Lanka. In this process Buddhism has received a marked influence from Christianity both Catholic and Protestant. At the same time it also has had a negative effect on Christianity in Sri Lanka because of the anti-Christian attitude of the revival of Buddhism. Since then the Christian church was forced onto the defensive. It was pushed down from a privileged position in the nineteenth century to that of a beleaguered minority in the second half of the twentieth century.

Some scholars who considered the impact of the urbanization of Buddhism on the Christian Church predicted that Christianity would disappear from Sri Lanka as it became materially disadvantageous to remain Christian. Contrary to this prophesy of doom by the secular historians, a remnant has remained vibrantly alive (de Silva 1976:394). It is those who took Christianity as a part of their life who remained in the faith while those who received material advantages slowly moved out of the faith when the Buddhists absorbed all the urban advatntages of Christianity in the second half of the twentieth century. Although politically speaking the Christians became a weak minority, theologically this group may be regarded as the remnant which continues to carry the torch to the next generation.

SECTION THREE

STRATEGIC MEANS

CHAPTER SEVEN

Reaching the Cities as Means to Reaching the Nations

STEPHEN M. SPAULDING

Opening the mail today, I was confronted once again with the pertinence and centrality of the thesis I share here. The CEO of a large North American mission agency was reflecting on what it is going to take to "reach the whole world for Christ." His outline was compelling, if simple: In order to reach the whole world, reach nations. In order to reach nations, mobilize the churches in those nations. In order to mobilize those churches, impact their leaders. This, I propose, is why we are all here at this time. Leaders, of churches, in nation(s), which we long to see touched and transformed by King Christ.

BUT, what is our rationale for this cause, and have we done due diligence to understanding our task, our target, our harvest force (or Temple, for sake of alliteration and theological correctness) and the trajectory which we expect to carry us forward across time? My studies over the past months and years would lead me to answer this largely in the negative. But my sense is a highly optimistic one—at this stage in church-mission relations. We are truly on the crest of a wave, a Spirit-wave and a *telos*—*kairos* wave, a moment in history with no rival on so many fronts.

The purpose of this paper is to explore primarily the biblical case for nations as the object and agent of God's grand purposes in the earth and across the ages. And I must confess that this paper is a work in progress, was originally presented in a DAWN Ministries leadership training to evangelical leaders mainly from WEF, primarily in Asian nations. But I share it shortened and evolved within the SEANET community because this is where my heart is, where God is moving in unexpected ways, and where we have yet to see much take place to his greater glory.

Defining "Nations"

First, a brief look at parameters for the term. In fact, my intent with the use of this term, over others, is partly to remain generic or even a bit "muddy" intentionally. So much energy has been given in recent decades in the interests of "strategic mission" (illustrated somewhat in this quote from North America), to encompass the best possible aggregation of humanity—it is difficult to know what one means any more by the term *nation.*

Our current 21st Century global context still puts "nation" in the same category as geo-political, sovereign "country." Hence, the U.N. as a body of sovereign countries with borders, visas, regional coalitions, multiple nationalities within, etc. More than any one modern feature, colonialism can be thanked for the world of 250 or so nations of this sort. Prior to the peak of post-colonial independent state-making, much of the world was still an agglomeration of loosely bounded or battling tribal states or feudal communities with the occasionally centralizing force of king, government or even empire to create that sort of state which we today take for granted. What we have today is a far cry in many cases from what "nations" would have meant—even on a similar hermeneutical footing—in biblical times and cultures. For one thing, the world's population today is easily 60 or 70 times that of the world in Christ's day. Extrapolated to the life, size, and complexity of "nations" it is clear that anything we are dealing with today is of a significantly different sort.

From a missions standpoint, Dawn Ministries founder Jim Montgomery, in collaboration with church-growth fountainhead,

Donald McGavran, paved the way for a new phase of strategic mission through the capitalization and exploitation of the modern geo-political nation, seen in his 1982 paper to the annual EFMA gathering: *The Challenge of a Whole Country.* The bulk of the global DAWN movement has been predicated on the genius of harnessing the resources, vision, disparate representative bodies of a political country for the "discipling of a nation" (including all the "nations" within that nation).

The future, though, is now also uncertain for us in this quickly shifting, globalized world. John Naisbitt, in the wake of the breakup of the Soviet Union, predicted that the UN by 2025 would have 1000 "nations" instead of the current 250 or so (1994) Balkanization and decentralization (think of the Soviet Empire and the Internet) was the order of the 1990's, and scores of the current skirmishes and all-out civil wars globally today are efforts by religious, ethnic or other disenfranchised groupings to secede from their oppressive nation-states and achieve geo-political autonomy—for better or worse. For political scientists like Harvard's Samuel Huntington, this is a scenario which will play out for some time into the future, with profound ramifications for global political stability (Huntington 1996). These men see human allegiances which have been nurtured for at least the past century on strong nationalisms, tending now both upward and downward from national loyalties toward more tribal, linguistic and clannish on the lower end and more civilizational (especially religious and worldview-oriented) on the upper end. Both mega-cities and major corporations have also taken center-stage as candidates for the replacement of nation-states as we've experienced them in the past one- to two-hundred years.

Missiology over the past 25 years has especially turned the attention of the worldwide missionary church toward "nation" as "people" or "people group." The biblical sanction for this is focused on the Greek translation of "nation" *ethne*, from which we of course get our "ethnic" groups. This has been seen as a major corrective in faulty limitations through the over-familiar geo-political categorization. Missiologist, Ralph Winter, and popular theologian, John Piper, have influenced many mission-minded groups toward an almost exclusive emphasis on nation as people, or cultural affinity grouping (See Lausanne).

Nuances, though, abound. What these factors illustrate is the importance of understanding the breadth and depth of the terms we derive from Scripture and utilize in church and mission strategy.

For our purposes, "nations" refer as in Scripture to a *range* of meanings on the collections of humanity into large self-identifying groups. These groups are mentioned throughout Scripture, often as a complementary set—beginning with the "table of nations" in Genesis 10 and moving on through the very last chapters of Revelation. The famous passages of Revelation present the simplest array, each time arranged in a different order, presumably not to allow for any one particular emphasis or sense of gradation/valuation, "tribe, tongue (language), people and nation"(Hayes 2003:193-199). Because of the demographics of the 20th and 21st Century world, we could include mega-cities (Bangkok, Metro-Manila) or city-states (Singapore, Hong Kong) in this collection of meanings with impunity. Indeed, Scripture seems to include city-states in its loose language of nations; consider Nineveh, Babylon, the "nations" of Canaan largely delineated by feudal/vassal territories around walled cities. Nations, from a scriptural and socio-spiritual standpoint, must also be seen as "powers," part of the institutional realms of secondary creation, an artifact/product of human culture and administration, which, as Walter Wink has poignantly made the case, are creaturely, fallen and, within the right course of events, eminently redeemable (See Wink).

Lastly, in defining nations from a scriptural standpoint, we need to underscore the "personality" of nations. This is necessary for two reasons: first, nations are corporate, and in a highly individualistic recent history of Christianity (discipleship, conversion and so many other concepts thought of in largely individualized application) the emphasis has been all on the personality of the individual. Secondly, because in modernity nations have become pre-eminently political and usually oversized bureaucracies with complex levels and structures of governance, they seem the furthest thing from "persons" in their essence. We hear of "Rage Against the Machine" from a younger generation which sees the large bureaucracies as utterly stifling of human survival, much less well-being.

Scripture paints a radically different portrait of "nations." A brief exercise will suffice to make the point. Answer the following list of rhetorical questions—from Scripture—ALL in the affirmative:

Can a nation be born? (Is.66 / Gen.12)
Can a nation conspire/plot, rage and hate? (Ps.2)
Can a nation die/be destroyed? (Ps.83:4)
Can a nation have no understanding? (Dt.32:21:Rom.10:19)
Can a nation know the power of God? (Josh.4:24)
Can a nation be healed? (Rev.22)
Can a nation receive a specific prophecy? (OT many)
Can a nation inherit the Kingdom (Mt.25:34)
Can a nation be judged? (OT many; Mt.25:41,46)
Can a nation borrow and pay back? (Dt. 15:6)
Can a nation rule? (Dt.15:6)
Can a nation be inherited? (Ps.2)
Can a nation show mercy? (Matt.25)
Can a nation/city-state repent? (Jer.18; Jonah)
Can a nation be disipled? (Mt.28)
Can a nation believe? (Rom.16)
Can a nation be taught? (Mt.28)
Can a nation obey/disobey? (Jer.7:28; Mic.5:15; Rom.16)
Can a nation respond to correction? (Jer. 7:28)
Can a nation be baptized? (Mt. 28/Rom 16)
Can a nation keep faith? (Is.26:2)
Can a nation break covenant? (Ezek.16:56)

It i s amazing that very few theologians have spent any time at all on this strong Hebraic/Semitic and divine tradition of personifying the large corporate and political entity, giving it apparently all the graces, corruptibility and Slavonic potential of individuals! These are not anthropomorphisms or simple grammatical personifications. The God of glory not only "takes historical development into account" but also seems to see nations as prime "personal" recipients and agents of his redemptive work in the world (Mouw 2002:86). This is a major thesis of this paper.

At a popular level, Dutch layman Pieter Bos has done the best work in laying out a "theology of the nations and their redemption." This includes a preliminary examination of nations as corporate personalities and the Scripture envelope providing the pluraform depiction of peoples as tribe/kinship, culture/language and state/government initially in Genesis 10, variously throughout redemption history and mirrored conclusively in Revelation (See Bos). Bos cites the DAWN vision near the end of his work as a case of "bottom-up" vs. "top-down" methodology/strategy in the discipling of the nations. While he commends this vision and strategy, he feels it is in a sense one half of a two-sided task, the other being his understanding of what can and should be sought with high-level officials, the "kings" referred to in this survey. As an urban planner and lay theologian, Bos brings a fresh, highly charismatic angle to this field and to his theology, with much experience at the national and urban levels of testing out his theology and theory (especially in Africa and Europe, but also with significant global exposure).

Finally, there is another tie between individuals called, saved and serving God and nations as persons. Throughout Scripture, individuals are singled out by God for a divine calling. Often this calling involves the formation of a nation or group of nations. Why did God call Abraham? To bless an individual or create a nation? What did God twice tell Moses in moments of crisis over idolatrous Israel's judgment? "Now leave me alone so that my anger may burn against them and that I may destroy them. Then I will make you into a great nation." The "patriarchs" were the fathers of nations. And with this, the bottom line of the Abrahamic covenant "that all the families/nations of the earth might be blessed" (Gen. 12 and 18). The individuals in this case seem to have been more means to an end, whether in election, salvation, judgment or other vocation.

A Biblical Survey Of "Nations"

Before embarking on a Genesis-to-Revelation biblical survey, it is helpful to consider just a handful of pan-biblical themes which need to be in the back of our minds throughout the study.

First, the revival in recent decades of the prominence of the Kingdom of God motif for all of biblical revelation is paramount to our consideration of "nations," since the two are in many ways a divine and human side to the same coin. The book of Revelation ends with the grand conclusion that the "kingdom[s] of this earth has [have] become the kingdom[s] of our God and of his Christ" (Rev. 11:15 [King James rendition in brackets]. This leads to a further under-developed scripture principal especially as "nations" relate to our discussion of church in mission. "Nations," throughout the Bible, whether ethnic enclaves, city-states or other large groupings of humanity, were so often lumped together with their kings that the political dimension of biblical nations is lost only on the most inobservant.

A perusal of word usage just in the OT prophets bears out the interrelationship between "peoples," "nations," "cities," "lands" and "kings:"

- 30 instances of the combined use of "peoples" and "kings"
- 27 instances of the combined use of "city" and "king"
- 19 instances of the combined use of "nation(s)" and "king(s)"
- 7 instances of the combined use of "nation(s)" and "city(-ies)"
- 5 instances of the combined use of "nations" and "lands"
- 3 instances of the combined use of "peoples" and "kings"
- 3 instances of the combined use of "peoples" and "cities"

Richard Mouw briefly treats the nature of ancient kings to educate us about the differences between monarchs of biblical times and political rulers today.

> The power and authority of ancient kings differed in two ways from our understanding of political rule today. It was, we might say, *more politically intensive* and *more non-politically extensive*. Within what we think of as the sphere of politics, ancient rulers possessed a very intensive kind of power. ... In

ancient times…it was assumed that political rulers had a right to function as dictators or near-dictators. But the authority of ancient rulers also extended well beyond the realm of politics. … The ancient king was more than a political ruler; …

"Politics" covered more territory for the ancients than it does for us today. The ancient office of kingship evolved out of the still more ancient roles of clan leader, tribal chief, leader of the hunt, and the like; and the office absorbed many of these functions. Kings were military leaders who often led their armies into battle. They were also the chief sponsors of the arts and sciences. In short, ancient kings served as the primary authorities over the broad patterns of the cultural lives of their nations. …to assemble kings together, then, was in an important sense to assemble their national cultures together (Mouw 2002:49-50).

Is it any wonder then that Israel, with God as her king, would have understood kingship and the "kingdom of God" in much more comprehensive terms and associations than we might, using the same terminology? But the main point here is that "nations" throughout scripture must generally not be dissociated from their rulers and kings, that "kings" in biblical times were more synonymous with their cultures, peoples, domains than almost any contemporary political rulers would be with theirs.

Along with this sub-theme, we should add the atmosphere which surrounded ancient kingship: that of glory and worship. Most ancient kings were demigods or in some way seen as divine. They elicited either all-out worship or fielty which would defy most modern secular forms of governance. They also spent large portions of their national wealth upon the buttressing of their own glory, their palaces, regal affairs and entourages—so that kingship was in the public imagination a kind of zenith in human-divine glory-encounters. As difficult as it is for the modern/secular mind to grasp these features of ancient national life, it is indispensable for a proper understanding of the original biblical writers' constant return to kingly and national themes whether in speaking of God Almighty or the affairs of "nations" and national life as they experienced it.

J. Daniel Hayes has provided a tremendous service, dealing with one dimension of this discussion of nations, that of ethnicity and race, doing an extensive survey of Old and New Testaments to discover a "theology of race," especially in the light of contemporary race relations both within and outside of the Church. A theology of "race" is another critical pan-biblical subject which must be addressed in seeking a fuller understanding of "nation" biblically and especially as pertains the mission of the Church among nations.

Old Testament Survey

The opening of the human drama in the book of Genesis has a not so subtle presage to the whole theme of nations, long before the first nation has taken shape. God's mandates to the first couple were simple in the extreme:

- Be fruitful and increase *in number* (after your kind);
- Fill the earth (see Mouw, 2002, pp 34-42 for an excellent excursus on this theme in relation to culture/nations)
- Subdue the earth (a welcome to among other things, science and technology?)
- Work, Care for, *Cultivate* your garden-surroundings (Establishing the first artifacts and traditions of *culture*, *agriculture*, *horticulture*, etc.)
- Exercise dominion (first by naming and subjecting living creatures—husbandry, etc....and then??)

Here was a short-list of responsibilities, some of which we seem to have pursued with holy abandon (i.e. increasing in number). But "ruling" was given to humanity from the outset—to *both* male and female (not just male). While the command was pertinent at the time for the animal kingdom, the function of ruling was clearly built into humanity from the outset, a political presage and necessity with the fulfillment of the other mandates—to increase in number and fill the earth. It was God who populated the earth with animals; the humans were given the task of populating the earth with people, for whom dominion and governance would be one of the primary distinguishing elements.

Whether the *imago dei* also had within it a prefiguring of the divine kingly rule, given the sorts of creation mandates delivered to Adam and Eve, is beyond the reach of this study but does warrant mention. Dominion is given the very first couple on the very first day: this is the first co-regency, co-rulership, co-kingship, even before there was any other human life to govern or culture to oversee.

In Genesis 10, close associations can be drawn between the severally repeated array of nation-terms and the nuances found in the Revelation grouping: family/clan/tribe, language, land/country/territory and nation (Gen. 10:5, 20, 31, 32). As Hayes puts it: "…the basis for the classifications of peoples in this chapter [Gen. 10] is a combination of anthropological, linguistic, political and geographical elements. Yet, all three genealogies [of Noah's sons] end with nations, perhaps indicating that political and national affiliations are the primary emphasis" (citing also Ross 1988:227-228). In light of the severity of the universal judgment in the flood, an immediate deduction from the nature of the judgment at Babel is the specificity; hence, mercy by limitation, with which judgment might thereafter be applied (as in the case of the nations of the conquest of Canaan). God had promised never again to so judge the whole world after the horrific loss from the flood (Gen. 8:21).

Apparently, many scholars have played down the significance of Genesis 10, doubtless due in part to its rather fragmentary and confusing listings. It has come under closer scrutiny in recent years. Scholars also have apparently dismissed it as any sort of influence on the understandings of "nations" by the NT writers. This, too, has begun to be re-examined. This writer's discovery of the similarity of categories between the four primary groupings of humanity in Revelation and the severally repeated groupings in Genesis 10 seemed to indicate some sort of biblical "envelope" encompassing the gamut of human "corporate history" from immediately after the re-formation of humanity with the flood to the very end of the book. And the context of Genesis 10 is the very hinge of history, with the Babel account as a backdrop for the table of nations and then, immediately following, the call of Abram to ultimately bless all the nations of the earth through his own nation's election and redemptive vocation.

The beginnings of salvation history, then, are rooted in the founding of a nation, not fundamentally the saving of a soul or even the calling of a leader. The Abrahamic covenant is all about nation(s). While the intermediate lines contain personal promises of blessing upon the man, the opening and closing lines refer to much grander purposes:

Top line:	I will make you into a great nation
Bottom line:	and all the peoples (families; see Gen 18:18 "nations") of the earth will be blessed through you.

Observe another rendition of the covenant with Abram: Gen. 17:3-6

As for me, this is my covenant with you: You will be the father of *many nations*. No longer will you be called Abram; your name will be Abraham, for I have made you a father of *many nations*. I will make you very fruitful (reminiscent of the Adamic covenant?); I will make *nations* of you, and *kings* will come from you.

God changed Abram's name to Abraham expressing the promise of his fathering many nations. The beginnings of salvation history in the postdiluvian world are introduced through the agency of a nation among the nations just enumerated. This is early cosmic-level evidence of the providence of God introducing in sharp relief a redemptive plan which emerged directly out of an act of global judgment—the dispersing of the people from Babel into languages, tribes, and nations all going their own way. Only the birth of the church would see the beginnings of a great international reversal on this judgment. But in the interim, God's redemption project would not only exploit but actually center in on the fragmentation of humanity into hundreds or thousands of nations.

The book of Exodus, after hundreds of years of "tribal formation" by the sons of Israel as slaves in Egypt, chronicles the story of a "nation" undergoing a massive liberation, one of the prime scriptural motifs/metaphors for salvation/redemption. This was the great Passover event, the freeing of a people to worship God, to settle a land, to have God as their king, to be taught—discipled and to live under all his good law.

In the climax of the exodus event, as Moses is being given the Decalogue, one of the Bible's more controversial divine-human dramas takes place, which again draws us into the centrality of nations in the overall program of God. Moses "stands in the gap" for the entire nation, at the moment condemned unconditionally by an angry Jehovah, over their fickle idolatry, immorality and short memory. God is about to "make of you [Moses] a[-nother] great nation." (see another repeat instance in Num. 14:12) Apparently nations really are the method God has prescribed for effective redemption in the earth! Yet Moses, meekest man on earth (see Ps. 2:9 and Matt 5:5) "inherits the nation" back from the brink of disaster (in classic Ezekiel 22:30 fashion) by appealing to none other than God's reputation among the Egyptians—the "nations" (Ex. 32:11-14; Deut. 32:27; see Num. 14:15). Later, Moses, appealing to God's glory and pleading for his presence to go with the nation, asks, "What else will distinguish me and your people from all the other people on the face of the earth?" God had promised to "do wonders never before done in any nation in all the world" (Ex. 34:10).

The conquering of the land of Canaan was a conquest of "nations" or city-states, all aligned in evil against the LORD God of Israel. From Leviticus onward, through the entirety of the OT, God is seen to be "discipling a whole nation." While individuals rise to prominence in the overall drama, it is the nation whose heart God is after. This is, after all, his showcase for the nations. His Bride (Hosea) is a model of not only individual followership, but of glorious corporate community under his kingship. The law given is less pietistic than social. The sum of the law is relational not spiritualistic: Love God with your whole being and neighbor as self. It extends to every corner of Jewish societal life. This is all a means to the end that *panta ta ethne* might be made to worship, praise and follow him in the footsteps of the model nation Israel.

In the poetry, the Psalmist is, imprecatory episodes aside, regularly interested in the glory of God among the nations. "All nations shall come and worship" is the high expectation of the poet/song-writer. Psalm 2, written by a king—for the Messiah, speaks the language of intercession for the inheriting of the nations. In fact, most of the Wisdom literature of the OT is written by kings, whether the subject is love (Song of Solomon), folly & philosophy (Ecclesiastes), ethics (Proverbs) or poetry/praise (Psalms). The Book of Proverbs is best understood in its fullest extent as a manual on national or societal ethics. Fully sixty verses speak specifically to the issues of kings and nation-states, beginning and ending with introductions of the primary authors (See 1:1; 8:15-16; 11:10-11,14; 14:28,34-35; 16:10-15; 19:6,12; 20:2,8,26; 21:1,31; 22:11,29; 23:1-2; 24:6,21-22,24; 25:1-7,15; 28:2-3,16,28; 29:2,4,12,14,26; 30:22,27-28-31; 31:1-9). This is the equivalent of two full chapters of the book devoted just to kings/rulers, not to mention the primarily society-wide anecdotes and proverbs applying to wealth and poverty, work and vice, integrity and immorality, crime and violence, health and education, law and business, labor and governance, child-rearing and marriage, justice and right living. In other words, this is much less a matter of personal piety as of community and national lifestyle and wellbeing—How should we live well in this world? Something like a secular Torah, Proverbs begins with a king and ends with a city-gate, the public square of monarchy-era Semitic life. It begins with a caricature of young men and ends with the portrait of mature womanhood.

The themes that run through the exilic literature are invariably national or nationalistic. Consider Esther, Ezra, Nehemiah, Daniel….

Books like Esther—which is the only biblical book not mentioning God—are reduced in meaning without the central role of nations and God's program to use, bless and move whole nations through the agency of his chosen people/nation. Esther, like Daniel, Nehemiah and others, is introduced as a representative of the people of God participating in the pinnacles of power, the greatest known empires (whether Egypt, Babylon, Persia and later Rome) in brokering the divine agenda in the midst of and often converting the great and godless superpower rulers of their day. Nehemiah operates as priest, prophet and king in post-exilic Israel, builder of walls, liaison with kings, prophet to his people, intervener in political affairs, defender of the law, restorer of order and justice.

The message of the major and minor prophets was directed primarily to NATIONS—rarely to individuals—unless to kings—or even clans; both ISRAEL (at times Judah, Samaria) as a singular audience with a will and often sundry other NATIONS in the vicinity—all are vital parts of God's judging and/or saving agenda for the earth.

◻ Think of all the oracles to nations in Isaiah (Assyria, Babylon, Moab, Damascus, Cush, Egypt, Babylon, Jerusalem, Tyre, Ephraim, David's city, the "obstinate nation" "those who rely on Egypt" ... "the nations")

◻ What about messianic prophecies: a KING is coming; the NATION will be restored:

◻ Is. 52:15 "So will he sprinkle many NATIONS, and KINGS will shut their mouths because of him." Messiah's redemptive work is directed at nations and their kings

◻ Is. 55:4 "See, I have made him a witness to the PEOPLES, a leader and commander of the peoples. Surely you will summon NATIONS you know not, and nations that do not know you will hasten to you, because of the LORD...."

◻ Is. 56:7 "for my house will be called a house of prayer for all NATIONS." A prime temple function, in God's vista, was intercession on behalf of the non-Jewish nations!

◻ Is. 66: A masterpiece on God's perfect future is all about NATIONS....

◻ Jeremiah's call to prophethood:1:9,10 "Then the LORD reached out his hand and touched my mouth and said to me [after the typical protest that he couldn't speak and was 'only a child']: 'Now, I have put my words in your mouth. See, today I appoint you over nations and kingdoms, to uproot and tear down, to destroy and overthrow, to build and to plant.'" Read on; the whole calling and the first chapter introduces Jeremiah to the nation, the whole land—its kings, officials, priests AND the peoples... (v. 18)

◻ Jeremiah 18—regarding God's pattern of judgment, strictly about "nation or kingdom" which receive his condemnation/warning (I judge—resent, they repent, I relent...) ; see also Jer. 26:3,19, Amos 7:1-6

◻ Ezekiel's famous passage on the man in the gap—God's willingness not to judge a wicked "Land"—and his forced choice to go ahead with judgment on the "land" after finding none to stay his hand (Ezek. 22); and his personifying speech regarding Sodom and Gomorrah as "your sister" (Ezek. 16).

◻ Daniel: exilic prophet, priest (intercessor) and king/governor—to/through the greatest empire on earth; a bridge person for the ages. Was there a parallel to Paul, sitting under house arrest, relating to members of Caesar's household, praying and preaching God's kingdom and the King Christ Himself?

◻ The example and story of Jonah, the paragon of OT mission, is a powerful testament to a holistic gospel, a holistic God, interested in the entire city-state of NINEVEH—not just its people, listed in four distinguishable social/political categories—but also its animals/beasts, both in their act of repentance but finally in God's stated concern for their welfare and ultimate saving, as the One who had indeed "tended it and made it grow." It seems that God is clearly saying to Jonah through the final lesson of the little vine, "Look, this is a city of my making; I've tended it and made it grow, and yet it's perishing; I must act on its behalf."

◻ Micah, another story of nations
◻ The "gospel" of Nahum 1 (oft-quoted in contemporary worship) is one of cessation of foreign invasion from Nineveh

New Testament Survey

The advent of the Christ, Messiah, comes upon the scene introducing simultaneously a KINGDOM and the KING...the centerpiece of history. His birth is attended by Eastern magi and violated by wicked King Herod—all purporting to worship this one who is "born KING of the Jews." The prophecies quoted at the time of Jesus' birth are pregnant with his anticipated kingship. "Son of God" is also to be understood primarily (in the 1st Century Jewish mind and expectation) as having more meaning in authority as king than in a sonship of divinity (See Wright). KING of KINGS is setting up his alternate society. Fulfilling OT prophecies of Davidic kingship, mentioned in the Magnificat, highlighted in Isaiah's potent naming of Messiah—Prince of Peace, on whose shoulders the government will rest—the increase of whose government and peace there will be no end.... He is the bringer of light to the nations/Gentiles (see Mt. 2:6; Lk. 1:52; 4:18; Is. 9:6-7; 40:1-4; 42:1-4; 49:6)

John the Baptist, admittedly an OT era prophet, had the audacity (and spiritual insight and obedience) to lay his life on the line asking none other than pagan Galilean King Herod Antipas to "act the Christian." The ethics of the Kingdom were brought to bear on a pagan king who reluctantly martyred the prophet due to his jealous, evil wife of adultery. John here was simply "teaching the nations to observe what I have commanded you," or, as one modern proverb puts it, "conforming the world to the word."

The temptation of Christ is climaxed by the offer of the arch-enemy, of all the "kingdoms of the earth" which are his by permission. This Jesus promptly, decisively resists, but later reflects in the introduction to the Matthean Great Commission [GC], in which "all authority" has been given to him—therefore the disciples are empowered to go—in his name—and teach these very same kingdoms (nations) to observe everything He's commanded. Between Christ (Messiah—Anointed One of prophetic Jewish expectation—of a KING), Lord *kurios*, Son of God (see Rod Allen's study on this for mission among more Semitic peoples/faiths) and King/Kingdom, the titles most common to Christ seem to converge more in his rulership than in any other one characteristic.

While this study cannot do justice whatsoever to even a brief excursus on the Kingdom of God in Jesus' life, ministry, teaching and vocation, it must simply be reiterated the Kingdom of God is, on one level the cosmic juxtaposition of all the kingdoms of this earth. It is the divine answer to human realms, the archetypal rule of goodness and light. And while the people of God are *the* prototypical nation, the new Israel, before which the nations of the earth are given a model of life, community and governance, yet the only ultimate kingdom by which humans can model their life is the unsullied reign, realm and good rule of God himself in Christ.

The passion of Christ is surrounded by talk of kings and kingdoms. For example, eleven times in John 18:33—19:21 "king" and "kingdom" are mentioned in Jesus' final hours before Pilate and on the cross. First, the singular trigger for Christ's self-aware announcement of the passion sequence, in John 12, is the advent of the Greeks to Jerusalem, querying, "Sir, we wish to see Jesus." This galvanized Christ into his final essays on the *raison d'etre* of his mission/vocation. Immediately he responds, "THE hour has come for the Son of Man to be glorified...!" It is a knee-jerk reaction to the internationalizing nature of the Greeks' request that puts Jesus on the final and irreversible trajectory to the cross. For (spoken just a few verses later) "I, if I am lifted up, will draw all men [not just Jerusalem Jews and pilgrim Greeks] to myself." Second, Christ's Olivet discourse and final words to his disciples seem especially conscious of his own kingship over the last days (Mt. 25). Thirdly, the triumphal entry into Jerusalem is Davidic, kingly, unmistakably a political threat to Jewish and other powers, for this announcement resounds through the streets of Jerusalem, "Hosanna; Blessed is the King of Israel!" …fulfilling the Zecharian prophecy, "Your king is coming, seated on a donkey's colt." Christ is then arrested in the swirl of accusations of inciting political rebellion (Lk. 23:2, 13 "We have found this man subverting our nation! He opposes payment of taxes to Caesar and claims to be…a king!"). Barabbas, the one released in his stead is a first-rate political conspirator (Lk. 23:19). This accusation becomes the axe the Jews grind before the Romans—strangely—in seeking Jesus' death. [Imagine, the chief priests claiming—in truly blasphemous fashion, "We have no king but Caesar!"] The parallel accusation is his claim to kingship.

Pilate—in Caesar's chair, probes and discovers not insurrection but an admission of Kingship and possession of a Kingdom. When Pilate discovers this due claim, Christ then summarizes his overall vocation in this status, "You are right in saying I am a king. In fact, for this reason I was born, and for this I came into the world.…" The Jews elicit from Jesus a claim to Messiahship—the Jewish equivalent of Davidic King, blasphemy in their judgment—and the secular leaders elicit a claim to kingship as well. Pilate chooses to post the claim—without dilution or explanation to Kingship (to the chagrin of the Jews)—in three languages(!) for all the world to read. This scene is spelled out in all four gospels. The mocking which occurs at the foot of the cross is mainly a throwing of this claim to kingship back in Jesus' face as he suffers and dies. Then, the thief upon the cross, overhearing the mockery and repenting, asks Jesus one favor, remember him when coming into his kingdom [or "in your kingly power"] (See Luke 23:42).

Jesus' death is explicable in a thousand shades and properly using multiple culpable parties. But, as Vishal Mangalwadi puts it so succinctly, to the first century followers of the Way, Jesus had obviously died at the hands of Jewish and Roman authorities for being a genuine troublemaker. He had called the bluff of oppressive regimes both within the Jewish religious hierarchy as well as within a host of oppressive powers, including spiritual authorities, grasping after gain and glory on the backs of the poor and downtrodden. He was associated with other renegade reformers, using violence on at least one occasion to correct gross injustice and abuse of God's people/presence. The greatest power encounter in history is of course the cross, in which the common people, the highest government officials, the religious and military establishments, and the hoards of hell all conspired as one man to put this man and his convicting/convincing message away.

The Great Commission in the post-resurrection appearances of Christ in the Synoptics makes unequivocal the prime "target" of the *kerygma*, THE NATIONS and THE KOSMOS/CREATION—not mentioning individuals (in Matthew and Mark); the task of preaching is directed at ALL CREATION (as opposed to our traditionally demographic interpretation of Mark), and the task of teaching/discipling is directed at ETHNIC NATIONS (as opposed, once again, to our persistent individualistic interpretations/implementations of "discipleship"). We will later return to this hinge of history in our discussion tying the overall biblical study to the mission of the church today. The Johannine post-resurrection appearance of Jesus to the apostles on the shores of Galilee contains a tentative allusion to the nations of the known world at that time with the particular count of 153 large fish. Peter's reversion to literal fishing at a time when he had been called to "fish men" was abruptly interrupted by the sovereign, risen Lord, who supernaturally provided the catch and immediately launched Peter into his pastoral and evangelistic career (John 21). Some scholars have postulated a symbolism in the number of fish caught, corresponding to the number of nations commonly known to exist, which point Peter and his fellow fishermen to the supernatural "catch" among the nations which God would grant the church in the ensuing church age (Wolfgang Simson).

Pentecost is marked by that bizarre presentation of the NATIONS to the birthday celebration of the [almost entirely Jewish] Church. Somehow representatives "from every nation under heaven" were gathered in the vicinity of the Pentecost-event (Acts 2:5). Of all things to punctuate the advent of the Spirit filling the church, the use of a score of the known world's languages simply accentuates the seriousness of Christ's commission: the priority of the nations, peoples, languages and countries of the earth as prime recipients of his mission. The last recorded words of Peter's otherwise very Jewish interpretation of the obviously international gift of the Holy Spirit at Pentecost seem to capture the meaning of the multiplied languages, but did not really offer an adequate answer to their question ("What does this mean? How is it that each of us hears them—these Galileans—in his own native language? We hear them declaring the wonders of God in our own tongues!"). "The promise is for you and your children *and for all who are far off….*"

The body of the Book of Acts is structured around the mission of Paul presented to Ananias, a message directed to three specific audiences: Jews, Gentiles AND their KINGS (Acts 9:15). As we discover later, Paul's understanding and use of "Gentiles" as read in most English translations may well have inferred "nations" more than generic "Gentiles" and in this case it seems Luke understands the term in the same way. The first chapters of the book are dominated by the Jerusalem church's founding, power encounters with the Jewish religious establishment and a large Jewish turning to Christ. The second third of the book is marked by the sending of the reluctant Jewish church into the *goyim* (Gentiles generically), with first the "deacons" of the Hellenistic church serving throughout Samaria and the vicinity of nations surrounding Palestine (eclipsing the intended work of the apostles who appointed them to serve tables so *they* could continue "ministry"), as well as the main missionary journeys of Paul into Asia Minor and southern Europe. The final third, to the disappointment of some, is the record of mainly the apostle Paul, inconveniently dragged before tribunals, interacting with military, political, and other governmental/institutional leadership; ending, of course, with Paul preaching both the KINGDOM and the KING in the shadow of Caesar's palace, the most powerful KINGDOM on earth at the time; one which would succumb, no doubt in some measure due to Paul's early influence, to the Christ-King under Constantine. This structure to the "acts of the apostles" not only corresponds with Paul's commission in Acts 9 but with the Matthean commission to disciple NATIONS, not just individuals, communities or generic Gentiles—which would have occurred through, say, Paul's apparent traditional means of power encounter, prayer, evangelism and church development or training.

The church, founded and built not by the apostles but by Christ—Messiah/King, is given the distinction of God's new NATION, priested with KINGS (1 Peter 2:9), that she might "declare the praises of God" purportedly before the *other* nations. 1 Peter 2 is illustrative of this connection between mission and national "ethics" by the apostle's church being a nation, called to proclaim the praises of God, then called to live righteously so the pagans will glorify God at his visitation...immediately followed by the commendation to submission to all earthly authorities, kings or governors.

The apostolic epistles (especially the Pauline) are addressed to churches, not local congregations, but collectives of house-fellowships identifiable by their host Roman province or city-state, their geo-political environs.

Paul's letter to the Romans, seen as a pinnacle of revelation by many within more propositional "modern" scholarship, begins and ends with magisterial summaries of Paul's mission. Rom.1:5 "Through him and for his name's sake, we received grace and apostleship to call people from among all the Gentiles to the obedience that comes from faith" Rom. 16:25-26. "Now to him who is able to establish you by my gospel and the proclamation of Jesus Christ, according to the revelation of the mystery hidden for long ages past, but now revealed and made known through the prophetic writings by the command of the eternal God, so that all nations might believe and obey him—to the only wise God be glory forever through Jesus Christ! Amen (NIV).

This envelope of his greatest epistle illumines a connection between Paul and the resurrected Christ—whose mission to him particularly included Gentile Kings. The language of 16:26 uses the same phrase, *panta ta ethne* as well as the *obedience of nations* as a parameter for mission which Jesus declares in the "bottom-line" of the Matthean commission.

It is interesting to note here that modern translators of the NT have almost entirely chosen a misleading or at least one-sided rendering in the English for Paul's treatment and understanding of nations within the program of God's mission. In Romans 15, for example, in discussing his ministry to non-Jews, Paul repeatedly mentions the "Gentiles" as the object of his ministry. Yet Paul is quoting here from passages which, in possibly every case are indubitably rendered "nations," not "Gentiles" in their OT source texts.

15:9 "Therefore I will praise you among the NATIONS (Gentiles—e.g. NIV, KJV, TEV); I will sing hymns to your name" (2 Sam 22:50; Ps. 18:49). 15:10 "Rejoice, O NATIONS (Gentiles—e.g. NIV, KJV, TEV), with his people" (Deut. 32:43). 15:11 "Praise the Lord, all you NATIONS (Gentiles— e.g. NIV, KJV, TEV), and sing praises to him, all you peoples" (Ps. 117:1). 15:12 "The Root of Jesse will spring up, one who will arise to RULE over the PEOPLES (nations—NIV); the NATIONS (Gentiles— e.g. NIV, KJV, TEV) will hope in him" (Is. 11:10).

It is J. D. Hayes who has uncovered more recent attention to this discrepancy and studied questions which this raises concerning Paul's understanding of the OT usage of "nation" within the 1st Century Jewish worldview and hermeneutic. J. Scott apparently concludes through extensive linguistic research that Genesis 10 did indeed provide a basis for [Paul's and his Jewish contemporaries'] geographical view of the world.

"Thus when Paul uses the term *ethne* he generally has 'nations' in mind rather than individual Gentiles."[12] In addition, Scott notes that Paul's use of the Abrahamic promise reveals an awareness of Genesis and the relationship between the Abrahamic promise and the Table of Nations (1995:129). Finally, Scott presents the idea that the Table of Nations in Genesis 10 lies behind Paul's missionary strategy, particularly as Paul outlines in Romans 15 (1995:136-147)

This lends new meaning to the title for Paul as "apostle to the Gentiles" since it could as easily have been understood by him and others as an apostleship to the [non-Jewish] nations. "Gentiles" can convey an unnumbered and monolithic or generic mass, whereas "nations" conveys a parsing of humanity into individually created, manageable/reachable, corporately identifiable units. This certainly is reflected in Romans as we've seen, and even in Paul's desire to go on through Rome to Spain, likely on the borders of Paul's conception of the "uttermost parts of the earth." A reading of Young's Literal Translation through Romans 15 and 16 is enlightening in this regard—in which every case of *ethne* is translated "nation" instead of "Gentiles."

Paul's treatment of election in Ephesians, on the face of it, appears individualistic in thrust ("for he chose us in him...that we might be holy and blameless in his sight."—1:4) But as the writer moves through the related soteriological themes, he comes to an ecclesiological climax in Chapter 2, in which he describes the Church as one "new man in Christ" where old enmities are done away through the Lord's peace-making work on the cross. Whereas before, these Ephesians were "separate from Christ, excluded from *citizenship* in Israel and *foreigners* to the covenants of the promise, without hope and without God in the world," now "you are *no longer foreigners* and *aliens*, but *fellow citizens* with God's people, and members of God's household...." (2:12,15,19) Then, Paul goes on to describe the mystery of the inclusion of *ta ethne* as "heirs together with Israel, members together of one body, and sharers together in the promise in Christ Jesus." (3:6) Even election is explicated here in corporate, national and instrumental terms—to the end that "now, through the church [this new nation/*ethne*] the manifold wisdom of God should be made known to the rulers and authorities in the heavenly realms...." (3:10)

Paul's late-in-life letter to Timothy, his beloved son in the faith, boldly proclaims that it is God's will that "all men be saved and come to a knowledge of the truth" (1 Tim. 2:3). But the context of this bold declaration is actually prayer for "all men everywhere, for kings and all those in authority." Somehow the peaceful national life, which political rulers hold within their purview, is connected to the desire of God for all to be saved; and the prayer for all people everywhere certainly ties to the same. Ed Silvoso has expounded further on this under-developed connection (See Silvoso). National well-being and universal salvation have some sort of cosmic symbiosis. This idea is continued in the verses immediately following, in which Christ is portrayed as the great mediator "who gave himself as a ransom for all men." And for this very purpose Paul was appointed a "...teacher of the true faith to the *ethne.*" Paul then seems to conclude with "I want men everywhere to lift up holy hands in prayer...." Intercession *everywhere* (in other words, a sort of "missionary prayer") is meant to occur within the vision of a world of "all men" and their kings/authorities coming to the knowledge of the truth, through the ministry of those who are teaching the true faith to the nations—a restatement of the bottom line of the Matthean Great Commission.

Peter, in describing the nature of the church as a "holy nation," moves immediately from the church's *national identity* to the requirements of this new people to submit themselves to every authority: kings and governors. When the same descriptors are used by John in the Apocalypse, he follows it with the co-regency of the people of God with the king of the universe—"And they will reign on the earth." As one popular author wrote in the 1970's, the holy nation of God's church is "destined for the throne," in some sense both now and later. The judgment of earth at the end of the age is also characterized by Jesus, in one discourse, as a judgment of the nations-as-persons (Mat. 25).

The dominant demographic motif of the Apocalypse is *nations* and their *kings* (see study), which at the close of this age experience the healing of God and bring *their glory* into the city of God. This is the consummation of redemption history—in which the kingdom(s) of this earth has (have) become the kingdom(s) of our God and of his Christ....

Richard Mouw, in his invaluable treatment of Isaiah 60, deals extensively with the relationship between the apocalyptic vision of this chapter (and indeed much of Isaiah's vision-life) and the vision of John in the book of Revelation (See Mouw). Apparently both men are being given a glimpse of the future of God's cosmic order, brought to restoration and fulfilment in the *eschaton*. But Mouw's contention, from solid exegesis and contextual scholarship, is that this vision is neither utterly other-worldly, nor utterly discontinuous with the present age. While not advocating a particular millennial theology,

Mouw is allowing the text and its context to point us in the direction of more practical understandings of these grand visions. Central to this thesis is the role of nations and their kings. These are not necessarily our idea of "Christian nations" or simply large agglomerations of saved people. Rather, there is a redemption of cultures and nations going on in the direction of the apocalypse which offers hope for the present world order. King Jesus has a project for the nations, just as he does for individuals. The book of Revelation is crystal clear on this.

This writer has examined the book of Revelation for clues as to both the "demographics of heaven" as well as hints concerning the governing metaphors for Christ in the apocalypse. One interesting sidebar of this study is to query the stereotypical understanding of Christ's titles and functions throughout Revelation, as opposed to the same in other Scripture contexts. A standard assumption in juxtaposing the first and second comings of Christ, for instance, tends to see the First Advent through the metaphor of the suffering Servant or the lamb slain for the sins of the world—contrary to all the heightened kingly expectations of the Jews of Jesus' day. The Second Advent is seen through the metaphor of *Christus Victor*, Christ the reigning King, the Lion of the Tribe of Judah. This portrayal is only partially correct, and the Book of Revelation demonstrates a character of the apocalyptic Messiah which is still very much rooted in the slain Lamb, NOT the Lion. And Mouw reminds us that the Lion is from and for the Tribe (nation) of Judah, while the Lamb, far and away the dominant Messianic motif in Revelation, is for the whole world and across all ages (see APPENDIX 1). And, though Lamb is the governing metaphor for Christ in the Apocalypse, Jesus is introduced at the beginning as "ruler of the kings of the earth" (Rev. 1:5) and in the end as "King of kings and Lord of lords" specifically in his engagement with the rulers of the earth (Rev. 19:11-21).

In the final city of God, "the nations" will walk in God's light, and in John's account all traces of a Hebrew-centered religion are erased. …The one who steps forth to open the scroll is a Lamb to whom the new song is sung… he appears neither very lion-like nor very Jewish. This point Mouw makes to contrast the highly nationalistic thrust of so much of the OT prophets' communication. Yet, Isaiah was confronted by visions which moved the purposes of God far beyond the locality and confines of the Jewish nation. And John's apocalypse bears this out only more fully (Mouw 2002:79).

Biblical Conclusions

1) Nations, understood biblically, encompass the larger groupings of humanity, whether within clan/tribe/kinship associations/allegiances, cultural/ethnic/linguistic enclaves, and/or political/civic/cosmopolitan/country boundaries.

2) Nations (often as political entities *with their rulers*) are central to the text and the overarching redemptive purposes of God in history. I propose here that they are in fact the prime recipients and agents of God's salvific work in the earth. Individuals within the program of God are subsumed within or under national/ethnic/ clan/tribe/linguistic categories, not vice versa. Bos sees this as a "greater glory" through a divinely ordained and trinitarian-reflective corporateness which spans all of Scripture (Bos 2002:23-50).

3) God has, in both covenant ages, chosen a nation, through an individual, to bless all the nations of the world with simultaneously a message, a working *nationhood* model, and a means/membership of salvation.

4) Election, then, may be less individualistic than national, corporate and instrumental (a means to an end); the elect, God's chosen nation, exist in good measure for the non-elect, or *ethne*, yet outside of their purchased covenant blessings.

5) Nations have unique, created, marred and (conditionally?) redeemed "glory," which their king-rulers will in real time bring into the city of God as a significant climax in the celebration of God's redemption of the cosmos.

6) Nations and their kings will be judged by Christ for what they have done in regard to him and his people.

7) The people of God in right standing with him have always been given or promised rulership over nature and the nations, as "kings and priests" with God.

8) Jesus Christ is both the desire of the nations (Hag. 2:7) and the light to the nations (Is. 42:1-4:49:6, others). For him, it was "too light a thing" to merely be the appointed/ anointed Servant to restore the tribes (nations) of Jacob... Rather, being a light to the Gentile nations would bring God's salvation to the very ends of the earth; this light he maintains and carries into eternity for the nations.

9) Whole nations, with their kings, will experience the healing of God and an eternal life within the city of God, in the presence of the Lamb; this is as much a part of the final picture of the ages as is individual salvation and eternal bliss.

10) The destiny of individual nations falls within a set of parameters in a divine-human interplay:

   ¤ Sovereign creation and specific intention for redemption, adoption, prayer, inheritance and worship (Gen. 10; Acts 17:26; Ps. 72:11;Is. 2:2; 42:1,6; 60:1-3; 66:18; Zech. 2:11; Rom. 3:29)

   ¤ Specific national identity and glory (Rev. 21:24,26)

   ¤ Demonic infestation and corruption or collaboration of "powers" with fallen human agents of the institutions of nations, creation of spiritual strongholds and oppressive realms/domains over against the good reign and realm of God (Gen. 3, Daniel 9, Rev. 16:12-14;17; 18:23; 20:8)

   ¤ Divine judgment upon all fallen structures, oppressive regimes, rebel rulers (Samuel, Nathan, Isaiah, Jeremiah, Daniel, Habakkuk, etc.)

   ¤ Human intercession as the great go-between and cancellation of judgment (Gen. 18; Ex. 32; Num. 14; Ps. 2; Ezek 22:30)

   ¤ The *kerygma* of Christ, including prophetic judgment, conveyed to all levels of society (Acts 9:15)

◻ The people of God as the visible model of proper national identity (2 Pet. 2:9)

◻ The Holy Spirit's conviction, outpouring and angelic intervention (the invisible "powers") (Dan. 9; Acts 10:45)

◻ National repentance (2 Kings 23-Josiah; Jer. 18:7-10; Jonah 4)

◻ The discipling of the nation ultimately yielding patterns of obedience to Christ's law of love (Mt. 28:18-20; Rom. 1:5; 16:26)

11) A significant part of the inheritance of the people of God is the "nations" and "the earth" or "the world" (Ps. 2; Is. 54:1-3; Mt. 5:5:Rom.4:13)

Missiology and the City

Urbanization is certainly one of about a dozen hallmarks of the age in which we live, which has completely redefined life on planet earth. I understand from a friend who knows China fairly well that one of their goals as a nation is to urbanize to the extent that China alone will have, by the year 2030, thirty cities, each with a population exceeding thirty million! We now may have just one urbanized nation at that size, but is China alone following this pattern? What about India? I have also heard that any city exceeding five million in population creates a bureaucratic nightmare, or something which no city-planning to this point has been able to master, organize or govern properly.

Urban squalor, the mass migration of the rural poor to become the urban poor, is a global nightmare. Almost every major city in the world over ten million has hundreds of thousands if not millions who live on that edge of global poverty, under one dollar-a-day, and consist of all manner of creative ways to make ends meet, many of them criminal in nature. And women and children inevitably become the most abused, oppressed or manipulated for evil intent in this process.

I tie the "discipling of the nations," as I've sought to lay it out in Scripture here, directly with the "discipling of a city" for several reasons:

1) "Nations" as we know them today are hardly recognizable in relation to "nations" in the times of the writing of the biblical scriptures. I believe this does not, by itself, undermine the conclusions I'm coming to in this paper, in part because it seems very clear that God has—through the various Scripture writers, allowed for a large degree of latitude in our understandings of the larger groupings of humanity, but at the same time not allowing for their obliteration-out-of-confusion. God is passionate about the discipling of these larger groupings of humanity—as distinct entities which all possess their own "corporate identity" and which will in some way participate in that final ingathering of humanity through these larger realities portrayed so clearly in Rev. 21.

2) Certainly, a few nations are cities and cities nations—worldwide. Just as there is in many cases plenty of overlap between "ethnic groupings" of humanity and the geopolitical nations of which they are a part (think of so many nation-states whose name reflects the dominant ethnic grouping within the nation), so there is also overlap, in some cases, between the geo-politics of certain nation-states and the dynamics or realities of city-life which defines that group as well.

3) Lastly, though, I borrow heavily from the work of Pieter Bos in laying out a dynamic relationship—in Scripture—between God's passion for "nations" and the distinct role of cities in relation to that wider, corporate passion of God for humanity.

Bos spends considerable time in his first book, *The Nations Called*, laying out the personality of nations—as they are described in Scripture (as I did at the beginning of this essay)—and then develops further material on their "corporate identity" by revealing both from

Scripture and then from extensive study of contemporary states an attempt to identify whole nation-states with their "corporate identity" as a particular group of people, whose culture and national identity is part of what is spoken of by God—through John—when it says in Rev. 21 that the "glory and splendour" of the *ethne* will be brought, by their kings, into the city of God.

Bos has devoted an entire second book, The City Called, to the notion that cities, typically the demographic smaller of these two groupings of humanity, also has a biblical calling, as an "Absolute Partner, or Helpmate, with God."

> According to the biblical evidence, cities are presented as feminine persons, who can speak, express will, welcome, mourn, have self-awareness, boast, kill, stone, rule, repent, be born, become a bride or a prostitute, be married and have sons, and who will be judged.

A person—like the nations—which was foreknown even at the time of the creation of the first couple, was a pre-fall concept, a fruit of God cooperating with humanity, both on this earth and on the new earth.

> Even his designed ruling partner, as nations gather in her place and invest themselves environment-wise, resource-wise, social-intercourse-wise and community-wise, so emphasizing the joy of eco-system, of labor, of culture and of being a people at a place (Bos 2002:24).

This language ties much material in Scripture together…certainly the case of Abraham, spoken of in Hebrews 11 as someone who was looking forward to the city with foundations, whose architect and builder is God….all the while living in tents! Bos sees the creation mandate as something within God's creation which was good but not finished. It was waiting for the full cooperation of humanity to finish his good beginning. As in the case of Adam naming the animals and

God ordaining that this would be his participation in the creation process. This also adds meaning to humanity being radically unique in the creation process—because he/she were made "in the image of God" which clearly implies their creative genes among other uniqueness.

God's city is where we are all headed. We may have begun in a garden but we are clearly headed for a city! And Bos points out that, as in the end, so it is with cities generically; while nations tend to be mono-ethnic in their make-up and identity, cities are multinational, multi-ethnic and so the picture of the last of the book is of the nations, bringing their glory and splendor *into the city of God.* Many nations, one city.

So urban missions and even "city-reaching" becomes a primary task of the church in this age...in what was inferred in the creation mandate, in the context of so much of God's language about cities throughout Scripture, in light of current global—urbanizing—context in which we find ourselves, and especially where we all are headed, into the *city of God!*

Missiology and the Buddhist World

Nation-states are very much in flux these days. It was futurologist John Naisbitt who claimed in his book *The Global Paradox* that by the year 2050 there could be 1000 nations in the U.N. as opposed to the 250 or so which were around when he wrote it—in the mid-1990's (1994:37ff). Some have pointed out that allegiances have tended to move either up or down in relation to old nationalisms: upward toward civilizational loyalties—like Islam, Catholicism, Buddhism or downward toward more tribal loyalties. In that respect Naisbitt was counting on many more nations emerging, as nation-states as we've known them become less relevant and tribal loyalties move our allegiances to our smaller, more ethnic units. If this actually happens it will assist in the final picture which John the Apostle draws of "kings bringing the glory and splendor of the nations (*ethne*) into the city of God" in the sense that there will be increasing numbers of nation-states whose borders, title, sovereignty, geo-politics and corporate identity are all wrapped up within their tribal AND national self.

The Buddhist world, mainly in the Far East, is as familiar with older-school kings and kingdoms as any part of the world in some ways. Bhutan, Thailand, Nepal, and older realms like Cambodia, Myanmar and Japan, have all experiences the good and bad of kingly rulerships, and the first two or three mentioned still have living kings who are very much a part of their national identity. Whereas we in the West are overly familiar with our several-hundred year old experiment with democracy, and thereby don't quite as easily embrace the nation of final-day "kings bringing the glory of their nations into the city of God" for many of those in Buddhist nations, a good part of their history, even recently, can understand the regal wonder of this procession.

The supreme difficulty for our more missionary perspective in relation to the Buddhist world is that for a very long time, "mission" has been largely nonpolitical. As Evangelicals we've tended to pride ourselves in the exclusivity of our claims and our message—Christ alone, which inferred a heaven-only outcome, a heavily dispensational theme of simple getting people saved and preparing them for heaven in our largely Western-style churches.

That reality is, I believe, a fact of the past. There is a massive and rapid revival of several overlapping themes which tie almost directly to the primary thesis of this paper:

1) The renewal of the centrality and primacy of the Kingdom of God, or, as one friend put it, the Overwhelming Transforming Influence of God, as our main objective in mission.

2) With this centrality of the Kingdom comes a renewed passion to see God reconciled to *all* things, that his will is that *all* be saved, and that he is ambitious to collaborate with humanity in restoring *all* things (individually, socially and environmentally) to his original purposes.

3) The refusal to continue a long dualism between the sacred and the secular, between heaven and earth, the spiritual and the physical; that holism or "wholism" as an approach

to people is much more consistent with all of Scripture and certainly with Christ's *modus operandi* than what we have tended to do in "ministry."

4) That the "ordained" is coming back to the "ordinary," and that ideas like "business as mission" are increasingly common-place, that what the church (laity) does for over 95% of its week—outside that Sunday service—is much more important, by sheer impact—in the long run, than what it does united in worship and the Word as the "church gathered."

For this to be meaningful especially within the Buddhist world I would propose that several fundamental changes have to occur in contemporary mission—if they are not already happening!

1) That our "target" in mission moves well beyond the mere individual to the family, the community, the tribe, the language and the nation…. That this shift will require some arduous work in strategizing for how we will in fact "disciple the whole *xyz*—clan, community, city or nation."

2) Following quickly on this, that our "task" is viewed as much more comprehensive and kingdom-related than the watchwords of "evangelism and church planting" of the past. While we will never downplay the importance of these activities, we have a view of God's kingdom coming to earth—within these same contexts—in ways which encompass all of reality, all the domains of life, including business, education, politics (the *kings*), media, family ,etc. because we have as our ambition the mission of Christ, *obedient nations* spoken of throughout the OT, inferred by Christ's kingship, exposed in the Great Commission, elaborated by Paul's conversion and calling, and climaxed in the great *eschaton*.

3) Thirdly, that the form of the church we'll pursue tends to look increasingly like something outside the churches of today, that it:

195

a) empowers the unordained, the *laos*—to do works of ministry;

b) celebrates its smallness so it can be eminently big (i.e. organic and reproductive);

c) learns to produce disciples—not converts;

d) is about multiplication and movement, not edifices and ministry professionals;

e) is a contextualized and relationship-based, corporate move to Christ and not a competitor religion; and it

f) infects all the major domains of life and their respective worldviews, whether that be labor (factories?), education, business and technology, politics, medicine, law, agriculture and land-ownership, media and the arts, sports and entertainment, the police and military, the press, recreation and the family—to name a few of the major ones.

5) That it's about story, not much about systematics. It engages people at the levels of real-life, and paints a picture of what God is like in the here and now. It's holistic which means it is not just about concern for the physically needy—which of course it must be—but it includes many arenas, like the realm of spiritual warfare, knowing full well that we are all dealing with an enemy who has come to "steal, kill and destroy," but also knowing that there are entities which exist today which are structural or systemic sources of oppression in these societies and which much be redeemed in order for society to function well, to be healthy. Individuals need demons cast from them—as do some larger powers.

6) That Christ must remain central to our every endeavor, that he is the King of kings, the lamb slain, the Servant-King, God's best for our worst, the author and finisher of our faith, that his act was the centerpiece of history, and that all history moves toward him...and that his is the Kingdom we all pray daily—and work hard—to see.

I apologize, sincerely, that this has not spoken to any one specific Buddhist context. I have spoken very broadly on a topic which I feel is foundational to mission among Buddhists. I feel that if we don't get this right, much of what we are currently doing may be not necessarily wasted time but certainly out of sync with God's passion for this world of ours. He is pointing us in new directions, filled with hope, truth, beauty and love...the things which our Buddhist world yearns for and has too often not seen—at the hands of Buddhists or even Christians.

Conclusion

What we may conclude hear are several items: First, it seems clear there's been some serious neglect in most evangelical missiology on taking seriously what Jesus said in his Matthean Great Commission by a task which is focused on the nations, which actually disciples them as nations and thereby incorporates their ruling elite in the process. As a recent writer-practitioner has said:

> There is a great deal of evidence we are doing something wrong in our missions work, and that merely planting more churches isn't enough. ...The real evidence of a nation's conversion to Christ is its godliness. ...Godliness comes when a nation's Christians make it their all-consuming passion to see God's glory reflected in every domain of the land, its arts, sciences, media, government, schools, businesses, families— in every domain. ...God has a destiny for the nations of the world, and, as hard as many churches have tried, that destiny is not being fulfilled in most cases (Layton 2000:19-20). ....preaching to a nation cannot substitute for discipling that nation (2000:58).

Or, as another writer put it in relation to the father of modern mission, William Carey's, work:

Carey's confidence was not in his social protest or social action, but in the gospel. This is the very opposite of those Christians who put their hope for change in their "social action." It is also different from the faith of those who believe that the world can improve only after the Lord Jesus Christ will return. Carey became a reformer because he understood the breadth of the theological concept of the "Kingdom of God." He believed that if we disciple nations, we will increasingly see God's will being done here on earth (Miller :180-181).

In light of this, secondly, our debates from the 20th Century are genuinely behind us, that we need not continue verbal battles as though it's really just about how conservative or how liberal one is, but rather what indeed is and has God been most passionate about? We need not deliver our tasks any more as slivers of Biblical truth but take the "whole counsel of God" and derive from it our own overall passion and pursuits. There will be increasing overlap, as I see it, between things like what we used to call "mission" or the "Great Commission," and the "Great Commandments" or what we increasingly strive for in "seeking first the kingdom of God and his justice." We are becoming increasingly holistic in the best and fullest sense of that word.

Lastly, given all the fruit of the past century or two of modern "missions," built upon the shoulders of the past which we stand upon, there will need to be increased synergy within the overall Body of Christ, nationally and internationally, so that, in the shadow of the cross of Christ, we'll be bold enough to craft plans—together, which will bring about the obedience of the nations which Christ was after in his final mandate. And our motivation can be enhanced by so much of what I've pointed out here from Scripture, including the final picture of the nations being brought by their kings into the city of God, experiencing final healing and celebrating that final feast of the good, pervasive rule of God. For, as Christopher Wright puts it so well:

God's mission is what fills the gap between the scattering of the nations in Genesis 11 and the healing of the nations in Rev. 22. It is God's mission in relation to the nations, arguably more than any other single theme, that provides the key that unlocks the biblical grand narrative (Wright 2006:455).

On that [final] day, with the discipling of the nations complete, the kings of the earth will bring the glory of the nations to the Lamb—our King, Jesus Christ. Until that ultimate day, we all have work to do!

CHAPTER EIGHT

Filipino Urban Missions in the Buddhist World Today

DAVID S. LIM

What is the present status of Filipino missions to reach the one billion Buddhists in the world today? Though there are no concrete data yet on how many Filipino Evangelical missionaries are in the Buddhist world, I estimate conservatively there may be about 2,000 of them, mostly tentmakers (Christians who support themselves through their employment but who evangelize and make disciples cross-culturally). Perhaps about 400 of them left with intentions to be church-supported "career missionaries" in Buddhist lands, but almost all of them soon found that finding employment (almost always in the cities) in their target country is the only way they can stay long-term.

Urban missiologist Ray Bakke observes, "Once cities were in the nations, now nations are in the cities!" The experiences of the Filipino diaspora churches scattered in the cities can serve as models of cross-cultural missions that other ethnic diasporas can use to reach the cities of the world.

Historical Context: Filipino Migration

In the last three decades, there has been a massive movement of Filipinos into more than 190 countries of the world. The causes are economic and demographic: the weak economy with high rates of unemployment and rapid population increase,[1] together with an inward looking industrialization policy. Thus, the economy has become more and more dependent on the remittance of these overseas contract workers (OCW) as a valuable source of foreign exchange currencies.[2]

Though it started mainly as "muscle drain" to work in oil fields, by 2002, thirty-five percent were "professional and technical workers" (engineers, pilots, physicians and nurses), which constitutes a large-scale "brain drain" (Wehrfritz and Vitug 2004:32). The main problem is low pay at home. For example, in 2002, nurses were paid $139/month in the country, but $650/month in Singapore, $982/month in Saudi Arabia, and $1,666/month in United Kingdom (2004:32-33). All the while, the Philippine economy earned $58.5 billion from 1990-2002, for an average of $4.5 billion/year from their remittances. In 2003, they brought in $7.2 billion or 20.6 percent of the country's export earnings or 6.2 percent of Gross National Product (GNP) (Baldoz 2004:47).

Another good reason why Filipinos can keep flowing abroad is their good reputation, especially in "people skills". They have been appreciated for their technical skills, adaptability, creativity and cheerfulness, their high level of productivity and quality in production and management, as well as their English proficiency and pleasant voice and disposition (Baldoz 2004:43-48).

With 7,582,504 Filipinos working overseas at the end of 2002 growing to almost eight million, with a record of over a million in each year of 2005 and 2006, the government continually aims to send at least one million annually. Geographically, they were distributed thus: American and Trust Territories (3,334,297), East and South Asia (1,453,296), Europe (1,371,621), Oceania (298,609), and Africa (66,243). The top

---

1. The National Statistics Office estimates a population growth of 1.95 percent, from 85.3 million in 2005 to 94 million in 2010. With reduced growth rate, the population is still expected to double to 141.7 million by 2040 (Philippine Daily Inquirer, April 5, 2006:A3).

2. Cf. Baldoz 2004:41-42; which also quotes the Pulse Asia, *1st Quarter* 2002 poll that shows almost 20 percent of Filipinos want to leave the country and stay abroad.

eight countries of destination in 2003 were (in numerical order):Saudi Arabia, Hong Kong, Japan, UAE, Taiwan, Kuwait, Singapore, and Qatar (that's 50% in the Buddhist-majority nations).

Though they contribute much to the Philippine economy through their remittances and donations, as well as gaining skills, know-how, and capital for the country, almost eighty percent of them suffer from the *social costs* of marital break-ups and juvenile delinquency, with hardly any help from government and society at large (Wehrfritz and Vitug 2004:33; Religion 2004:22). The percentage of women has increased persistently: twelve percent in 1975, forty-seven percent in 1985, sixty-one percent in 1998, seventy percent in 2000, and seventy-three percent in 2003 (Baldoz 2004:41). This is bad news for the social and moral fiber of Philippine society which has traditionally been quite matriarchal.

Philippine Protestant Evangelical Religious Profile

The Philippines is the one major Asian nation with a Christian majority: eighty-four percent Roman Catholic, eight percent Protestant (including Aglipayans or Filipino/Independent Catholics), three percent Iglesia Ni Cristo (INC), three percent Muslim, and two percent others. Evangelicals (a subset of Protestants) are about seven percent, just over five million in an estimated population of eighty five million. The most visible evangelical group, with perhaps the most diaspora churches, the Jesus is Lord Church (JIL), whose influence extends far beyond its membership, has 300,000 members, 0.3 percent of the population.[3]

The first Protestant missionaries arrived with the American occupation forces in 1898. The churches they planted eventually became the mainline Protestant churches that constituted the National Council of Churches of the Philippines (NCCP) in 1965. In that same year, the Philippine Council of Evangelical Churches (PCEC) was formed by the

---

3. This is higher than Harper's (2000:249) conservative estimate of 150,000, but much lower than JIL's claim of two million internationally (2000:262).

churches that were established through Christian and Missionary Alliance (entered the country in 1928) and many post-World War II evangelical missionaries, many of whom were re-assigned to the Philippines when China turned Communist in 1949. With the charismatic revival of the late 1970s and the 1980s, the leading Full Gospel church called Jesus is Lord (JIL) gathered the others together to form the Philippines for Jesus Movement (PJM). DAWN 2001 Survey reports that Protestant churches are categorized thus: PCEC = 28%, NCCP = 13%, Baptist = 16%, Independent = 19%, and Full Gospel = 24%. The same survey shows there were 5.5 million Protestants who make up 7.2% of the population.

Philippine Protestantism has experienced relatively rapid church growth[4] in two main waves. In the first, the main evangelical denominations have tried to plant as many churches as possible following the "saturation church-planting" strategy which has promoted by Discipling a Whole Nation (DAWN), which began as Christ the Only Way (COW) Movement in 1968 and became DAWN in 1975.[5] The second was the charismatic revival of the 1980s and continuing to the 1990s, which attracted many in the developing or aspiring lower classes to form or join Full Gospel fellowships that eventually became churches.[6] In 1980, Filipino church leaders aimed to plant 50,000 churches by 2000. In 2001, DAWN reported that this target was reached. Many have considered this a religious revival, and it is in this context that Filipino missionaries are being mobilized. Yet till the present, as in almost all global cases, cross-cultural missions have been marginal in the life of the churches.

Filipino Missions

The main coordinating body for Filipino missions is "Philippine Missions Mobilization Movement (PM3)," which was formally organized at the

---

4. On the growth of Protestantism (see Vencer 1988:5-7) and of PCEC churches (see Aragon 2001:371-382).

5. On the birth (1974) and growth of DAWN in the Philippines, see Montgomery (1989:21-36) and Aragon (2001:384-386).

6. On the economic status of most new charismatic groups, cf. Martin (2002:1-7, 167-176) and Jenkins (2002).

March 17-19, 2005 Mission Consultation, with about forty church and mission leaders coming together for a historic strategic planning workshop. Its mission statement reads, "as a global movement of the Filipino church and partners, we shall seek to mobilize, train and send 200,000 tentmakers and career missionaries to reach the unreached people groups for Christ by 2010." The Philippine Missions Association (PMA, founded in 1983) through its new National Director, Bob Lopez,[7] volunteered to serve as its secretariat.

As of October 10, 2006, the "Status of Philippine Missions" Research Report has covered 1,900 missionaries in seventy countries, with 1,055 working overseas and 143 not indicating the nations they are working in. 338 are listed as "career missionaries," only sixty-five as tentmakers and nine as short-termers (both very under-counted), and 117 as missionary mobilizers and trainers. It has also found 360 mission agencies, seventy-two missionary-sending churches, 188 Global Filipino churches, and nineteen OFW pastors. Most Filipino mission leaders believe that these statistics cover only about twenty to twenty-five percent of the actual situation, but these can serve as a very reliable data-base and sample for this article.

So far, the top twenty countries of *documented* Filipino missionaries are (Buddhist nations in italics): *China* (159), *Thailand* (126), USA (106), *Cambodia* (81), Indonesia (67), Malaysia (39), *Japan* (24), *Singapore* (24), *Vietnam* (20), Afghanistan (15), Canada (15), Austria (14), Bangladesh (14), Nepal (11), *Hong Kong* (11), Kuwait (10), United Kingdom (10), *Mongolia* (9), UAE (8), and India (7).

These are joined and often supported by perhaps 30,000 Christian Filipinos overseas contract workers (OCWs) who are members in the various diaspora Filipino congregations (and international fellowships) in the major cities with significant Buddhist populations (like Hong Kong, Singapore, Taipei, Yokohama, Bangkok). They are part of the global labor-export industry of the Philippines since the mid-1970s,

---

7. Lopez came from the corporate world, a self-supporting pastor and one of the first ACM trainees, who sought to win the Sikhs, and was appointed Administrative Director of ACM (1999-2003). As he was moving to transfer his base to the Middle East in 2004, the PMA Board asked him to succeed Corpuz in 2003.

which now consist mainly of medical professionals (like nurses, doctors, medical technologists, physical therapists), various professionals (executives, engineers, teachers), skilled workers (entertainers, seamen, care-givers) and domestic helpers. This article considers only 2,000 from among them as missionaries in the Buddhist world, as those who have actually made conscious cross-cultural efforts to reach their Buddhist hosts, neighbors and/or colleagues for Christ.

The concept of tentmakers is new for most church leaders, so PM3 has to exert effort to inform and persuade them to work towards mobilizing their members to go as OFWs and serve as "lay missionaries" in their host countries. Almost every church has members who have relatives or friends working overseas. Given the poverty and unemployment situation in the Philippines, tentmaking is almost the only option for the local churches to play any significant role in world missions. According to a PCEC survey, about 80% of the pastors in Luzon receive less than $20 per month from their churches.[8]

Strategy: Integration of Four Streams

The Philippine missions movement has benefited from the integration of three main strategies, represented by four streams: Evangelical, Charismatic/Full Gospel, Transformational, and Diasporal.

Evangelical. The first stream is the mainline evangelical groups who have traditionally used the Western evangelical model of "evangelism and church-planting" in mission. Many of them frame their work using the fundamentalist and pietistic language of "saving souls". They constitute the majority of the membership of Philippine Mission Association (PMA), which includes the mission committees of local churches and denominations, as well as all kinds of mission groups: indigenous missions, foreign missions (especially American and Korean), missionary training institutes, and campus/youth ministries.

Among the churches, the Christian and Missionary Alliance of the Philippines (CAMACOP, organized in 1962) sent their first

---

8. Kim 2004:195, fn.1 also mentions the average attendance per church is about 35 adults.

missionaries (two couples) to Indonesia in 1968 (Guillermo 1983:84), and by 1988, they had eleven working in Bolivia, Palau, Thailand, Hong Kong and Uruguay also (Pate 1989). In 1973, the Assemblies of God sent their first missionaries (a couple) to Vietnam. They stayed until the fall of Saigon (1975), barely escaping to return safely (Javier 2002:75). In 1982, the Conservative Baptists (CBAP) sent two couples and a lady to Bangladesh, Guam and Nepal (2002:219-200,235), while the Assemblies of God sent a couple to Singapore and a lady each to Taiwan and Hong Kong (2002:316). Caloocan Bible Church supported one Campus Crusade for Christ (CCC) couple to serve in Thailand (2002:414). By this time, the Foursquare Church had eight missionaries in Asian mission fields (2002:158).

Among the mission agencies, the most prominent in the 1990s was the Philippine Home Council (PHC) of Overseas Missionary Fellowship (OMF), which was formed in 1966. By 1988, they had twelve missionaries serving in Japan, Thailand, Taiwan, Indonesia and Malaysia (Pate 1989:221), and 50 by 2001 (Manzano 1998:31). Together with two other west-based agencies, SEND International and World Team (formerly Regions Beyond Missionary Union, RBMU) and their partner church, the Alliance of Bible Christian Communities of the Philippines (ABCCOP), they formed Global Alliance Philippines Ministries (GAP) in order to field international missionary teams (Smith *et. al.* 2000:753).

PMA member churches with significant members of (partially) supported overseas missionaries are: Diliman Bible Church, Faith Baptist Church, Greenhills Christian Fellowship and Shekinah Christian Church. PMA also benefits from the presence of the major Western agencies, which often have their base for Asian or Asia-Pacific operations in Metro-Manila. The regular fellowship and interaction among these leaders has enhanced the healthy cross-fertilization of ideas and strategies as well as developed partnerships in the sharing of personnel and resources. Almost all of these missions operate with the typical evangelical paradigm of doing "evangelism and church-planting," and in recent years moved towards "church planting movements" (CPM), which is an approach different from that used by the next stream.

Charismatic/Full Gospel. The second stream, which may be growing the fastest, may be labeled "Charismatic/Full Gospel."[9] It has a similar church-planting emphasis but has a different strategic approach; they not only emphasize power evangelism through healing and deliverance ministries, they also adopt a more short-term approach to empowering local believers for ministry, thereby effecting a more "total mobilization" of the churches for faster church growth (or multiplication).

The two most prominent organizations in this stream are Desired of All Nations Missions Network (DOAN, formerly Asia Missions Network or AMNET) and Asian Center for Missions (ACM). DOAN is a loose association of independent churches from the Full Gospel tradition, formed through the initiative of Tribes and Nations Outreach (TNO) in 1996. TNO was founded by Brother Joseph in 1985, after he left Open Doors with whom he orchestrated the "smuggling" of one million Bibles at one time into China (Zaide 1994:32). He developed a CPM strategy that became a thirteen session training manual in their School of Workers (SOW) program. This has been implemented successfully in Mindanao, Indonesia, Myanmar and Indochina (Vietnam, Cambodia and recently in Laos). In recent years, they have developed an Asia Strike Force program to bring relief and the gospel to disaster-hit areas, as well as agricultural development programs to help make barren trees productive through organic farming methods.

DOAN gained quick prominence because it adopted the successful mission model of TNO, and utilized the management skills of its first General-Secretary, Chito Navarro, who had worked closely with Jun Vencer and trained national leaders from 100 nations. Its strategic thrust is called "Project END," to "Empower Nationals for Disciple-making" by sending church leaders in short-term mission teams to train local church leaders in their effective ministries for contextual application in their own milieu (Lim 2003a:205). It now looks forward to expanding the END strategy from twenty to (mostly Buddhist) twenty-five nations in Asia.

---

9. The Pentecostal denominations especially Assemblies of God, Foursquare and Church of God (Pentecostal) have followed the main evangelical paradigm, but their newer churches are adopting the Full Gospel approach.

Through DOAN some country-focused partnerships were organized. Bamboo Ministry was formed to reach Vietnam in June 1998. Soon after that, Torch Ministry was organized also to evangelize Myanmar. The latter raised funds to support some Burmese partners in the effective ministries. Their most successful venture is in medical missions, led by its Executive Director, Kara Dimacali, a dentist who rejoiced to see the Burmese forming their own medical teams and resourcing medicine and funds from their local sources in 2005. Similar to the DOAN strategy, but working from its three bases in Thailand, Ethnos-Asia led by Sonny Largado has been mobilizing Filipino and other Christians to do both short-term and long-term missions in the South-East Asian region, China, Myanmar and Nepal.

The other major group is ACM, which has become the training ground of those who have determined to go into career missions from the charismatic stream, with a few from the evangelical stream.[10] By 2005, ACM had trained 660 missionaries with over 290 deployed to twenty-six countries (Benigno 2005:14). These missionaries have undergone a five-month practical training at almost no cost to the trainee if they make a clear commitment to serve as career missionaries.

In the early years, ACM discovered that there were not enough mission agencies to deploy their graduates to their intended mission fields, so it became a sending agency also, with local churches asked to be partners in supporting these missionaries. Up to twelve extension training centers were set up (nine in the Philippines, three overseas in Varanasi, in Jakarta and in another city which can't be specified due to security reasons (Shubin 1998:39-40).

But this scheme did not work out well, for the churches just could not follow through on the pledged support for their missionaries and the expected local resources could not cover the budget. So the sending role was stopped and the training centers were decreased. Yet another

---

10. It was founded in 1995 by Atty. Gordon Robertson, founder and CEO of CBN-Asia and son of televangelist Pat Robertson. His burden for missions was kindled when he witnessed first-hand India's great need for the gospel in spring 1994. He found a kindred spirit in Miguel Alvarez, the then president of the Asian Seminary for Christian Ministries (ASCM) of the Church of God Cleveland; they gathered the key leaders of PCEC and PJM to establish ACM.

reality soon manifested itself: it was very difficult to raise funds without connecting potential donors to actual missionaries, so the center has been adopting and supporting partially yet significantly some of their better graduates to be its own missionaries (cf. Benigno 2005:14).

By the beginning of 1999, for strategic positioning due to financial considerations, Navarro left DOAN leadership. With the help of four DOAN Board members, he formed its transformational development arm called "Foundation for Transformational Development" (TransDev). It has provided models and given seminars on cooperative formation, low-cost housing construction, gardening for family sustainability, not just in Southern Luzon and Western Mindanao, but also in Mongolia and Sri Lanka. This connects to the other stream of PM3.

Transformational. The third stream may be labeled "transformational," which has emphasized contextualization (culture-sensitivity) and community development approaches in missions. Often using the Lausanne Covenant as their theological basis, these "radical evangelicals" have advocated for the integrity and quality of mission. In many ways, they have served as the thinkers and friendly critics of the evangelical (including its missionary) movement, and since 1998, as co-leaders of evangelicalism (including its cross-cultural missions) in the country.

The beginnings of the transformational stream may be traced to the third IVCF-Philippines triennial missions conference in December 1970, which tackled national and social issues. It was held amidst the brewing activism in the college campuses nationwide which culminated in the declaration of Martial Law in September 1972. Out of the desire to stir the church out of its conservative stance of acquiescent submission to authoritarianism and to highlight contextualization issues, Melba Maggay, an IVCF staff, with her two American friends (Bill Dyrness and Mac Bradshaw) set up the Institution for Studies in Asian Church and Culture (ISACC) in 1978. In the same year, the Asian Theological Seminary (ATS) started to offer "Church and Culture" as a required course in its Master of Divinity (M.Div.) program, perhaps the first among evangelical seminaries. Soon, the PCEC General Secretary Jun Vencer, using the resources of World Vision, tried to train Bible school faculty for the introduction of "Community Development" as a required course in evangelical Bible schools nationwide. Sadly this important attempt lasted for only two years.

The 1980s saw the birth of several indigenous Christian development organizations (CDOs), including the Institute for Studies of Asian Church and Culture (ISACC, 1978), Mission Ministries Philippines (MMP, 1983) Penuel School of Theology (1986), and most prominently the Center for Community Transformation (CCT, 1992). The latter has grown to be one of the most successful CDOs in the nation, enhancing the lives of more than 150,000 families in seventy urban poor communities, including Muslim ones, nationwide.

Two networks of CDOs have been formed since: the main Evangelical one called Alliance of Christian Development Agencies (ACDA, 1995), and the Ecumenical one that works in partnership with Roman Catholics called the National Coalition for Urban Transformation (NCUT) in 1996. Besides holding Consultations on Urban Ministries, the latter has been promoting indigenous models of Transformational Development (TD) for ministries in the cities, as they also contribute to the global urban ministry networks of Ray Bakke (International Urban Associates) and Viv Grigg (Servants Among the Urban Poor).

Then in late 1999, with the seed money pledged by the Christian Reformed World Relief Committee (CRWRC), a training consortium called Asian School for Development and Cross-Cultural Studies (ASDECS) was formed. It became the first major official link of PMA and some key leaders of PM3 (like OMF and WCG) to the transformational stream. Informal linkages were formed at the PMA-facilitated Missionary Trainers Fellowship that the author led from 1998-1999. ASDECS also brought the missions department of the major evangelical seminaries[11] together to offer three Masters programs

---

11. These are Alliance Graduate School (Quezon City), Asia-Pacific Theological Seminary (Baguio City), and Koinonia Theological Seminary (Davao City). Asian Theological Seminary is informally involved through Corrie DeBoer who heads its Masters and D.Min. in Urban Ministry. The IRM Bible College has adopted the MDM to be the graduate training program for its denomination.

(in Development Studies, Cross-cultural Studies and Development Management) for their students. When the author reluctantly took on the leadership of the school in August 2002, it started to hold extension programs in Cambodia, Laos and Vietnam (and soon in Thailand and Myanmar) to empower church leaders and missionaries in those countries in doing transformational missions (TM) in their contexts. It is looking for local partners in each Asian nation to equip nationals for TD or TM locally and globally.

All these three streams are represented in the leadership of PM3. Thus, Filipino missions promises to be an integration and mixture of these three types of mission strategies (cf. Tizon 1999:12-21). This paradigm shift is most welcomed by the transformationists fed mainly by the writings of Maggay and the author.[12] In this paradigm there is no need for a cross-cultural missionary to stay long-term in an area. Their mission is to simply make a few converts and then disciple those converts to become able evangelists and disciple-makers like themselves. Then they can move on to another place to multiply disciples and "house churches" (or "simple churches" or "small Bible communities") for CPMs, contextualization and community transformation to happen almost naturally without having to build complex church structures.

This integration has been working since the 1990s in actual mission work. Prominent evangelical church leaders, especially from Assemblies of God and CAMACOP got involved in short term pastoral leadership training modules in Indochina, sponsored mainly by Open Doors and also facilitated later by TNO and Ethnos-Asia (cf. Javier 2002:81). In recent years, the author and his mission, Chinese Ministries International-Philippines (CMI-Phil) started doing END in China in 1994. For strategic reasons since 2001, he decided to focus on missionary training and mobilization of tentmakers, of which eighty three were raised and sent to China by December 2007. He even includes Roman Catholics who have led group Bible studies in charismatic renewal communities in his mission.

---

12. The author labeled the traditional paradigm as "a third world church trying hard to do first world missions" (Lim 2003:200, n. 26.), and considers the tentmaking paradigm to be "the only way to disciple nations" (ibid:196-197, 200-201).

Interestingly, the Southern Baptists produced three important ingredients in this integrated mission strategy:(1) their western missionaries (like Robert Clark and Paul Stevens) have led in advocating for CPMs; (2) an ex-OFW couple, Art and Linda Elbinias through their "OFW Care" structure has provided a model for integrated missionary care; and (3) recently a Korean missiologist teaching at their seminary in Baguio City has spearheaded an ambitious short term mission program called "Asia Vision –STM 2015," which aims "to send 300 short-termers annually between 2006-2015 from Asia (especially the Philippines) to Asia;" that is a total of 3,000 to be mobilized by 2015. The program was pilot tested in summer 2003 when thirty-seven were sent to Indo-China (all raised their own funds), and repeated in summer 2004 when ninety-nine went to China, Cambodia, Thailand, Laos, Bangladesh and the Burmese Karen refugee camp, and Chinese Muslims in northern Thailand (2004:205-206); about 20 from the 2004 batch decided to become long-term missionaries in Laos, China, Cambodia, Thailand and Indonesia (2004:200). The plan was to mobilize 180 short-termers in 2005 (2004:211).

Moreover, this confidence has also been built through actual ministry in using the integrated mission approach to reach out to local UPGs especially Muslims in Mindanao, Metro Manila and other key cities where Muslims have relocated in recent years.[13] The most prominent are:(1) Love Your Neighbor founded by Florentino de Jesus, Sr. in 1980, which started as a department of Open Doors (Guillermo 1983:542); (2) SERVE-Philippines of the OMF-PHC, which was founded in 1997 to mobilize Filipino missionaries to reach out mainly to Muslim UPGs; and (3) more recently, the Bridge of Love Foundation that has effectively used the transformational development approach to reach Muslim communities.

In the 1990s, there were dozens of independent missionaries who left for the mission field without church or mission support. They left "by faith" and those who remained in the field became tentmakers (of course). Almost all of them developed their evangelistic skills as

---

13. Due to security reasons, instances of work among Communists and Muslims, especially in Mindanao and the Middle East have been given minimal mention in this work.

active members of their respective campus ministries (mostly CCC and Navigators) or charismatic local churches.

Diasporal. Though sharing in the same vision and mission, there is yet a fourth major stream that has yet to be fully integrated into PM3.[14] Nevertheless, the diasporal or OFW churches have been interacting with churches in the Philippine, and their theological ethos and missional paradigm are akin to the evangelical and charismatic/Full Gospel streams. While they have strong links (usually on the giving end) with their "denominational affiliations" in their motherland, most of them have been connected loosely (and conscienticized to go into cross-cultural missions) through the Filipino International Network (FIN). These churches have half-consciously ministered cross-culturally wherever they exist, but have been slowly moving to a more conscientious role in cross-cultural missions.

The person most active in promoting this is Rev. Joy Tira, a Christian and Missionary Alliance (CMA)-Canadian pastor, who was able to convince his church, First Filipino Alliance Church (FFAC) to give him the time and resources to organize and manage the Filipino International Network (FIN). He considers April 1994 in his participation in a conference on mobilizing the diaspora (not only of Filipinos, but also Koreans, South Asians and Africans) of CCC leaders from USA, Europe and Philippines, as the start of his call to this ministry. As he went on to survey the needs in the Middle East, he found that Filipinos were among the "most aggressive" and effective evangelists to Arab Muslims through "Operation Trojan House" (Manze 2004:240). This motivated him to meet the leaders and attend the conferences of the European Filipino Christian Workers Network, Filipino Japanese Network and those in Singapore and Hong Kong.

FIN held its first mission consultation on the "Filipino OCW Churches" in Cyprus in May 1995, which ended with the signing of the "Larnaca Covenant" which committed the participants "to recruit, train, and mobilize Filipino believers as tentmakers and career missionaries to the 10/40 window and the world…" (2004:156-157).

---

14. By "full integration" is meant the inclusion of the OFW church leadership in the Facilitation Team of PM3.

The second one was held in the Philippines in September 1996, with the participation of evangelical church leaders and Philippine government officials, and issued the "Puerto Azul Declaration." Tira was present at the PMA-sponsored 2nd National Tentmaker Conference in December 1996, where the greater role of the Philippine Overseas Employment Administration (POEA) was affirmed (2004:158-159,169-170). The present administrator of POEA, Atty. Linda Baldoz, is an evangelical Christian who sees herself as a key partner in PM3.

In 1997, FIN held a Filipino North American Prayer Advance in Midland, Texas, and in 1988, three Consultation in Singapore, Bahrain, and Camp Nakaman, Alberta, Canada; the last was for International Diaspora leaders which included South Asians, Chinese, Vietnam, Blacks, Persians, Japanese, Koreans and Spanish/Latinos (2004:160). FIN held another consultation in Singapore in July 24-26, 2002, with Thomas Wang of AD 2000 Movement and founding General-Secretary of Chinese Coordinating Center for World Evangelization (CCOWE) as main speaker. He congratulated the Filipinos as the second Diaspora group strategically organized for world missions (2004:160)

Since its start, FIN has aimed to mobilize the Christian Filipino Diaspora as "peace-makers" and "gatherers" trained to "multiply disciples" among the nations, (2004:164-165). It has five main ministries: Prayer *Advances* (a new spin on *Retreats*), Family Life Conferences, New Life Training Curriculum (forty training units on how to multiply disciples using CCC materials (Tan 2004:184-195), Jesus Film distribution (over 50,000 in video and DVD formats distributed), and regional and international mission consultations.

In anticipation of the Lausanne International Forum to be held in Pattaya, Thailand in September 28-October 5, 2004, FIN held the "Seoul Consultation" on "The Filipino Diaspora and Missions," hosted by the Network of Filipino Evangelical Ministries in Korea (NFEMK) and some Korean partners. All the major papers were compiled and edited into a book entitled *Scattered*; this was given as a free gift to each participant at the Lausanne Forum. Although FIN started mainly with the traditional evangelical mission paradigm of a Western evangelical denomination (C&MA) and a Western campus ministry (CCC), it has learned from the positive and negative experiences in evangelism of their constituents, so they will hardly have difficulty in working with the transformational mission paradigm of their Philippine-based partners.

The success of PM3 will depend a lot on its ability to quickly mobilize and train these churches into cross-cultural missions in close partnership with FIN. On the whole, mission awareness (much less proper missionary training) is still relatively low in most of the Filipino diaspora churches. So the PM3 vision and goal to mobilize and train Christian OFWs already there would still require some efforts.

Perhaps half of these OFW congregations are intentional church-plants of forward-looking denominations in the Philippines as they followed the migration of their members and leaders. By 1998, Jesus Is Lord (JIL) had seventy-two churches abroad (plus 476 in the country) and Jesus Christ Saves Global Outreach had five abroad (plus seventy-eight in the country).[15] Victory Christian Fellowship had twenty-four churches, including Bangladesh, Guam, Russia, Taiwan, Cambodia and Dubai, with plans to plant churches in thirty-four more nations in the next ten years (1994-2004) (Perry 1992:97-98). Others include Free Believers, Take the Nations for Jesus, Bread of Life, Love of Christ, and so on.

Yet the other half came to birth almost naturally through the gathering and growth of cell groups and fellowships started by ordinary witnessing believers at their residence or workplace, as shown below in the following depictions of their ministries country-by-country in the major destinations of OFWs. Filipino congregations globally started with effective ministries to reach out to their fellow OCWs. Not a few of their members have also been sharing their faith with their neighbors and colleagues from other nationalities, including those from among their host countries, "naturally" with hardly any cross-cultural training at all. They would have been much more effective if they received such training. This is now being remedied through the training teams sent out by PM3 and the new yet fast-growing Philippine house church movement.

---

15. Directory in Evangelicals Today Centennial Issue 1998:89.

Filipino Urban Missions by Country

Hong Kong. The second largest number of OFWs (after Saudi Arabia) is in Hong Kong, mostly working as domestic helpers (DH). In 2002, those were about 143,000 registered out of the 237,000 from all nationalities, and in 2004, there were only 126,500 left, yet still constituting the largest expatriate community in Hong Kong (Felomino 2004:210-212).

The first Filipino Protestant church there was born in 1978, and by 2004, there were more than 100 (including Roman Catholics). In a 2004 survey of sixty of these churches, there were about 150 services and fellowship times with a total membership of about 5,000. About a quarter of them are led by tentmakers (DHs or professionals who lead their congregations), because many of these DHs are from the teaching professions since Hong Kong employees want them to also "tutor" their children (2004:209,214).

Almost all major churches there are supporting church planters and also donating towards land purchase and building construction of churches in the Philippines (2004:218, 221-222). His Sanctuary Services has ministries to Indonesians and Sri Lankans. Ixthus sends tentmakers into China, and C&MA, too, which had plans to send to Taiwan, Korea and Japan in 2004. Free Believers, JIL, Grace of Jesus Fellowship and His Sanctuary, Revival Christian Church have already extended to Macau, while the first two have also established churches in Taiwan (2004:219).

Japan. The third largest OFW community is in Japan, where about 240,548 were documented in 2001. 95 percent of them are female entertainers earning $800 per month, and these 185,000 send home a total of $200 million per year (Galvez 2004:255).

Most of the thirty Filipino churches belong to the Network of Filipino Ministries Japan (NFMJ) and work closely with Japanese churches. Most of them provide holistic care that seeks to transform oppressed entertainers into servant-leaders in establishing churches in Japan and beyond (2004:264-266). A significant number eventually marry Japanese nationals, bear Filipino-Japanese children and reach out to the families and business networks of their husbands (2004:259-262, 266). One night club singer became a female minister in a Japanese church, and another entertainer became a prayer mobilizer for Intercessors for Japan (IFJ).

Taiwan. Taiwan had about 91,000 OFWs by December 2004, mostly as factory workers in electronics, computers and machineries (55,000), caregivers (33,000), DH (1,000), fishermen (600) and construction workers (400) (*Philippine Star*, April 12, 2005:9). They are the second largest expat community (next to the Thais) and are preferred because of their skills and diligence.

There were about 7,000 church-going Roman Catholics and 4,000 Protestants with about 100 meeting points on Sunday by early 2004 (Adhikari 2004:28). The three largest groups are Jesus Is Lord (JIL, with twenty-four fellowship groups), Word for the World and Free Believers Fellowship.

One Filipino missionary team has planted a Chinese church in Taichung, and many have won their Chinese spouses to Christ. But most found difficulty reaching out to local Chinese, because of the language barrier, miscommunication and ignorance of Chinese culture and religion. The lively Filipino worship services and Sunday Schools are good mainly for youth who are trying to learn English and some old people in wheel chairs brought by their caregivers (2004:281,284). Many of them are determined to play an important role in cross-cultural missions when they learned, in 2004, that two pastors have been tried, sentenced and heads shaved in preparation for execution in Riyadh (2004:282).

Singapore. The fifth largest concentration of OFWs is in Singapore, with over 50,000 as of 2003, mostly medical personnel, Information Technology (IT) professionals, Domestic Helpers (DH) and construction workers. Though informally linked since the late 1980s, the KSPS was formally organized in July 1998. Five are led by Hawaiian-Japanese, eight by Singaporeans, and only one has been accredited by the government. Three large churches have Filipino fellowships (Solano and Ysip 2004:273-274). Their main goals are to evangelize Filipinos through prayer gatherings, evangelistic meetings and sports festivals, raise funds for Philippine calamities (like the 1990 earthquake and 1991 Mt. Pinatubo eruption), help the Philippine embassy take care of OFW needs, and organize the Filipinos through the United Council of Leaders in Singapore (Solano and Ysip 2004:274-276; Dimangondayao 2004:308). They have also planned to became a "strong mission base in Far East Asia" (Solano and Yap 2004:278).

South Korea. And the sixth largest OFW community is in South Korea, where in 1994 the Philippine ambassador to the 30,000 OFWs there was also a pastor of a Filipino church there (Dumapias 2004:318-319). Ambassador Rodolfo Dimapias helped in organizing the Evangelical Ministers Fellowship in Korea (EMFK) with the support of partner Korean churches which had Filipino congregants (2004:319-320). It has since been an active member of FIN and hosted the 2004 Consultation that produced the book *Scattered.*

The life and ministry of these diaspora churches will surely continue to influence the Philippine churches and PM3, since there is a lot of travel and communication back and forth as well as the financial capacity of OFWs and rising dependency of the homeland churches on their remittances. With these four streams coming together, Filipino missions will consist of a three-pronged approach :(a) "CPM by tentmakers" of PMA & FIN; (b) power evangelism and short-term training seminars of the charismatics; and (c) contextualized holistic approach of the transformationists.

Specific Cases Per People Group

Here are six "snapshots" of Filipino missionaries in the Buddhist world. Because of the sensitive nature of some contexts, some names of persons and places are not revealed, and not all details can be given.

Singapore & Hong Kong. In these two predominantly Chinese (folk Buddhist) societies, Filipino OCWs have brought their non-Filipino "bosses" and colleagues to the Lord and to join their churches. Many of their non-Filipino converts have joined other churches where they could feel more comfortable in worship and fellowship.

Though several Filipinos work as professionals (mainly in middle management positions), the majority went in as domestic helpers in these two cities. They, especially the latter, have done excellently. Many have been converted through the Filipino churches there, and these new believers have been trained to use the "Jesus" film to reach entire households for Christ. One who worked in the household of a Christian expatriate in Hong Kong shared her burden to reach the mainland Chinese with her "masters." They supported her to learn Mandarin in Beijing for two years, and she ministered in a city in central China for three years.

Thailand. Thailand is a Buddhist country where it is almost unthinkable for their citizens to convert from Buddhism; "To be Thai is to be Buddhist." It is with this major unreached people in mind that Dr. H left his prestigious work in one of the top universities in the Philippines to teach in an equally prestigious university in a major Thai city some years ago. He had developed his campus evangelism skills during his student days. So one of his favorite ministries in Bangkok is to serve as an adviser and mentor to the student evangelism movements there.

Meanwhile, his main witness is to share his expertise in his field of study, and share Christ with his professorial colleagues, most of whom are scholars in their own fields. He sees himself as a Christian serving a Buddhist nation to help train its next generation of leaders and help develop its potentials as a people. At the very least, he has helped encouraged and train the future leaders of the nation to have a positive view of Christianity.

Cambodia. Many short-term mission trips have been made into Cambodia since 1900s. Not a few Filipinos, particularly medical and educational personnel have stayed on for longer term ministries. Perhaps the most effective one has been that of Mr. and Mrs. R who arrived in Cambodia with their two children with minimal provisions for their stay and without any supporting group. They went just because of a clear call to minister in that land. The husband was mainly trained as a church-planting pastor while the wife is trained in community development.

They proved that God's resources are found in the harvest. In just five years, their holistic approach has produced forty-seven churches in the villages surrounding their town. These churches had social impact in their respective communities; thus they have gained connections to top leaders in their province. Signs and wonders added to the rapid evangelization of their area. Most of their leaders have been trained in their simple yet effective missionary training institute.

During one of the great floods that devastated their region a couple of years back, their exemplary relief and rehabilitation efforts were noticed by the government and secular media. Recently they received a donation of a huge property from a prominent Cambodian believer for them to develop into a model farm or the like. They hope that this will serve as a good training ground for Khmer missionaries to go to other unreached peoples in Indo-China and beyond.

Myanmar. Though there are hardly any jobs available in this fellow ASEAN country, Filipinos have been sending effective mission teams. One of the major groups is called Torch Ministry, which views its mission as "empowering nationals for disciple-making." Teams have gone in to train local Burmese Christians on how to conduct effective holistic ministries, Sunday Schools, youth fellowships, church planting movements, etc.

In their latest trip, they saw the local believers themselves organize their own medical mission teams and raise funds to purchase medicine for these teams. They also witnessed the growing confidence of these nationals to make plans and launch programs to reach the unreached in their city and surrounding villages.

Japan. Filipinos have gone into Japan to work mainly as factory workers, entertainers, and English teachers. Most of them went in as non-Evangelicals and were "born again" through the witness of several Filipino churches and fellowships there. One of the major ministries is Filipino Christian Ministry Network (FCMN) led by Ms. Hannah Galvez. They have specialized ministries to first-timers, returnees, those married to Japanese and mothers of Filipino-Japanese children (Japinos).

Most significant may be their ministries among Filipina entertainers, many of whom were converted after they became wives to their Japanese customers. Galvez sees this as God's plan to raise missionaries from among the lowly, semi-educated women (cf. 1 Cor.

1:27-28). These singers, dancers and bar girls have become evangelists inside the closely-knit, homogeneous Japanese families.

For instance, a certain Shirley was a former model and nightclub worker who is now managing a construction business. She was instrumental in planting two Filipino-Japanese churches in Saitama and Kanagawa Prefectures. She is married to an Okinawan who now supports the Filipino ministry by offering their house for worship and outreaches.

China. Miss N is one of the dozens of Christian Filipino English teachers in China, where about 1.2 billion (out of 1.35 billion) are still unevangelized, in spite of the revival of the past thirty years. She felt God's call to China about six years back, and went before making her decision to do it in a more permanent basis. She was able to recruit three other churchmates to go in with her, and they intentionally planned to work in different schools and regions.

Since she went in four years ago, she had the benefit of being trained to be an effective cross-cultural disciple-maker (especially to lead church planting movements, CPMs). Within a year, she had fifteen baptized disciples; actually ten are disciples of three of her five disciples . Her teammate had another six direct disciples. When they returned to that city two years later, they found that their disciples have grown to nine known house churches, not counting those that may have been born in the cities where their other disciples may have gone as teachers.

Recently, one of her graduated disciples is now teaching in a rural school. She was invited to teach English in that school, two hours by car, one day each weekend. The government officials in the village told her that she is the first foreigner to ever step into that area. Meanwhile, she has met a Chinese house church leader in her area, and introduced six of her disciples to him for absorption into the house church networks there. All her six disciples like attending the meetings of the underground house church and are, therefore, learning the Word more deeply in their own language and are in fellowship with their own people.

Conclusion

We hope that as more Filipinos go abroad for work, more Christians will join them as tentmaker-missionaries, like the above cases, among the Buddhist peoples and cities. The Philippine Mission Mobilization Movement (PM3) is aiming to recruit at least 200,000 such tentmakers by 2010; hopefully 50,000 will target the Buddhist world. May they be equipped to make disciples in effective ways as they evangelize among the Buddhist cities and nations. May Christians and churches worldwide support us in prayer as we seek to fulfill our role in world evangelization.

CHAPTER NINE

Buddhadasa, Tamma, Jesus, and the Promise of New Creation: A Holistic Contextualized Gospel for Urban Buddhists in Thailand

DAVID VON STROH

Good news! This is our message to the world as followers of Jesus. What the good news is varies depending on what band of Jesus-followers one gathers with and is influenced by. In fact, there are many gospels proclaimed by the universal body of Christ, most of which can claim fairly strong biblical foundation. It is not my task here to judge between these gospels, nor is it my intention to create argument between followers of Jesus. However, I will assert here that depending on which gospel we proclaim, we will find more or less common ground with Buddhists and opportunity to effectively teach and disciple Buddhists in the Way of Jesus. In other words, we need to ask, "What is good news for Buddhists?" Moreover, when working with the urban poor, the question is intensified, "Jesus proclaimed good news for the poor, but what is good news for the poor?"

Similarly, we must ask which Buddhism we are discussing and what kind of Buddhists we are dialoguing with. There are many versions of Buddhism followed in Asia. This is quite well documented and not my concern here. Within Thailand too, though, there are many versions of Buddhism. Most existing discourses on the variations within Thai Buddhism, however, focus simply on the differences between folk

Buddhism, with its animistic tendencies, and a generally conceived standard Theravada Buddhism. I appreciate this helpful scholarship. The focus of my research goes past this to ask what is the pure, true Buddhism, or in other words the religion and worldview that Buddha himself proposed to the world, distinct from both folk Buddhism as well as the mainstream formulation of Theravada Buddhism in Thailand. My guide and primary source in this research is the now deceased Thai Buddhist monk, Buddhadasa.

My thesis is that to the extent we access the fullness of the holistic message of Jesus and to the extent that we access the fundamentals of what Buddha himself put forth, we find a large common ground and opportunity for fruitful ministry together. This common ground centers around the equivalent concepts of *Tamma* and *Logos*, the pursuit of which leads us presently to the end of suffering, as Buddha would say, and to the new creation of God, the new heavens and the new earth, as both Isaiah and John would say in Isaiah 65-66 and Revelation 21-22, respectively. In speech and writing, I refer to the central Buddhist concept of Tamma, though in most English language writing, the same concept would be rendered Dharma. I prefer speaking of Tamma, rather than Dharma, for two reasons. First, in this way I reflect how the word is pronounced in Thai language. Second, and more importantly, in this way I distinguish what I am referring to as the Theravada Buddhist concept of Dharma which may differ greatly from understandings of Dharma in other branches of Buddhism.

Stated negatively, my thesis is also that to the extent we present a truncated gospel that focuses merely on where we go after we die and to the extent that we place ourselves in competition with folk Buddhism and popular conceptions of Buddhism, which also have a large focus on what happens to us after we die, there is very little common ground for contextualization. I propose that the process of contextualization necessarily forces us to understand better our own faith in the message and worldview of Jesus, even as we seek to analyze and understand Buddhism. This process serves as a filter through which only the most holistic versions of the gospel can pass.

Contextualization breeds holism. In the process of contextualization, we come away with only the very best news.

My Context Among Bangkok's Urban Poor

From September 2003 until June 2007, I lived in a slum community named Permsup in Bangkok, Thailand, among the low-educated and underemployed, where alcoholism is rampant. Over ninety percent of the Permsup residents were migrants from rural northeast Thailand, or Isaan, who have lived in Bangkok for about fifteen to twenty years, on average. My immediate neighbors were the drug dealers who are supplied by the local police. Our houses are made of scrap wood and tin and built on stilts over swampy garbage, dense and packed so that I could hear explicitly every domestic quarrel and drunken rage of my neighbors. As squatters, we have been under threat of eviction for four years and the community will soon be bulldozed for construction of a new road. About seventy percent of the community has already moved out. I have daily seen the despair in my neighbor's eyes, beaten down by years of scraping to get by. I despair myself when I see this hopelessness and the young naked children playing on the thin paths around dog feces with no one caring for them. A gospel that is just about where an individual's soul goes after one dies just does not seem to be relevant here and I have longed for a coherent message of hope and holistic transformation.

Of course, I came to Bangkok full of hope and committed to holistic mission among the poor. But even while I have deep values for social justice, inner healing, community empowerment and leadership development, as well as economic development, reconciliation, and city and community transformation, I had never in my past been equipped to share them as part of the story of the good news. Even as I shared the traditional evangelical gospel with people, I just had to hope they would see these other important things by the witness of my life. Not a bad way to go, but I thirsted for a story that incorporated all these things and put them at the core of what God was doing. Besides my living in Permsup and simple relational ministry with the neighbors, we (our Thai Peace Foundation and house church network) have been involved in Permsup with house church planting and leadership development, small business development, and community organizing of savings groups to prepare for relocation ahead of eviction.

I moved out of Permsup ahead of the eviction, and for the last six months, I have lived in another slum community named Samaki Patana. (I will refer to it simply as Samaki, as it is commonly shortened for ease of reference.) The Samaki community is just down the road a couple of kilometers from Permsup. Samaki is much larger with migrants from all corners of Thailand. The average resident has lived in Samaki for about ten years. Samaki, despite being much larger and more diverse than Permsup, has for many years progressed in development through an organized and proactive leadership. Samaki has its own direct legitimate connections to electricity and running water. Permsup, in contrast, pays a much higher fee for these services to nearby businesses and neighborhoods to extend informal connections, which often experience cuts in electricity and days without water. Samaki also has a paved *soi* or road through the center of the community, allowing much greater access, whereas Permsup is just a maze of footpaths. While many of the residents of Samaki are better off than the residents of Permsup, many of the same dynamics are present and some sections of Samaki experience greater poverty than Permsup.

Migration from Rural Isaan to Bangkok Slums

In Permsup, Samaki, or in any number of slum communities throughout Bangkok, the urban poor are predominately rural migrants. They may be living in the city, but their hearts are still in the village, especially for the Isaan. On many occasions, I have enjoyed the invitation of neighbors to join them on trips upcountry to their home villages in the provinces of Isaan for New Years and Songkran festivals or other reasons. Their previous life experience is agricultural. Planting rice, harvesting rice, fishing, cooking, cleaning and constructing houses are their primary work skills. Many have only a fourth to sixth grade education. Upcountry, they have always enjoyed living in community with extended networks of relatives and friends who have been neighbors for generations. The social fabric and mutual obligation to each other is strong. Meals and rounds of drinks are always open to neighbors, friends, and often even strangers dropping by. The ethic of *namjai* or generosity, is primary in Isaan society.

Most of my Isaan neighbors in Permsup followed other friends or relatives to Bangkok and the specific location of Permsup. In several instances, an initial family came and discovered open land to squat on in a good location, and they then sent word to their siblings and cousins that were also desiring to move to the city in search of jobs and perhaps better schooling opportunities for their children. In this way, several cliques or networks of relatives arrived in Permsup, including one from Kalasin province, one from Ubon Ratchathani province, another from Khorat, as well as many others. Upon arriving in the city, they naturally try to maintain and continue their lifestyle and values. They continue their *namjai* ethic, enjoying communal meals and drinking sessions within their cliques from the same province, and sometimes crossing between them.

My Isaan neighbors have come to the city for economic reasons. Agriculture upcountry is often no longer viable to support all of them, particularly when droughts hit, when banks repossess land, or when parents' land is divided between too many heirs or unequally among them. Also a significant factor is the growing appetite for material goods, like televisions, VCD players, stereos and karaoke machines, refrigerators, and nice houses. Most Isaan migrants to the city intend to send money back home to build a nice house for their parents or a house that they will live in when they return home. (It should be noted that the definition of a nice house is certainly relative. Nevertheless, the expectation to provide for such construction is a significant burden.) They see their time in Bangkok as a temporary sojourn, and never cease to long for the village life. When times are rough, they frequently consider packing up and moving home, even though they may have lived in Bangkok for fifteen to twenty years. A couple times per year, when relatives and friends upcountry request help with the rice harvest or rice planting, they may travel back for a week or two. Even though they and their immediate family may not otherwise be active in agricultural use of the land in Isaan, they rarely seriously consider selling their land, if they are lucky enough to still be landowners, in order to have capital to invest in making a nicer, more permanent home in Bangkok or to invest in a small business in Bangkok. The land in Isaan is their root, their home, the village and community there is where their heart is. Life in Bangkok is seen as a temporary phase, lasting perhaps until their children finish school. Often within a married (or unmarried) couple, one spouse will maintain their official residence status upcountry so that they can vote in elections there, continue membership in inexpensive life insurance programs, and perhaps for legal reasons related to their land holdings. The other spouse would register their residence in Bangkok in order to have house registration as a semi-legal squatter and to be able to send their children to Bangkok schools. The spouse whose registration is upcountry suffers in regard to health care, however, for the registration in Thailand's universal health care program is such that one can only use hospitals in their home district.

The employment prospects of these migrants in Bangkok are limited. Most end up working in the informal economy, selling food from street-side stands, coffee from motorcycle carts, brooms from bicycle carts, selling cheap flowers at street corners, doing construction and odd-jobs for hire, driving taxis, and cleaning houses. Working stable minimum wage jobs at 7-11 or stores in the mall are usually out of reach because they do not have the minimum grade nine education. (Their children can sometimes attain such jobs as they progress in their education farther.) Much of their informal economy work depends on the weather and their health. If it is raining many of them stay home and receive no income for the day. Rainy season can be a struggle economically. If any part of their body is sore from the previous day's work, they may stay home for a day or two, further forgoing income. Also, sometimes they are just burnt out from the daily grind of seeking cash income through these activities and prefer to attain their family's evening meal by going fishing with neighbors.

In addition to the individual family and personal economic struggles, the *namjai* ethic also often obligates anyone in the community, especially within a given regional clique, who has a little extra cash, to share with those who are not presently able to make ends meet. Struggling neighbors may ask presently successful neighbors for a loan, for example when their children's school fees come due, but it is often not repaid as a loan would be. However, it is understood that the same would be done for the other if the situation were reversed. This directly reflects the agricultural society upcountry that depends on neighbors helping each other out with farm tasks. Labor is joined together to plant one rice field and then the next. Later labor is joined to harvest one rice field and then the next. When houses or any building is constructed, everyone joins in. This cooperative agricultural life seems to predate the modern cash based economy. Certainly the owner of the field or the new house would provide food and drink for their friends, relatives, and neighbors who helped out, but otherwise there likely would not be any cash exchange. This is reflected in the Thai language as the word for work, *tam ngaan*, literally means to make a party. You work together in order to have a party together afterwards. I assume the Isaan/Lao equivalent, *het wiek*, has the same meaning and connotation, though I am not as familiar with the Isaan/Lao language.

This *namjai* ethic is seen even in the process of the Permsup residents moving out of the community ahead of eviction and building new houses on new squatter sites or lands that they can rent. Many neighbors gather together to help build the new houses, even those who are not moving to that particular location. Those who are most indebted may proactively contribute the most to the work, but in general it is a shared activity. In Bangkok, as the cash based economy defines daily life, cash payments for helping out in such work are sometimes also made. This is becoming more common as patterns of city life replace the patterns of village life.

Addictions, Family Breakdown, and Fatalism

Other significant factors in the life of the poor in Bangkok slums, including the Isaan migrants, are common substance abuse and gambling addictions, family breakdown, and a fatalistic worldview. A majority of the men in the Permsup community and a significant number of men in the Samaki community are alcoholics. Some of this is due to the culture of near daily social drinking that they bring with them from the village and which is prevalent throughout many segments of Thai society. Drinking is how Thai men socialize. My friend Komsorn, a devout Buddhist, often talks about the *sin haa*, the five moral directions for Buddhist lay people, including the prohibition of drinking alcohol or taking other intoxicating substances. But he also drinks with everyone, saying that to reject offers to drink would be to reject the society and the friendship, which is where one can have an influence on people. Otherwise, he says, there is no opportunity to influence and teach people. In my own experience, I have sometimes drunk with the circle of men and other times sat with them without drinking. There is certainly no shunning towards me when I would reject their offers to drink, but accepting their offers to drink does seem to endear one to the circle and put everyone at more ease, often causing them to open up in conversation more quickly towards me. All this to say there is a significant social inertia towards regular drinking and expectation that the social fabric is cemented through drinking together.

Because of the high value for tolerance of others' behavior within Thai culture, which is attributed to Buddhism, there is also very little, if anything, spoken against excessive drinking and drunkenness. By my observation, perhaps as many as a third of the men in the Permsup community are/were chronic drunks. (Many of them have since moved, ahead of the eviction.) Most of them are functional during the day, but may get drunk every evening. Another third of the men are probably alcoholic in the sense that they have withdrawal symptoms if they go without alcohol for a day or two, similar to caffeine addicts. This third of the men may rarely get drunk, but in a very significant sense, they are tied to drinking. It would be interesting to do more research and compare the drinking cultures and the occurrence of chronic drunkenness and the lower level alcohol addiction that exist in the upcountry villages and in the Bangkok slums. Besides just the social inertia towards drinking, many in the slums do explain that they are driven to drink because of worries about their family finances and how they are going to make ends meet. I wonder how much the despair and depression caused by living in a poor slum affects the drive to drink. Obviously, the high level of alcohol consumption is a significant economic factor for families in the slums as well. The worst drunks will spend half of their income on alcohol. The more moderate alcohol addicts may still spend as much as a sixth to a quarter of their income on alcohol.

Each of the slum communities I have lived in has a significant drug-dealing ring. In Permsup, it was known that the local police were actually the supplier to this drug ring. *Ya ba*, literally crazy drug, or methamphetamine, is the main drug sold. However, to my observation, there were very few residents in Permsup who were users of this drug themselves. I knew of only a couple men in Permsup who drove taxis who would use these drugs to stay awake on overnight shifts. The drugs were sold primarily to those who would come in from outside the community to buy. There may be more of a user rate in the Samaki community, but my observation so far is that it is a similar dynamic, where the drugs are sold to those from outside. In each place there are some adults who seem to be behind the drug-dealing ring, but the active selling agents are all youth who hang out at one of the entrances to the community. Many people in each community are opposed to the drug-dealing activity, but at least in Permsup, felt mostly helpless to do anything about it, since it was known that the local police were the supplier. On a couple of occasions, one of our community leaders was able to determine which high ranking offer was clean and get them to organize a raid using police officers from another district. For the most part, though, the drug-dealing activity is looked upon with fatalistic acceptance.

Glue sniffing and paint thinner sniffing is, however, a significant problem, especially among the youth in Permsup. Sniffing is much more dangerous than alcohol abuse and even, I think, methamphetamine use, as it destroys brain cells and brain function while it gives a high. A couple adult men in Permsup were regular sniffers, always attached to a bag of glue or a rag of thinner. Their brain function consistently deteriorated over time, causing them to not only be chronically incoherent, but to fall off the raised concrete pathways in the community into the swampy garbage under the houses. These sights, along with the youth who were sometimes incoherent and high off the glue or thinner, were a regular reminder of the literal human decay going on in the slum community, further contributing to poverty induced despair and depression and reinforcing a fatalistic outlook.

For the women in the slum communities, alcohol abuse is present, but much less prevalent. To some extent, this may reflect gender roles that are predominant upcountry. In villages upcountry, and still to a large extent in the slums of Bangkok, men and women are separated into drinking and cooking circles respectively. The men sit around and drink together, with food occasionally brought to them by the women. The women do not sit with the men, but hang out together while cooking or cleaning. When they sit and eat, they usually do so without alcohol, perhaps because they are also looking after the children. On upcountry trips with my neighbors, if I was tired of sitting with the drunk men, I would sit and eat with the women and children, which could also feel awkward. If I ever tried to help with washing dishes or anything, I would be rebuked and asked not to do so not only because I was the guest, but also because "the neighbors will think you are gay". Thus, the prevalence of male alcohol abuse and the lesser prevalence of female alcohol abuse are tied to some extent to gender identity and expectations of gender roles.

The women in the slum communities, while drinking significantly less than the men, still find their social activity commonly attached to another addicting, income draining activity, gambling. In the slum communities, while the men sit around and drink together, the women will also sit around together and play gambling games. It would seem that gambling together with neighbors would not cause a net economic drain on the community, as money is just changing hands between different neighbors and ultimately cycling around. But I have heard of women racking up large gambling debts in excess of $1000. I do not fully understand the dynamics of the women's gambling activities, but apparently there is a long-term net loss for some individuals, and I would presume, net gain for others.

In addition to drinking and substance abuse, as well as gambling, the buying of lottery tickets is another activity that drains money from poor people in the slums and plays into the despair and fatalism that people experience here. Since people are beaten down, not expecting that they can climb their way out of poverty through hard work, getting lucky on a lottery is their one hope of gaining some money they would otherwise never have access to. But, of course, the fatalism that induces people to buy lottery tickets is reinforced by the economic drain the regular purchase of lottery tickets creates for them. And if one wins a cash prize in the lottery, the money is often blown on food and drink, or unnecessary material goods like stereos, within a very short time. Because of the existing fatalism, people are not making plans of what to do with the money if they do win anything. Another example of this is when the majority of the people in the Permsup community received cash compensation from the government in agreement for moving out ahead of the eviction and the coming road construction. Depending upon the size of their house, each family received on average perhaps $2500-$3000. Ideally, this money would have been saved to plan for relocation. However, much of the money was whittled away over the months on unnecessary expenses. There appears to be a lack of confidence in being able to successfully execute plans for the future, so no plans are made and what enjoyment can be found in the present moment is taken.

Beyond all these factors, you see the common occurrence of infidelity and family breakdown among the poor in the slums. Marital infidelity is extremely common throughout Thai society. It is probably less common in the slums, simply for the financial reasons that poor men have less cash to maintain mistresses or to use on prostitutes. Nevertheless, while many families are intact, single parent families are common as men have fathered children and then left for another woman. This reinforces the down-and-out fatalism that says, "This is all we have and all we can expect from life." Boys grow up in this environment and expect that they will do the same things as the unfaithful men they saw around them or the absent fathers and husbands they did not see. Girls grow up in this environment and are already familiar with the *mia noi* (minor wife) phenomena, just accepting it as *reuang bokiti* (the usual story) and possibly their future fate. In fact, the refrain *reuang bokiti* is repeated often for anything for which there might be lament, but fatalistic acceptance. It may also be repeated as an excuse for one's own behavior. Another *reuang bokiti* related to children and family is the common story of children being raised in the villages upcountry by their grandparents while their parents work in Bangkok or elsewhere. In this way, many children may grow up for many years only seeing their parents once or twice a year. It is unfortunate that this is how things are, that economic pressures force parents to leave their kids behind with reliable caretakers while they seek money in the city, but that is just the way it is. *Reuang bokiti.*

Within folk Buddhism and popular conceptions of Buddhism in Thailand, there are many reasons and explanations for poor people having the lives they do. Folk Buddhism, with its fear of the local spirits and adherence to various superstitions to gain luck as well as favor with the spirits, attributes misfortune to waning diligence in paying homage to these spirits. When several members of a family in Permsup started following Jesus three years ago, they encountered a series of misfortunes. The father, Ratchai, had some difficulties with his business, selling brooms from a motorcycle cart. The police on several occasions unjustly fined him for driving in certain areas and this nearly sunk his business. Their teenage son, Nat, had a motorcycle crash when driving too fast in which he was badly injured, even knocking out his front teeth. Then one evening, they had a strange intruder from outside the community, likely one of the customers of the drug-dealing ring, sneak into their one-room house in the night and lay down next to their teenage daughter, Pat, as if he was going to molest her or worse. Fortunately, Ratchai woke up as he heard the guy sneak in and beat him off. But the mother, Pai, was badly shaken and wondered why all this misfortune came upon their family. Pai reasoned that it was because they had become Christians and abandoned the offerings to the idols and spirits and the making of merit at the temple. They were now in bad luck and the spirits were angry and retaliating, Pai assumed, and thought that maybe they should reject their new faith and go back to folk Buddhism. Pat and Ratchai, who had been believers longer, reassured Pai that Jesus was stronger than any spirits and had authority over them, and exhorted her that following Jesus was the safest place to be and that these misfortunes were not due to a new bad luck, but the actions of bad people unrelated to them or in the case of Nat's motorcycle accident, personal foolishness. Pai was won over by her husband and daughter and emerged from the crisis of faith stronger. But the sense of being trapped in obeisance to the spirits and the need to make merit to maintain good luck was clear. For others not of Jesus-following-faith, it is a natural reflex to redouble efforts to appease the local spirits or to *tam bun* (make merit) whenever misfortune strikes. The very acts of making offerings to the spirits or to making merit at the temples or in other special ways can be financially draining for the poor who have little to begin with. Thus, their efforts to change their luck can be factors contributing to their poverty.

Another woman in the Permsup community, Watsana, knows that she has a demon inside of her. Sometimes it torments her and she wishes that she could be rid of it. She is now about 40 years old, but she remembers this demon entering her when she was a child. She has tried to get rid of it before, but the demon torments her more when she does so. Watsana has thus decided to just live with it and try to not make it angry. She knows that we Christians can pray in Jesus' name and cast out demons. She is intrigued by the hope that she could finally be rid of the demon. But she is too afraid to try, knowing that the demon will torment her extra again if she allowed us to pray for her in this way. She has just accepted her fate.

Popularly conceived Buddhism, with its emphasis on making merit so that one's next life will be better than the present, attributes lives of poverty to the accumulated merit and demerit people have carried from their past lives. Thus, people are encouraged to simply live quietly and meekly, accepting their current life and circumstances and doing good where they can to make merit for the next life. Merit-making, however, takes many forms, most including the giving of money to the temple for different occasions or projects or the funding of expensive parties to commemorate the anniversary of the death of a loved one or to commemorate the temporary monkhood of oneself or one's son. The focus on reincarnation reinforces fatalism and passivity about one's prospects for progress in this present life and causes the allocation of significant financial resources to activities for which their may be some social benefit but little if any developmental impact. The fatalistic worldview founded upon both the animistic elements of folk Buddhism as well as the focus within popular conceptions of Thai Buddhism on merit making for improving one's present karma as well as prospects for a better reincarnation reinforces poverty by draining resources and hope for transformational development and improvement of one's situation in this life. Of course, these elements are only several among many factors that affect the outlook of those living in poverty in Bangkok slums. General discouragement and pessimism from failed attempts to improve one's business or education are also quite significant. Addictions, family breakdown, fatalistic thinking due to religious aspects, or general discouragement from failed attempts at development, cause many people living in Bangkok slums to experience a deficit of hope, an abundance of despair, and a fatalistic outlook. Good news is needed.

Buddhadasa and the Search for Buddha's Buddhism

The culture and context in which I share the gospel of Jesus is ostensibly Buddhist. As mentioned previously, most of my neighbors in the slum communities have been migrants from Isaan, the rural northeast region of Thailand, and are predominately folk Buddhists. My understanding of Buddhism, however, and indeed, even of Christianity, has been significantly impacted by the writings of Buddhadasa (pronounced "Buttataat", meaning "Buddha's slave"). Buddhadasa, who lived in a forest monastery in Surat Thani province, in the south of Thailand,

and died in 1993, was essentially the Martin Luther of Theravada Buddhism. Buddhdasa was the first monk in 1500 years to have engaged a thorough research of the voluminous canon of Buddhist scriptures in the original Pali language rather than just accept the commentaries of other monks and scholars, which in most cases are just based on other commentaries, an iterative string stretching back hundreds of years (Jackson 2003:2,11,18). The fruit of Buddhadasa's work, much of which was published in newsletters and books with the help of his brother, a layman, is monumental (2003:13-14).

Buddhadasa illustrated for the broader population that popular religious practices in Thailand such as the honoring of idols and worship of local spirits, ceremonies to make merit, superstitious rites to determine lucky lottery numbers or to divine auspicious days to get married or give birth, and even the belief in reincarnation are not Buddhism at all (2003:4,33). These practices are related more to the Hinduism and Brahmanism which Buddha himself was protesting against. For those who would read Buddhadasa's writings, primarily the middle and upper classes of lay people as well as some of the more learned monks, Buddhism was saved from being seen as a superstitious irrelevancy in the modern era and given a practical face that could motivate social action to improve society, the environment, and the economy in the here and now (Jackson 2003:3,4,33; Buddhadasa 1992:8-9). The popularity of Buddhadasa's work among the educated classes is evident by the wide availability of is books. One can go to any Thai language book stand in any of the many shopping malls throughout Bangkok or in some provincial cities and easily find upwards of twenty different titles by Buddhadasa, much more than any other author. Some of his books are thin treatises on specific topics of interest. Others are thick academic volumes. For those who read, Buddhadasa is likely the single most influential religious figure in recent Thai history. Many of his books are now translated into English as well.

In his research, Buddhadasa rejected one of the three major sections of the Buddhist canon, the *Abhidhammapitaka,* since it is not written in the Buddha's words (Jackson 2003:70). He also judged the most important commentary since the fifth century CE as not even valid as a representation of Buddhist thought. This work, the *Visuddhimagga*, commentaries and instructions on obscure spiritual practices written by Buddhaghosa 1000 years after Buddha himself, contrasts with the sections of the canon Buddhadhasa accepts by interpreting everything through Brahmin and Hindu lenses which demanded an eternalist perspective that maintained the doctrine of reincarnation. Trying to appropriate the record of Buddha's own discourses as much as possible, Buddhadasa disavowed the doctrine of reincarnation and asserted that the core of Buddhism is simply an attempt to end suffering in this world through the seeking of and practice of *Tamma* (truth or wisdom) and the release of greed, lust, and all selfish notions (Buddhadasa 1992:8,10,21,22,60-61,65-69,79-81).

Buddhadasa eventually wrote several articles and books explaining his understanding of the common ground between Christianity and Buddhism. He argued against the notion that Buddhism is not a religion at all, but simply a philosophy of life since it ostensibly has no God. According to Buddhadasa, Buddhism does indeed have a notion of God, the important concept of *Tamma* (Buddhadasa 2004:9).

Tamma, Logos, and God

The idea of Tamma is the force behind the universe, the right order of things, the path of righteousness, Truth, Wisdom, etc. When I look up *Logos* in the Greek lexicon on my computer Bible program, the definition is eerily similar. *Logos* is the important concept in the New Testament that we usually translate as Word, like when we say that Jesus is the Word of God. *Logos*, however, was an important foundational concept in Greek philosophy long before Jesus and the writers of the New Testament. The importance of Tamma in Thai society and Buddhist thinking is seen in the Thai language, as it is the root word in Thai behind the words for nature (*tammachat*), righteousness (*kuamchobtaam*), normal (*tammada*), morals (*silataam*), culture (*watanataam*), religious truth (*kristataam* or *putataam* for Christian and Buddhist respectively), scripture (*prakristtaamkampi* or *praputtaamkampi*), and the community of saints (*tammikachon*). John makes the leap in John 1 to say that, "In the beginning was the Tamma, and the Tamma was with God, and the Tamma was God. He was with God in the beginning. Through him all things were made.....The Tamma became flesh and made his dwelling among us..." This is not how the official Thai Bible translates it. The official Thai Bible uses a royal language word, *prawata*, to translate Logos that essentially means the "word from the throne". But the concept of *Logos* in Greek is certainly much bigger than the literal word of a king. *Tamma* is a much more fitting translation. Translating *Logos* as *prawata* reflects an English language bias, trying to represent the English translation, Word, rather than being true to the concept of *Logos* in Greek and the genius of John's contextualization. By forgoing the natural translation of *Logos* as *Tamma*, the church in Thailand misses a wonderful opportunity for dialogue about who Jesus is in relation to the teachings of Buddha.

My light bulb went on as to how I could communicate the concept of God with Buddhists. Through a regular dialogue I had with our slum community president, Komsorn, a 50 year old father who had previously been a monk for 10 years when he was younger, I learned that, unlike most monks and former monks, Komsorn is actually very learned in Buddhism, especially the teachings of Buddhadasa. We would regularly *kui Tamma* (talking about Tamma or God) for hours at a time. Informed by his previous study of Buddhadasa, Komsorn had no problem with my use of the word *Prajaow* (God) and proactively contextualized toward my Christian terminology, using *Prajaow* and *Tamma* interchangeably. Whenever I would say that God is a person, however, he would laugh off and rebuke the idea, saying that God could not possibly be a person (echoing Buddhadasa, I would later learn). "If God is a person, then what is his name?" Komsorn would ask. I would try to explain that God's name is Yahweh in Hebrew, which means "I am". Komsorn was not won over by this explanation, though. We went back and forth on this sticking point for two years. But then one day, he explained to me in such a way, "God cannot possibly be a person because God is infinite and eternal, there is no beginning and no end to God, he does not have a day he was born and a day he will die and be no more, he is all powerful and all knowing…" Hearing Komsorn say this was an epiphany for me as I thought, "Wow! This is exactly what I believe about God. He is Yahweh, the Alpha and the Omega…." I asked him, "Do you believe that you can pray to God as you conceive him?" He answered yes. We were on to something. He was not opposed to the idea of God being relational, he was opposed to the idea of God being finite, as if God were just another human being like you or I. Every time that I previously insisted that God is a person, he must have thought it absurd that I, and Christians in general, apparently had such a low view of God. Again, the concept of Logos/Tamma came in handy.

From my background in physics, I already had the concept that God was the force that holds the universe together—that in the electromagnetic and gravitational and nuclear forces, within the quantum mechanics of the quarks and protons, neutrons and photons, in the infinite complexity, we are seeing none other than the hand of God. So if God is a Force, bigger and broader and beyond our imagination than we could conceive of as a person, this is a beautiful thing. If God is indeed the Alpha and Omega, the Great I AM, the one in whom we "live and move and have our being" (Acts 17:28), then of course he is more than a person. And, amazingly, I can read Paul saying something very similar in Colossians 1, "The Son is the image of the invisible God, the firstborn of all creation. For in him all things were created: things in heaven and on earth, visible and invisible, whether thrones or powers or rulers or authorities; all things have been created through him and for him. He is before all things, and in him all things hold together….For God was pleased to have all his fullness dwell in him…Now I rejoice…by the commission God gave me to present to you the Tamma of God in its fullness—the mystery that has been kept hidden for ages and generations, but is now disclosed to the Lord's people…" (Colossians 1:15-17,19,24a,25b-26) We reclaim the miracle that though God is more than a person, he wanted us to know him and knew that the only way we could know him in his fullness is to relate to him as a person. And so it is an absolute mind-boggling miracle that God, Tamma, in all his fullness, squeezed into Jesus so that we might know him. And then that we are told God's Spirit comes to live in us, in our hearts. If we indeed believe that all of God's fullness is in the Spirit, then we ought to burst into flames.

Jesus, Buddha, and Tamma

From all this, we can emphasize how Jesus was a teacher of Tamma, the same Tamma that Buddha taught. We can talk about Jesus' life and how he was the only one who ever fully lived out this Tamma. We can emphasize Jesus' teaching to repent and believe the good news, that the Kingdom of Tamma is at hand. We can explain how Jesus taught that he was the Way, the Truth, the Life (i.e. the full manifestation of Tamma, just as Colossians teaches). I asked my friend Komsorn, "Do you believe that Jesus is the Son of God?" He answered yes. To clarify that we were on the same page, we defined "Son of God" as the only one who fully walked out Tamma, the full manifestation of Tamma. He still clearly and confidently refers to himself as Buddhist, but I think we both understand each other to have little difference in our beliefs. Komsorn has since composed worship songs for our house church in the Isaan *sarapan* and *laae* styles, even writing one *laae* about the creation from Genesis and another series of *laae*s that made up an entire Christmas play, taken from the gospel of Matthew.

Some Christians may take issue with the assertion that the Tamma of Jesus and the Tamma of Buddha are one and the same. This is an appropriate concern and so it is important to spell out in detail the nuance of this statement. I believe that there is one universal truth and one God of the universe. Thus, whoever seeks the divine or seeks out what is true, wise, just, and righteous, will be, to varying degrees, seeing, understanding, and relating to this one universal truth and this one God of the universe, even if "as through a glass darkly" (as I recall one translation of 1 Corinthians 13:12). It is my proposal that the teachings of Buddha, the wisdom and truth that he did discover, not unlike the wisdom and truth that Solomon discovered and wrote about in Proverbs and Ecclesiastes, are indeed a portion of the divine Logos. Buddha's understanding of this Tamma was no doubt incomplete, just as any human's understanding of God is. However, I suggest that this was none other than the Tamma which inspired Moses in the burning bush and inspired the prophets of the Hebrew scriptures. That Buddha, or Moses, David, Solomon, Isaiah, or even Mohammed for that matter, spoke of and taught what they understood of the divine Tamma, in no way impinges on the uniqueness of Christ. As John states, Jesus is Tamma. Buddha taught what he understood of Tamma. Jesus is the full manifestation of Tamma. Tamma became flesh and dwelt among us.

Finding Common Ground:
Popular Teachings Versus Scriptural Fundamentals

Some Christians, as well as Buddhists and Muslims, would argue with these statements, claiming that the teachings of Buddha and Mohammed, respectively, are in direct contradiction with the teachings of Jesus and the Hebrew and Christian scriptures in many instances. For helping me untangle this problem, I owe a huge debt to both Buddhadasa as well as several dear brothers who serve in Muslim contexts and with whom I have had the privilege of conferencing with in Bangkok annually the past few years. One brother at the Muslim contextualization conference, whose name he would probably prefer I not mention for security reasons, taught using a geometrical illustration that if one takes the popular understandings of Christianity and Islam, they are at complete odds with each other, 180 degrees apart. But if one takes the popular commentaries within the two religions, they are a little closer, but still very far apart, perhaps 120 degrees askance. If one goes further to investigate the teachings of some of the better scholars, pastors and imams, the two religions appear to be getting quite close, perhaps just 60 degrees apart. However, if one goes all the way to analyze just the Bible and the Koran in their original languages, it is hard to find any contradictions and they appear to be teaching completely complementary messages. The Koran even has quite a bit to say about Jesus as a very unique figure and ultimately exhorts readers to consult the Hebrew and Christian scriptures if there is anything in the Koran that leaves them confused. As a result, they are able to teach Muslims to follow Jesus straight from the Koran and to remain under the identity and label of Muslim rather than converting to being a Christian, which would cut them off from their family and friends and all opportunity to be a witness for Jesus. From the example of these brothers ministering in Muslim contexts, I was inspired to consider the opportunities for deep contextualization with Buddhism as well.

However, most people I was in contact with to that point in time saw very little opportunity for similar contextualization with Buddhism because Buddhism did not apparently share any common monotheism or Abrahamic background and common scriptural legacy like Islam does with Christianity. Buddhadasa, however, by researching the fundamental roots of Buddhism, Buddha's Buddhism, if you will, has shown that the above geometrical illustration can also be used for finding common ground between Christianity and Buddhism as well. Popular conceptions of Buddhism are completely at odds with popular conceptions of the Christian message. If we dig deeper into what Buddha's own message was and what the gospel really is according to Jesus himself, we do find the common ground to make these messages complementary to each other and not contradictory.

Ironically, I was pleased to also meet and get to know some dear brothers and sisters working in Thailand at these Muslim contextualization conferences, including Banpote Wetchgama and Tongpan Prometta. Banpote and Tongpan, of Udon Thani in northeast Thailand, have been researching and practicing contextualization strategies throughout the Isaan region for over thirty years. They teach and proclaim *Put run mai*, or "new generation Buddhism." Essentially, this is the equivalent of the deep contextualization that is able to occur with Muslims. Banpote and Tongpan have been teaching Buddhists to follow Jesus, as Buddhists, and not encouraging conversion to Christianity. A key facet of their evangelism revolves around the Buddhist prophecy of the *Phra Sri Ariya Mettrai* (The Most Beautiful Love), or *Phra Sriahn* for short. This messianic prophecy, attributed to Buddha, was especially well-known to the Isaan people in past generations. Understanding Jesus as the fulfillment of this Phra Sriahn prophecy is a major part of Banpote's personal journey to faith and has been a path to faith for many people throughout Isaan. Banpote has also gained much from Buddhadasa's writings which have undergirded his efforts at contextualization of the gospel of Jesus. I had already begun to discover the writings of Buddhadasa on my own when I met Banpote. Dialoguing with him, however, spurred on my understanding of the value and potential of Buddhadasa's work for our contextualization efforts, especially regarding the key dynamics inherent in the concept of Tamma.

Through my own ongoing reading of Buddhadsa's work, dialogue with Banpote and Tongpan and others on the Christian side, and dialogue with Komsorn and others on the Buddhist side, I began to understand that Buddhism and Christianity could actually enjoy a large common ground similar to the shared monotheism, Abrahamic background and common scriptural legacy between Islam and Christianity. We have one God in common. Christians may call him *Prajaow*. Buddhists will call him *Tamma* (Buddhadasa 2004:9). We can together reject the notion that God is finite or non-eternal in any way. We can together affirm that anything and everything that is good, wise, just, or righteous is of God. Beyond just the similar moral teachings of Buddhism and Christianity, as well as the amazing similarities between the Hebrew messianic prophecies and the Buddhist prophecies of the *Phra Sri Ariya Mettrai* (which unfortunately are less well known among younger generations), we can also stake out common scriptural legacies together, according to my friend Komsorn. I have inquired several times about how to acquire a copy of the *Pratraibitok*, the Buddhist cannon of scripture. Apparently, there are only a very few temples in all of Bangkok that even have a complete set of the many volume *Pratraibitok* (40 volumes, if I recall correctly). One can easily find "peoples' versions" at bookstands, like the ones that sell Buddhadasa's books, but they are just compilations of excerpts that are thought to be worthwhile to the general reader.

Coming from Protestant Christianity, with a heavy emphasis on the written Bible as the foundation for all belief and practice, I was preoccupied with finding the full version of the *Pratraibitok* so that I could find and study key texts for myself, like the *Phra Sri Ariya Mettrai* prophecy, for example, as well as Buddha's exhortations to do away with idol worship, to abandon belief in reincarnation, and to focus all efforts on seeking out Tamma and practicing Tamma. Komsorn instructed me, however, that Buddha taught that any teaching should not be accepted simply because he or anyone else of stature presented it or because it was written down in any book, but that each person should test and analyze for oneself each teaching and only accept it if one could discover its self-evident truth for oneself. In this way, Komsorn emphasized that all truth, all Tamma, is self-evident enough that one does not need to appeal to some notion of scriptural authority. The authority is in our conscience, essentially, and the agreement of the teaching with other teachings we know to be true.

This, in fact, is quite similar to how the New Testament canon was constructed and approved. There were many writings during the days of the early church, but only those that were gathered into the New Testament received approval based on the common agreement of the early church leaders that these teachings were indeed true and consistent with the life and message of Jesus and the message of God stretching back to the Old Testament (Wright, 2005). Komsorn essentially proposed an open Buddhist Bible that could include Christian teachings and scriptures. Propose the truth of Jesus' teaching and if it is self-evidently true and right to each person who hears it, they will accept it. Our scripture, according to Komsorn, is the Tamma. This might be similar to a Christian saying, "the Word is the Word" in which they essentially mean that the authority of teaching and practice is rooted to Jesus himself primarily and not just to a printed book. The book helps people of scriptural orientation to know Jesus, but Jesus is the one to be known and followed, not the book. I think this is what Komsorn is saying for Buddhism: The book, the *Pratraibitok*, does not matter so much. Seeking out Tamma, understanding Tamma, and following and practicing Tamma are what is important and are not tied to access to a book.

Orthopraxy Vs. Orthodoxy

Within Western Evangelical Christianity, we usually place having the right beliefs as the first priority and the prerequisite to salvation, however salvation is defined. However, as Peter Jackson notes, within Thai Buddhism, focus is placed on right action (orthopraxy) over right doctrine (orthodoxy) (Jackson 2003:19). Whether you do the right thing is more important than whether you believe the right thing. This is reflected in the popular saying: *Tuk satsana sorn hai tam dii. Tuk satsana ga dii. Tuk satsana meuan gan.* "All religions teach people to do good. Therefore, all religions are good. All religions are the same." So goes the universal reply of any Buddhist in Thailand if religious or spiritual topics are engaged in conversation. It is at once affirming of other religions and avoiding conflict with other religions. It is also implying that it does not matter what one believes, whether one be Buddhist, Christian, Muslim, etc. as long as one does good. This saying affirms the common belief that, indeed, all religions do teach people to do good and thus defines what a religion even is for Thais. In the West, we would emphasize that a religion must necessarily have some entity that is worshipped, revered, and followed. A religion must have a god or it is no religion at all, or so it is thought. In Thailand, religions are seen to address the problem of suffering in this world, they teach good morals and practice to eliminate suffering in this world. Each religion has great value and together, religions are seen as brothers in common cause rather than competitors. Just as some westerners might argue that Buddhism is not a religion and simply a moral philosophy, since on the surface it seems to have no god in which to have right belief, some Thais, if they were fully aware of the worldview of certain streams of evangelical Christianity, might label them as not religions either, as they focus almost exclusively on having right belief for salvation into the afterlife, rather than focusing on good deeds that can help the world now.

Since all religions have value to Buddhists, no religion is rejected. Though some people may be bored of and disinterested in religious discourse for other reasons, Buddhist beliefs reinforce a respect for other religions, including Christianity. Thus, a teacher of Christianity is generally welcomed and listened to. A traditional evangelist overtly tries to get people to change their affiliation from Buddhist to Christian and learn the right beliefs and may experience frustration at their lack of fruit in this endeavor, determining that the Thai people are hard-hearted towards the gospel or dominated by minions of Satan. Most Thai Buddhists see little need to change their religious affiliation—"our religion is good enough, why change?"—but will gladly listen to the teachings of the Bible and of Jesus especially.

What Is Good News? – A Prescription

Considering everything written above, I propose that any message that will be received as good news by urban poor Buddhists in Bangkok slums must contain several important elements, including the affirmation of Buddhist identity, an understanding of salvation that is communal and global as well as individual and which is very much placed in this world and at least begins on this side of death, affirmation and vigorous empowerment of experiences of community and manifestations of the *namjai* ethic, active engagement of fatalism through the recruitment and commissioning of each person as having a crucial role in a larger movement of transformation, and eager partnership in good deeds with those who may have different beliefs.

Buddhadasa's scholarship has made an enormous impact on the understanding of Buddhism in Thailand. The refrain, "All religions teach people to do good. Therefore, all religions are good. All religions are the same" may even be traced back to Buddhadasa, as he was a pioneer in emphasizing the common ground between Buddhism and other religions. (I would be interested to research the source of that universal refrain.) However, the leading edge of his impact on the beliefs and practices of Thai Buddhists is with the educated upper and middle classes, not with the undereducated poor who are more active in folk Buddhist practices. Does Buddhadasa's work have any relevance for ministry among the poor in the slum communities of Bangkok? His interpretation of Buddhism became central to my discussions with Komsorn, the community president in the Permsup community. Komsorn is fairly well educated for a slum dweller, however, and is more learned into Buddhism than probably 95 percent of monks, let alone lay people. He may enjoy *kui Tamma* (talking about Tamma and God) for hours on end, but few others in the slums do. Though some people were edified by overhearing our discussions, they were mostly over the head of our other neighbors, and rarely would anyone else actively join in our discussions. So what value are the high level ideas of Buddhadasa for ministry with the majority of slum dwellers?

I see this question as to the value of Buddhadasa's ideas for ministry among the poor answered on two main levels: Buddhadasa's value as a bridge builder between Buddhism and Christianity, and his prophetic voice against animistic elements of folk Buddhism as well as prevailing Hindu and Brahman influences within popular Buddhism that emphasize reincarnation (Jackson 1992:253-256,259-261). Buddhadasa shows us where the common ground between Buddhism and Christianity is so that we can confidently affirm Buddhist identity. As a minister of the gospel of Jesus, I no longer have to see Buddhism as the enemy or to try to convert people to become Christians. I can exhort people to grow in their understanding and practice of Buddhism, centering around the concept of Tamma and also to consider Jesus as the full and complete manifestation of Tamma. I can analyze the many social ills in Thailand and determine that they are not caused by Buddhism but because the Thai people are not Buddhist enough. I can use Buddha as an ally in exhorting people to abandon their animistic and superstitious practices in favor of the pursuit of Tamma. I can refocus discussion of Buddhism away from making merit and thoughts of reincarnation towards a present focus on how we can work for the ending of suffering on this earth (Jackson 2003:33, 34). I can affirm the potential of Buddhist institutions like the temple and the monkhood, even while lamenting their current failings. I can talk about the present access to *nibban* (nirvana). In essence, Buddhadasa opens up many conceptual doors that would otherwise be closed. His research into the historical roots of Buddhism and journey to discover what Buddha himself actually said and what he meant by it is a project that does not need to be repeated or fully understood by the people in the slums that I work with. But the fruit of his research allows directions in ministry that simply would not be possible otherwise. Buddhadasa's legacy ultimately makes space for the biblical vision of new creation to be relevant to Buddhists.

Holistic Gospel Of New Creation

As I stated at the outset, contextualizing the gospel with Buddhists around the concept of Tamma necessarily leads us to a more holistic gospel. Traditionally, the Christian gospel is presented by the four spiritual laws/bridge diagram model which focuses on the individual sin and guilt of each person and the work of Christ as an atoning sacrifice for each person's sins so that they can be reconciled to God and go to heaven after they die instead of to hell. This is the gospel I shared with people when I first came to the Permsup slum community. It seemed to fall on deaf ears for the most part. I felt a distinct dissonance between the hope I had for seeing the slums of Bangkok transformed and the focus of the message in this gospel that I felt obliged to share and proclaim. Evangelism felt forced. I did not feel in my gut that this message was actually good news. As I sat in the midst of poverty and brokenness, I was not excited by this message. "Who cares where people go after they die, if they are living in hell now?" I thought. I knew that God cared about the poor. I knew that the Kingdom of God included such important things as justice, putting others before oneself, love of neighbor, laying down one's possessions and ambitions in order to be freely available to God's call of discipleship, prophetic accountability for those in positions of power, healing of diseases and ailments, the casting out of demons, reconciliation between people, even across significant lines of division, judgment of oneself and not of others, the counting of what it would cost to devote oneself fully to the Kingdom, generosity to those less well off rather than to those better off, humility, perseverance in prayer, the forgiveness of sins, and the call to repentance. Why did the traditional gospel message only focus on the forgiveness of sins part? Why did the rest seem like extra credit?

Jesus himself rarely, if ever, shared such a presentation like the traditional gospel message we have in evangelical Christianity today. Instead, he frequently proclaimed with joyful authority that the Kingdom of God is at hand and pleaded with people to repent and receive this good news. A mentor of mine back in the States, James Choung, who is an Intervarsity staffworker in San Diego, was struggling with similar issues regarding the relevance of the truncated gospel message we had to share with people and its dissonance with the larger themes of the Kingdom of God, which we were more excited about as good news. James insightfully pointed out that Jesus himself, when calling his first disciples, did not say, "Come and follow me...and I will give you a ticket into heaven after you die." Nor did Jesus say, "Come and follow me...and I will make you happy...or prosperous." Jesus said, "Come and follow me, and I will make you fishers of men." (Mark 1:17) From the very first, Jesus gave his followers a mission. He immediately made them his partners, his co-workers. Why then do we not usually use the call to mission and an orthoprax life of service as part of our evangelistic message?

As I sought to learn about Buddhism and opportunities for contextualization, and zeroed in on the concept of Tamma, I was also beginning to experience a revolution in my understanding of what God is doing in this world and what his ultimate purposes are. I had always been enthralled by passages in the Bible like Isaiah 65 and 66 and Revelations 21 and 22 that spoke of a new heavens and a new earth, a world full of justice, peace, health, and intimate relationship with God. However, I had consistently been led to believe by most Christian teachers and authors that the hope of a world full of shalom was not to be fully realized until Jesus came back in judgment, destroyed this current space-time universe, and started anew from scratch. It was a consistently fatalistic message that encouraged the emphasis on a truncated evangelistic message for the primary purpose of saving souls since, after all, this world is decaying and we should not therefore waste time on what is passing. This fatalistic message then left no room for common ground or contextualization with Buddhists and could not possibly be heard as particularly good news for Thai Buddhists or the poor living in Bangkok's slum communities. Even some of those who advocated all the holistic values of the Kingdom of God and ministries of justice, reconciliation, and care for the poor still felt compelled to toe the party line and at the end of the day speak fatalistically of how while we live between the Now and the Not Yet of the Kingdom, we can do these works of justice and holistic healing and transformation in the world only as signs that point to the coming Kingdom. They obviously hope for the fullness of new creation and shalom, but ultimately, they lament, this will only be realized when Jesus comes back. This pulling back from hope was discouraging for me.

Through my own Bible study, however, and reading many books by authors like N.T. Wright, Brian McLaren, Dallas Willard, Andrew Perriman, and Greg Boyd, I began to see a different eschatology as possible. There is not space in this paper to go into this literature, but suffice it to say that I found a biblically sound and orthodox foundation for an orthoprax agenda of engineering the eschaton. That is, there is definitely biblical support for believing that what we do here and now to bring about healing, reconciliation, repentance, discipleship, and transformation has lasting value beyond just souls going to heaven after they die and little tastes of heaven being offered here. I have come to believe that the vision of new creation in Isaiah 65 and 66 as well as Revelation 21 and 22 is not a picture of what we will experience after God destroys this existing space-time universe and places us in a new one that he creates, but it is a picture of what God, even through us, is currently creating on this earth. Humankind can move up or down, towards this vision of shalom or away from it, however, depending on whether people repent and seek out the Kingdom of Tamma or whether we go our own way. This is not a naive vision of human progress, like the many failed –isms of the twentieth century, but rather the faith that Jesus actually meant what he said when he announced that the Kingdom of God is at hand. Only as humankind, person by person, community by community, daily and continuously repents and submits to the Kingdom of God will the new creation be realized in growing measure and the abundant "life of the ages" enjoyed (as Dallas Willard translates "eternal life"). The promise of resurrection is then made even more special as we will not then lament the loss of our earthly home and everything familiar to us, but we will ultimately see and experience the fulfillment of all things, the redemption of so many places dear to us to be transformed into how they were always meant to be.

Having retrieved a Christian orthodoxy that fit with the orthoprax needs of ministering to Thai Buddhists in the slum communities of Bangkok, I had new motivation for ministry, including evangelism. I had a story to tell now. The gospel was good news again. Very good news! My friend James Choung has developed a new gospel diagram presentation as an alternative to the bridge diagram which he uses with much success on college campuses in San Diego and which he has written about in his forthcoming IVP book, *True Story: A Christianity Worth Believing In*. His diagram draws four worlds, which he labels, "Designed for Good", "Damaged by Evil", "Restored for Better", and "Sent Together to Heal". This is a tool I am able to use with ease in my context as well (the storyline more so than the diagram). James and his wife Jinhee came to visit me in Bangkok during the summer of 2006 and we invited him to share his formulation of the gospel with our monthly church leaders training. Our various house church leaders responded to his message quite positively, expressing how it emphasizes how the gospel is good news for the whole world, not just for individuals who would respond to it. It freed them from having to condemn a person as a lost sinner before giving them the supposed good news of Christ's atoning sacrifice. Instead, it allowed them to start with Buddha's diagnosis, that there is suffering in this world, which receives universal agreement and is simply an empathetic acknowledgement of the experience of peoples' lives, and then move on to genuinely good news that it is not meant to be that way and that Jesus came to show us the way of *Tamma*, the way to end suffering (individually, communally, and globally) and the way to restore and heal *tammachat* (nature, the environment). Moreover, it does not end with a static salvation, but it is a dynamic missional call to partner with God in healing and restoring the earth and humanity to the image of *Tamma*.

As I began to share this story with neighbors in Permsup, even young drug dealers, I not only felt free and excited myself, but I could see in their eyes that this message was resonating and made sense. There was still a hesitance to believe and accept this message, but it was not because it was irrelevant. Rather it was because it was telling them they were worth something, that God wanted their company in his mission to heal the world and believed they had something of value to offer this mission and bless others—and this seemed too good to be true. I saw in young men's eyes something rising that had not been touched in a long time. With this message, I was telling them that they were worth something, that they could actually be a blessing to others. This was an idea they had long given up on, assuming that they were worthless and hopelessly selfish and self-serving.

Although I will not go into a full explanation of the biblical orthodoxy of the holistic gospel of new creation, I will engage the Isaiah 65 text to explain the orthopraxy inherent in this vision of a new heavens and a new earth, which can be naturally received by orthoprax Buddhists seeking the Tamma for ending suffering on this earth. I began suspecting that this was a vision for us to pursue here and now from my own reading of the text and also with the help of N.T. Wright's immense scholarship, most succinctly summarized in his capstone book, *Simply Christian: Why Christianity Makes Sense*. But I owe a debt of gratitude to David Lim for being the first person I have seen boldly and without apology teach and exegete this passage as a manifesto for what the church should be busy pursuing presently. The full text of Isaiah 65:17-25 bears quoting here:

> For behold, I create new heavens
> and a new earth,
> and the former things shall not be remembered
> or come into mind.
> But be glad and rejoice forever
> in that which I create;

for behold, I create Jerusalem to be a joy,
    and her people to be a gladness.
I will rejoice in Jerusalem
    and be glad in my people;
no more shall be heard in it the sound of weeping
    and the cry of distress.
No more shall there be in it
    an infant who lives but a few days,
    or an old man who does not fill out his days,
for the young man shall die a hundred years old,
and the sinner a hundred years old shall be accursed.
They shall build houses and inhabit them;
they shall plant vineyards and eat their fruit.
They shall not build and another inhabit;
    they shall not plant and another eat;
for like the days of a tree shall the days of my people be,
and my chosen shall long enjoy the work of their hands.
They shall not labor in vain
    or bear children for calamity,
for they shall be the offspring of the blessed of the Lord,
    and their descendants with them.
Before they call I will answer;
    while they are yet speaking I will hear.
The wolf and the lamb shall graze together;
    the lion shall eat straw like the ox,
    and dust shall be the serpent's food.
They shall not hurt or destroy in all my holy mountain,
                says the Lord.

As David Lim so forcefully illustrates, this passage focuses on so many of the issues impinging upon the urban poor. Health care is a major concern. Infant mortality is no more. Disease and frailty are pushed back by increasing gains in science and medicine so that life expectancies far surpass one hundred years. No longer will the poor be exploited as underpaid construction workers, building others' houses and shopping malls and skyscrapers while they live in squalor in one room shacks in the slums. They will build beautiful houses and be able to live in them themselves. No longer will the poor be exploited as sharecroppers and slaves and underpaid migrant farm workers, enriching the wealth of landowners while they struggle to find enough to eat themselves. Now they will be able to eat richly of the fruit of their own labors, no longer oppressed. There shall be equity in the economic system. No longer shall children be born into situations where they will be abused, neglected, or enslaved. There shall be justice and parents shall love their children rather than abandoning them in search of drink or illicit sex or money. No more will there be debilitating birth defects. Medicine will be far advanced. People will enjoy intimate relationship with God such that he answers their prayers before they even voice them. God will indeed be Immanuel. There shall be peace and an end to war. No longer will people live in fear of one another or nation in fear of nation. No longer will there be an unequal access to resources and fearful hoarding. The strong and the weak will trade together, access resources together and be at peace with each other, no longer seeking to exploit or needing to protect. And yet it is clear that this vision is not some final perfection that comes only after God has destroyed this fallen world and started over. People still die. People are still building and dwelling, planting and eating, marrying and bearing children. It is very much a picture of this world, only as it should be. "So do you believe this is possible?!" David Lim preaches. "If so, how will we make it so? What should we be doing to pursue this vision?"

Eschatalogical Engineering

If we have a worldview which really believes that as we submit ourselves to the Kingdom of Tamma, we will make progress in transforming our own lives and our relationships, our communities, our cities and our globe to reflect the new heavens and the new earth promised in Isaiah 65, and indeed that it is the task God has bestowed upon us to be his willing hands and feet in recreating this world, then we each have an important role and would do well to strategically plan how we will move forward. We can thus eagerly exhort each person to recognize their value and importance not only to themselves but to the community around them and affirm their crucial role in moving the community forward to a state closer to shalom. We must also gather people together and eagerly affirm existing manifestations of mutually dependent community and the *namjai* ethic of generosity. Both of these affirmations are unmistakably good news to the urban poor Thai Buddhists. Even more powerfully, we can exhort existing community groups, or at least cohesive regional origin cliques within slum communities, of their capacity to not only join forces to help themselves and lift their own community up, but to consider the opportunity that they ultimately have to be a blessing to neighboring communities. Thai people, especially the poor, are not selfish by nature. Any encouragement to maintain and improve upon healthy community dynamics will be received with open arms.

There is a significant factor of pessimism and fatalism that is fostered by years of poverty and living in the slums. Hope is needed. Good news is needed. But no one is going to reject this message. They only need to be exhorted consistently to have hope and believe in these possibilities. If we do not put up barriers to faith in Jesus and the Kingdom of God by needlessly framing a competition between Buddhism and Christianity, like most mission work had done in the past, people will eagerly respond to the message of hope and give it a fair hearing. Because despair and pessimism have been engrained for so long, however, it is necessary to do more than simply proclaim the message, we must begin living and modeling it both in the areas of spiritual formation as well as in community development and community organizing.

Tamma of Jesus and Tamma of Buddha

If we understand that the gospel is "Jesus is Lord" and that the Kingdom of God is at hand and that this news is good news for this earth here and now, that God's purpose is to send us out as healing agents in this world, that he endeavors to bring about a new creation, a new heavens and a new earth, we can make the Tamma of Jesus and the Tamma of Buddha equivalent. If we believe, however, that God would just have us proclaim a message of four spiritual laws and an individual salvation for the afterlife, it is very hard to show how this is good news because sin and guilt are not the primary concern of Thai Buddhists. It is then necessary to have people convert from the religion of their fathers and their country to the foreigners' religion and be seen as essentially becoming a foreigner. Buddhism is from square one all about ending suffering. If we believe that God is about ending suffering and bringing about a new creation, even presently, the Tamma that Buddha sought and tried to explain is the same as the Tamma of Jesus and we can see Jesus as the special one, the Annointed One, or as the Buddhist messianic prophecy would put it, The Most Beautiful Love (*Phra Sri Ariya Mettrai*), the fulfillment of Buddhism and the one whose reappearing will set the world to rights and coincide with our coming to live in harmony together in what can be summarized with a Judeo-Christian term as shalom. We do not then even need to have people change their affiliation from Buddhist to Christian and will succeed in evangelism as well as concrete personal and community transformation all the more by avoiding such dividing distinctions and rather taking opportunity to point to the story of Tamma and Jesus' life.

REFERENCES

Chapter 1

Bakke, Raymond J. *A Theology As Big As The City*. Downers Grove: InterVarsity Press, 1997.

Blandford, Carl E. *Chinese Churches In Thailand*. Bangkok: Suriyaban Publishers, 1975.

Bowring, Sir John. *The Kingdom And People Of Siam* Vol.1, London: John W Parker and Son, 1857.

Burnett, David. *The Spirit Of Buddhism*. London: Monarch Books, 2003.

Dhammananda, K. Sri. "Do You Know?" *Buddhist News*. Available from: <http://www.geocities.com/~buddhistnews/page207.htm> (accessed Dec. 30, 1998).

Diamond, Jared. *Guns, Germs, And Steel: The Fates of Human Societies*. New York: W.W. Norton & Company, 1999.

Ellison, Craig Ed. *The Urban Mission*. Grand Rapids: William B. Eerdmans, 1974.

Government of Thailand. *Thailand Official Handbook*. Bangkok: Government House Printing Office, 1964.

Greenway, Roger S. *An Urban Strategy For Latin America*. Grand Rapids MI: Baker Book House, 1973.

Graham W. R., *Siam*. Vol.1. London: Alexander Moring Limited, The De La More Press, 1924.

Higgins, Kevin. "The Key To Insider Movements: The 'Devoted's' of Acts." *International Journal of Frontier Missions*. 21: 4, (Winter 2004): 155-165.

Hinton, Keith. Growing *Churches Singapore Style: Ministry In An Urban Context*. Singapore: Overseas Missionary Fellowship, 1985.

Jesuit Fathers, ed. *The Catholic Directory Of Thailand*. Bangkok: Xavier Hall. 1967.

Jocano, F. Landa. *Slum As A Way of Life*. Quezon City: University of the Philippines Press, 1975.

Johnstone, Patrick. *Operation World*. Pasadena: William Carey Library, 1986.

_____. *Operation World*. Grand Rapids: Zondervan Publishing, 1993.

Johnstone, Patrick and Jason Mandryk. *Operation World*. Gerrards Cross: WEC International, 2001.

Jusmai, M. L. Manich. *Popular History Of Thailand*. Bangkok: Chalermint, 1972.

Kauffman, Donald T. *The Dictionary Of Religious Terms*. New Jersey: Fleming H Revell Company, 1967.

Lim, David. "The City in the Bible" *Urban Ministry In Asia*. (1989): 20-41.

McGavran, Donald A. *Understanding Church Growth*. Grand Rapids: William B. Eerdmans Publishing, 1970.

_____. *Understanding Church Growth*. (Fully Revised) Grand Rapids: William B. Eerdmans Publishing, 1980.

McManners, John ed.. *The Oxford Illustrated History Of Christianity*. New York: Oxford University Press, 1990.

National Statistical Office, 1970. *Preliminary Report Of The 1970 Population And Housing Census Of Thailand*. Bangkok: Office of the Prime Minister.

Pantoja, Luis Jr., Sadiri Joy Tira and Enoch Wan eds. *Scattered: The Filipino Global Presence*. Manila: Lifechange Publishing, 2004.

Ro, Bong Rin. *Urban Ministry In Asia*. Taiwan: Asia Theological Association, 1989.

Skinner, G. William. *Chinese Society In Thailand, An Analytical History*. Ithaca, New York: Cornell University Press, 1957.

Smith, Alex G. *Strategy To Multiply Rural Churches: A Central Thailand Case Study*. Bangkok: OMF Publishers, 1977.

_____. *Siamese Gold: A History Of Church Growth In Thailand - An Interpretive Analysis 1816-1982*. Bangkok: Kanok Bannasan (OMF Publishers), 1982, 1999.

_____. "Family Networks: The Context for Communication." Paper Presented, SEANET 8 Forum, Chiang Mai, Thailand, 15 January 2006.

Toynbee, Arnold. *Christianity Among The Religions Of The World*. New York: Charles Scribner' Sons, 1957.

Victoria, Brian Daizen. *Zen At War*. Oxford UK: Rowman &Littlefield Publishers, 1997.

_____. *Zen War Stories*. London: Routledge Curzon, 2003.

Wong, James. *The Church In the Midst Of Social Change*. Singapore: Church Growth Study Center, 1973.

Wyatt, David K. *Thailand: A Short History*. Bangkok: Trasvin Publications, 1984.

Chapter 2

"*Buddhism In Cambodia: The Impact of Buddhism In Khmer Society*" <http://www.watdamnak .org/watdamnak/buddhism.html> (accessed January 5, 2008).

"*Executive Summary, Conference On Youth, Poverty And Conflict In Southeast Asia Cities*" Bangkok, April 8-9, 2003.

Online NewsHour Forum: Robbert Coles – The Moral Intelligence Of Children. Public Broadcasting Service, March 3, 1997 .

Bailey, Stephen. "Communication Strategies For Christian Witness Among The Lao." In *Sharing Jesus Effectively In The Buddhist World*, D. Lim and S. Spaulding, eds.. Pasadena: William Carey Library, 2003.

_____. "World Christianity In Buddhist Societies." *Communicating Christ In The Buddhist World*, P. De Neui and D. Lim, eds. Pasadena: William Carey Library, 2006.

Bausch, William. *Storytelling, Imagination And Faith*. Mystic, Connecticut: Twenty-Third Publications, 1999.

Birch, Carol. *The Whole Story Handbook: Using Imagery To Complete The Story Experience*. Little Rock: August House Publishers, 2000.

Bradshaw, Bruce. *Change Across Cultures: A Narrative Approach To Social Transformation*. Grand Rapids: Baker Academics. 2002.

Carter, Denise. "New Locations: The Virtual City." *Anthropology Matters Journal*. 6, (2004): 1.

Curtis, Brent and John Eldredge. *The Sacred Romance*. Nashville: Thomas Nelson Publishers, 1997.

Dorji, Kinley. "*Pretty Woman*." Paper presented, 3rd International Conference on Gross National Happiness, Bangkok, 26-29 November 2007.

Edirisinghe, Padama. "Religious Values Vs. TV Ads." Buddhist Spectrum, *Daily News*, Colombo, Sri Lanka, 13 June 2007.

Ellis, Elizabeth and Niemi, Loren. *Inviting The Wolf In: Thinking About Difficult Stories*. Little Rock: August House Publishers, 2001.

Evans, A. Steven. "Globalization And Its Challenges To Christian Media." Plenary Presentation, Arabic Media Convention, Beirut, 11-14 March 2001.

Forest, Heather. *Wisdom Tales From Around The World*. Little Rock: August House Publishers, 1996.

Friedman, Thomas. *The Lexus And The Olive Tree*. New York: Anchor Books, 1999.

Gabler, Neal. *Life The Movie: How Entertainment Conquered Reality*. New York: Vintage Books, 1999.

Kitiarsa, Pattana. "Faith And Films: Crisis Of Thai Buddhism On The Silver Screen." Paper Presented, Conference on Religion in Contemporary Myanmar-Burmese Buddhism and the Spirit Cult Revisited, Stanford University, 22-23 May 2004.

Kraidy, Marwan. "The Global, The Local And The Hybrid: A Native Ethnography Of Glocalization." *Critical Studies in Mass Communication* 16, (1999).

Lasn, Kalle. *Culture Jam: How to Reverse America's Suicidal Consumer Binge – And Why We Must.* Harper, 2000.

Lham-Dorji, Lam. "Believe In Yourself And Let Others Do Their Own," In *Voices Of Bhutanese Youth: Through Their Dreams, Experiences, Struggles And Achievements*. Thimphu: Centre for Bhutan Studies, 2007.

Lim, David. "Towards A Radical Contextualization Paradigm In Evangelizing Buddhists." In *Sharing Jesus Effectively In The Buddhist World*, P. De Neui, D. Lim, and S. Spaulding, eds. Pasadena: William Carey Library, 2005.

Mejudhon, Nantachai. "Meekness: A New Approach To Christian Witness To Thai People." In *Sharing Jesus Effectively In The Buddhist World*, P. De Neui, D. Lim, and S. Spaulding, eds. Pasadena: William Carey Library, 2005

Miksic, John. "Southeast Asia: Ancient Centre Of Urbanization?" *IIAS Newsletter*, no. 35, (June 2005).

Naisbitt, John, Nana Naisbitt, and Douglas Philips. *High Tech High Touch: Technology And Our Search for Meaning*. New York: Broadway Books, 1999.

Pek-Dorji, Siok Siam. "Opening The Gates In Bhutan – Media Gatekeepers And The Agenda Of Change." Paper Presented, 3rd International Conference on Gross National Happiness, Bangkok, 26-29 November 2007.

Peterson, Eugene. *Stories Of Jesus*. Colorado Springs: Navpress, 1999.

Roger, Everett and Arvind Singhal. *Entertainment – Education: A Communication Strategy For Social Change*. Mahwah, New Jersey: Lawrence Erlbaum Associates, 1999.

Simmons, Annette. *The Story Factor: Inspiration, Influence And Persuasion Through The Art Of Storytelling*. Cambridge: Perseus Publishing, 2001.

Smith, Alex. "Missiological Implications Of Key Contrasts Between Buddhism And Christianity." In *Sharing Jesus Effectively In The Buddhist World*, D. Lim and S. Spaulding, eds. Pasadena: William Carey Library, 2003.

Sobol, Joseph. *The Storytellers Journey*. Chicago: University of Illinois Press, 1999.

Søgaard, Viggo. *Media In Church And Mission: Communicating The Gospel*. Bangalore: Theological Book Trust, 1993.

Taber, Michael. *Globalization, Mass Media And Indian Culture*. Delhi: ISPCK, 2003.

Tan, Kang-San. "Genesis 1-11 And Buddhist Scriptures: How The Gospel Can Transform Buddhist Worldviews." In *Communicating Christ In The Buddhist World*, P. De Neui and D. Lim, eds.. Pasadena: William Carey Library, 2006.

Tan, Kang-San. "The Power Of The Kingdom For Encountering Buddhist Worldviews." In *Sharing Jesus Holistically With The Buddhist World*, D. Lim. and S. Spaulding, eds. Pasadena: William Carey Library, 2005.

Twitchel, James. *Lead Us Into Temptation: The Triumph of American Consumerism*. New York: Columbia University Press, 1999.

Van Rheenen, Gailyn. *Communicating Christ In Animistic Contexts*. Pasadena: William Carey Library, 1991.

Wolkomir, Richard and Joyce. "You Are What You Buy," *Smithsonian*, 31(7), (2000).

Marshall McLuhan. *The Gutenberg Galaxy: The Making of Typographic Man*. University of Toronto Press, 1964.

Chapter 3

Albright, W.F. "Some Remarks On The Song Of Moses In Deuteronomy XXXII" In *Essays In Honour Of Millar Burrows*. Leiden: Brill, 1959, 343-344.

Baker, David W. *Nahum, Habakkuk And Zephaniah: Tyndale Old Testament Commentaries*. Leicester: InterVarsity Press, 1998.

Bartholomeusz, Tessa J. & De Silva, Chandra R. *Buddhist Fundamentalism And Minority Identities In Sri Lanka*. Albany: State University of New York Press, 1998.

Bechert, Heinz. "The Beginning Historiography In Ceylon: The Mahavamsa Political Thinking." In *Religion And The Legitimation Of Power In Sri Lanka*, B.L. Smith, ed. Chambersburg: Prima Books, 1974, 48-72.

Betz, H.D. *Essays On The Sermon On The Mount*. Philadelphia: Fortress Press, 1985.

Blomberg, Craig L. *Matthew: The New American Commentary*. Nashville: Broadman Press, 1992.

Brown, Colin. Ed., *The New International Dictionary Of New Testament Theology vol 1*. Carlisle: Paternoster Press, 1976.

Bruce, F.F. *The Book of Acts: The New International Commentary On The New Testament*. Grand Rapids: Eerdmans Publishing Company, 1988.

Carson, D.A. *Matthew: The Expositor's Bible Commentary vol 8*. Grand Rapids: Zondervan Publishing House, 1984.

_____. *Love In Hard Places*. Wheaton: Crossway Books, 2002.

Cole, R. Alan. *Galatians: Tyndale New Testament Commentary*. Leicester: InterVarsity Press, 1991.

Davis, John J. *Paradise to Prison: Studies In Genesis*. Salem: Sheffield Publishing Company, 1998.

De Silva, Chandra Richard. *Sri Lanka: A History*. New Delhi: Vikas Publishing House, 1997.

De Silva K.M. *Reaping The Whirlwind: Ethnic Conflict, Ethnic Politics In Sri Lanka*. New Delhi: Penguin Books India, 1998.

_____. *A History Of Sri Lanka*. Chennai: Oxford University Press, 1981.

De Silva, K.M., Duke, Pensri. Goldberg, Ellen S. & Katz, Nathan. ed., *Ethnic Conflict In Buddhist Societies: Sri Lanka, Thailand and Burma*. London/Boulder: Printer Publisher/Westview Press, 1988.

Dharmadasa, K.N.O. *Language, Religion And Ethnic Assertiveness: The Growth Of Sinhalese Nationalism In Sri Lanka*. Ann Arbor: The University of Michigan Press, 1992.

Divayina 7 Sep. 2003

Dunn, James D.G. *Galatians: Black's New Testament Commentary*. Peabody: Hendrickson Publishers, 2002.

Filson, Floyd V. *Matthew: Black's New Testament Commentary*. London: Adam & Charles Black, 1971.

France, R.T. *The Gospel Of Matthew: The New International Commentary On The New Testament*. Grand Rapids: Eerdmans Publishing Company, 2007.

REFERENCES

Free, Joseph P. *Archaeology And Bible History*. Wheaton: Van Kampen Press, 1950.

Garland, David E. *2Corinthians: The New American Commentary*. Nashville: Broadman & Holman Publishers, 1999.

Geiger, Wilhelm. *Mahavamsa: The Great Chronicle Of Ceylon*. Dehiwala: Buddhist Cultural Centre. 2003.

Gunasingam, Murugar. *Primary Sources For History Of The Sri Lankan Tamils*. Sydney: South Asian Study Centre, 2005.

Hagner, Donald A. *Matthew 1-13: Word Biblical Commentary vol 33A*. Dallas: Word Books Publisher, 1993.

Ham, Ken, Carl Wieland, and Don Batten. *One Blood: The Biblical Answer To Racism*. Green Forest: Master Books Inc., 2001.

Harris, Ian. ed., *Buddhism And Politics In Twentieth Century Asia*: London/ New York: Continuum, 1999.

Harris, R. Laird, Gleason L. Archer, and Bruce K. Waltke. *Theological Wordbook Of The Old Testament*. Chicago: Moody Publishers, 1980.

Indrapala, K. *The Evolution Of An Ethnic Identity: The Tamils In Sri Lanka C.300 BCE To C.1200 CE*. Colombo: Vijitha Yapa Publications, 2007.

The Island, 28 Jan. 1993

Karunaratna, Charles Winston. *Buddhism And Christianity In Colonial Ceylon: The Portuguese And Dutch Period*. London: SPS Communications, 2000.

Kink, R.L. "The Legend of Prince Vijaya: A Study Of Sinhalese Origin" *American Journal Of Physical Anthropology* 45, (1976): 91-100.

Lester, Robert C. *Theravada Buddhism In South East Asia*. Michigan: The University of Michigan Press, 1973.

Leupold, C.H. *Exposition Of Genesis Vol. 1*. Grand Rapids: Baker Book House, 1942.

Mathews, Kenneth A. *Genesis 1-11:26: The New American Commentary*. Nashville: Broadman & Holman Publishers, 2001.

McGavran, Donald. *Understanding Church Growth*. Grand Rapids: Eerdmans Publishing Company, 1970.

Megoran, Nick Solly. *The War On Terror: How Should Christians Respond?* Nottingham: InterVarsity Press, 2007.

Morris, Leon. *Matthew: The Pillar New Testament Commentary*. Grand Rapids: Eerdmans Publishing Company, 1992.

_____. *Galatians: Paul's Charter Of Christian Freedom*. Leicester: InterVarsity Press, 1996.

Papina, S.S., S.S. Mostara, and H. Jeyasekara. "Genetical Variation In Sri Lankan Population." *Human Biology* 5, (1996): 707-737.

Perera, H.R. *Buddhism In Sri Lanka*. Kandy: Buddhist Publication Society, 1988.

Pytches, David. *Upside Down: Living The Beatitudes In The 21ˢᵗ Century*. Eastbourne: Kingsway Publications, 2007.

Roberts, Michael. ed. *Collective Identities, Nationalisms And Protest In Modern Sri Lanka*. Colombo: Marga Institute, 1979.

Sailhamer, John H. *Genesis: The Expositor's Bible Commentary vol 2*. Grand Rapids: Zondervan Publishing House, 1990.

Seneviratne, H.L. *The Work of Kings: The New Buddhism In Sri Lanka*. Chicago/London: The University of Chicago Press, 1992.

Singer, M.R. "Sri Lanka's Tamil – Sinhalese Ethnic Conflict: Alternative Solutions" *Asia Survey* 32 no. 8, (1992), 711-722.

Singer, S. *The Authorized Daily Prayer Book*. London, 1939.

Stott, John R.W. *The Message Of Ephesians*. Leicester: InterVarsity Press. 1989.

_____. *The Message Of Acts: To The Ends Of The Earth*. Leicester: InterVarsity Press, 1990.

Swamy, Subramanian. *Sri Lanka In Crisis: India's Options*. New Delhi: Har-Hand Publications, 2007.

Szeles, Maria Eszenyei. *Habakkuk & Zephaniah: International Theological Commentary*. Grand Rapids: Eerdmans Publishing Company, 1987.

Tambiah, Stanley Jeyaraja. *Buddhism Betrayed? Religion, Politics, And Violence In Sri Lanka*. Chicago/London: The University of Chicago Press, 1992.

Wickremeratne, Ananda. *Buddhism And Ethnicity In Sri Lanka: A Historical Analysis*. New Delhi: Vikas Publishing House, 1995.

Wijayathunga, Harishchandra. *Religious Freedom And Fundamental Rights*. (Sinhalese) Colombo: S.Godaga and Brothers, 2003.

Wilkins, Michael J. *Matthew: The NIV Application Commentary*. Grand Rapids: Zondervan Publishing House, 2004.

Wilson, A Jeyaratnam. *The Break-Up Of Sri Lanka: The Sinhalese – Tamil Conflict*. Honolulu: University of Hawaii Press. 1988.

Young, R.F. & Jebanesan, S. *The Bible Trembled: The Hindu – Christian Controversies Of Nineteenth Century Ceylon*. Vienna: De Nobili Research Library, 1995.

Young, R.F. & Somaratna, G.P.V. *Vain Debates: The Buddhist – Christian Controversies Of Nineteenth Century Ceylon*. Vienna: De Nobili Research Library, 1996.

Chapter 4

Amarasekara, Daya. *Naweekaranaya Saha Pansala.* Warakapola:Ariya Prakasakayo, 1981.

_____. *Bududahama Saha samajaya.* Warakapola: Ariya Prakasakayo, 2005.

Darmakeerthi, Sri Nivandama. *Sasanika Ithihasaya.* Dehiwala: Buddhist Cultural Centre, 1996

Darmananda, K. Sri. *What Buddhist Believe.* Expended 4th edition; Kuala Lumpur: Buddhist Missionary Society of Malaysia, 2002

De Silva, Lynn. *Buddhist Belief And Practices In Sri Lanka.* Battaramulla: School Of Technology. 1978.

De Silva, Ranjith *Disciplining the Cities in Sri Lanka*, Peredeniya: Lanka Bible College, 1985.

Dharmabandhu, D.S. *Panca Mahavadaya.* Colombo: Gunasena and Co., 2002.

Gay, Bennett . *Family In Sri Lanka.* London: Lerner Publications Company, 1985.

Perera, Madura Priyadarsana. *Bouddha Deva Sankalpaya.* Dehiwala: Buddhist Cultural Centre, 2004.

Chapter 5

Ahuja, Namrata Biji. "AIIMS Dalits Are Treated As 'Untouchables.'" asianage.com/presentation/leftnavigation/news/stop-story/aims-dalits-are- treated-as-'untouchables'. aspx. (accessed 11 May 2007).

answers.com/topic/dalit-buddhist-movement. (accessed 1 July 2007).

Aryan, Pastor Amit, in discussion with author. 16 May 2007.

Christopher, P.J., in discussion with author. 21 September 2007.

Desai, Darshan. "Embracing Buddhism" www.countercurrents.org/dalit-desai080503. htm. (accessed 6 December 2007).

"English Stumps Engineering Students" timesofindia.indiatimes.com/ articleshow/ 1518501.cms. (accessed 7 May 2006).

Everyculture.com/South-Asia/NeoNeo-Buddhist.html. (accessed 1 July 2007).

Gaddalwar, Praful, in discussion with author. 15 November 2007

Guha, Ramachandra. *India After Gandhi: The History Of The World's Largest Democracy.* London: Pan Macmillan, 2007.

Ilaiah, Kancha. *Buffalo Nationalism: A Critique Of Spiritual Fascism.*
   Kolkata: Samya, 2004.
Interview with Kancha Illiah. swaraj.org/shikshantar/resources_ilaiah.htm.
   (accessed 19 October 2007).
"Landlessness True Index for Poverty" hindu.com/2007/12/09/stories/2007
   120953911200.htm. (accessed 9 December 2007).
Luce, Edward. *In Spite Of The Gods: The Strange Rise Of Modern India.*
   London: Little Brown, 2006.
Manokaran, J.N. *Christ And Cities: Transformation Of Urban Centres.*
   Chennai: Mission Educational Books, 2005.
Masih, Pastor Ajay, in discussion with author. 27 May 2007.
Misra, Neelesh. "They Have Sacked The Priests And They Are Doing Fine."
   Hindustan Times (2 October 2006).
Mokkil, Vineetha. "Serenity Hunters In Buddha Bar." *Tehelka*, (31 July
   2004): 30-31.
Parveen, Aurangabad, in discussion with author.16 May 2007.
Pinglay, Prachi. *One Lakh People Convert To Buddhism.* hindu.com/2007
   /05/28/stories/ 20200752806851200.htm. Accessed 28 May 2007.
Sen, Amartya. *The Argumentative India: Writings On Indian History, Culture
   And Identity.* London: Penguin Books, 2005.
Srinivas, M.N. *Social Change In Modern India.* Hyderabad: Oriental
   Longman, 2001.
Vijay Mohod, Bharatiya Sevak Sangati, in discussion with author. 27 May
   2007.

Chapter 6

Balding, John William. *The Centenary Volume Of The Church Missionary
   Society In Ceylon, 1818-1918.* Madras: Diocesan Press, 1922.
Bechert, Heinz and Richard Gombrich. *The World Of Buddhism.* London:
   Thames and Hudson, 1995.
Ceylon Independent Sept, 12, 1904
Colombo Observer Mar. 27, 1992 .
Copleston, Reginald Stephen, *Buddhism Primitive And Present In Magadha
   And In Ceylon.* New Delhi: Asian Educational Service, 1908.
Deegalle, Mahinda. *Popularizing Buddhism: Preaching As Performance In Sri
   Lanka.* New York: Taylor & Francis, 2007.

REFERENCES

Denham, E.N. *Ceylon At The Census Of Ceylon Of 1911*. Colombo: Government Press, 1991.

De Silva, C.R and T. Nartholameusz. *The Role Of The Sangha In The Reconciliation Process*. Colombo: Marga Institute, 1991.

De Silva, K.M. *University Of Ceylon: History Of Ceylon,* Vol. III. Peradeniya: University of Peradeniya, 1973.

_____. *Sri Lanka: A Survey.* London: Oxford University Press, 1976.

_____. "Religion In The Nineteenth Century Sri Lanka; Christian Missionaries And Their Critics." *Ethnic Studies Report*, Vol. XVI, No I, (January 1998): 104-138.

De Votta, Neil. *Sinhalese Buddhist Nationalist Ideology: Implications For Politics And Conflict Resolution In Sri Lanka,* Policy Studies, 40, Washington: East West Center, 2007.

Dewaraja, Lorna. *The Muslims Of Sri Lanka: One Thousand Years Of Ethnic Harmony*. Colombo: The Sri Lanka Islamic Foundation, 1994.

Dharmadasa, K.N.O. "Buddhism and Politics in Modern Sri Lanka." In *Bhikshuva Saha Samajaya*, edited by Maduluvave Sobhita, et al. Colombo: Systematic Print Ltd., 1997.

Disanayake, J.B. *Introducing Sinhalese Culture: The Vesak Full Moon Festival*. London: Pioneer Lanka Publishers, 1993

Ferguson, John. *Ceylon In The Jubilee Year With An Account Of The Progress Made Since 1803, And Of The Present Condition Of Its Agricultural And Commercial Enterprises*. London, 1883.

Gombrich, Richard, *Buddhist Precepts And Practice*, London: Kegan Paul, 1995.

Gunasekera, Susan W. *The Sinhalese Have Met The Modernists*. Colombo: Stamford Lake Publications, 2003.

Harris, Elizabeth J. *Theravada Buddhism And The British Encounter: Religious, Missionary And Colonial Experience In Nineteenth-Century Sri Lanka*. New York: Taylor & Francis, 2007.

Jayawardena, Kumari. *The Rise Of The Labour Movement In Ceylon*, Colombo: Sanjeeva Prakashana, 1972.

Johnstone, Patrick, *Operation World*, Gabriel Resources Center, 1986

Kariyavasam, A.G.S. *Buddhist Ceremonies And Rituals Of Sri Lanka*. Colombo: Wheel Publications, 1982.

Koscherke, Klaus, Frieder Ludwig and Mariano Delgado. *A History Of Christianity In Asia, Africa And Latin America, 1450-1990*. Grand Rapids: Eerdmans, 2007.

Malalgoda, Kitisiri. *Buddhism In Sinhalese Society, 1750-1900: A Study Of Religious Revival And Change.* Berkeley: University of California Press, 1976.

Obeyesekere, Gananath. *Buddhism Transformed.* Delhi: Mothilal Banarsidas, 1988.

_____. "Is The Sri Lanka War A Buddhist Fundamentalism" In *Buddhism, Conflict, And Violence In Modern Sri Lanka*, Deegalle,ed. New York: Taylor & Francis, 2007.

Pannasiha, Madihe Thera, ed. *Sri Vijragnana Sahityaya.* Colombo: Ahasa Press, 1967.

Peiris, Patrick. *A Study of the Use of Indigenous Art by the Church in Ceylon.* Colombo: Wesley Press, 1973.

Perera, Nihal and Mark Selden. *Society and Space: Colonialism, Nationalism, And Postcolonial Identity In Sri Lanka.* San Diego: Westview Press, 1998.

Peter D. Hershock. *Buddhism In The Public Sphere: Reorienting Global Interdependence.* New York: Routledge, 2006.

Premasiri, P.D. "Righteous War In Buddhism?" in *Buddhism Conflict And Violence In Modern Sri Lanka*, edited by Degalle. London: Routledge, 2006.

Prothero, Stephen R. *Henry Steel Olcott (1832-1907) And The Construction Of "Protestant Buddhism".* Ph.D. dissertation, Harvard University, 1991.

_____. *White Buddhist Asian Odyssey Of Henry Steel Olcott.* Indianapolis: Indiana State University Press, 1996.

Smith, Bardwell, ed. "Buddhism Without Bhikkhus: The Sri Lanka Vinaya Vardana Society." In *Religion And The Legitimation Of Power In Sri Lanka*, Chambersburg P.: Anima Books: Pa., 1978, pp. 212-235, reprinted by Columbia University Press, 1989.

Somaratna, G.P.V. *Kotahena Riot 1883.* Nugegoda: Deepanee Publishers, 1991.

SPG, *Report For The Y Ear 1900 Of The Society For The Propagation Of The Gospel*, London, 1900.

Toupe, David. *Wesak And The Recreation Of Buddhist Tradition.* Montreal Religious Site Project, 2001.

Whalen Lai, Michael Von Bruck, and Michael Von Bruck. *Christianity And Buddhism: A Multicultural History Of Their Dialogue.* Maryknoll: Orbis Books, 2001.

Wickremeratne, Ananda and Paul J. Griffiths. *The Roots Of Nationalism: Sri Lanka*. New Delhi: South Asia Books, 1996.

Wickramasinghe, Nira. *Sri Lanka In The Modern Age: A History Of Contested Identities*. Colombo: Vijitha Yapa Publications, 2006.

Chapter 7

Adelaja, Sunday. *Church Shift: Revolutionizing Your Faith, Church & Life For The 21ˢᵗ Century*. Lake Mary, FL: Charisma House, 2008.

Bos, Pieter. *The Nations Called: A Theology Of The Nations And Their Redemption*. Kent: Sovereign World Publishers, 2002.

Haugen, Gary. *Good News About Injustice*. Downers Grove: InterVarsity Press, 1999.

Hays, J. Daniel. *From Every People And Nation: A Biblical Theology Of Race*. Downers Grove: InterVarsity Press, 2003.

Huntington, Samuel P. *The Clash Of Civilizations And The Remaking Of World Order*. New York: Simon & Schuster, 1996.

Layton, Douglas. *Our Father's Kingdom*. Nashville: World Impact Press, 2000.

Mangalwadi, Vishal and Ruth Mangalwadi. *William Carey And The Regeneration of India*. New Delhi: Nivedit Good Books Distributors, 1993

Mangalwadi, Vishal. *Truth And Social Reform*. London: Spire / Hodder & Stoughton, 1989.

Miller, Darrow. *Discipling Nations: The Power Of Truth To Transform Cultures*. Seattle: YWAM Publishing, 2001.

Mouw, Richard J. *When The Kings Come Marching In: Isaiah And The New Jerusalem*. Grand Rapids: Wm. B. Eerdmans Publ. Co., 2002.

Naisbitt, John. *Global Paradox*. New York: Avon Books, 1994.

Roberts, Bob Jr. *Glocalization: How Followers Of Jesus Engage A Flat World*. Grand Rapids: Zondervan, 2007.

Silvoso, Ed. *That None Should Perish*. Ventury: Regal Books, 1994.

Stier, John; Poor, Richlyn; & Orvis, Lisa, editors. *His Kingdom Come*. Seattle: YWAM Publishing, 2008.

Wagner, C. Peter. *Dominion: How Kingdom Action Can Change The World*. Grand Rapids: Chosen Books, 2008.

Walls, Andrew F. *The Missionary Movement In Christian History: Studies In Transmission Of Faith*. Maryknoll: Orbis Books, 2003.

Wink, Walter. *The Powers That Be: Theology for a New Millennium*. Galilee Trade, 1998.

_____. *Engaging The Powers: Discernment And Resistance In A World Of Domination*. Minneapolis: Augsburg Fortress Press, 1992.

Wink, Walter. *Naming the Powers: The Language of Powers in the New Testament*. Minneapolis: Augsburg Fortress Press, 1984.

Winter, Ralph D. *Lausanne Paper*. 1974.

Wright, Christopher. *The Mission Of God: Unlocking The Bible's Grand Narrative*. Downers Grove: InterVarsity Press, 2006.

Wright, N.T. *Evil And The Justice Of God*. Downers Grove: InterVarsity Press, 2006.

_____. *Jesus And The Victory Of God*. Minneapolis: Fortress Press, 1996, p. 485ff.

Chapter 8

"ABS-CBN/SWS May 14, 2001 Day-of-Election Survey," 2001. http://www.sws.org.ph/exit01/ex01rpts.htm: 13.

Adhikari, Ronald. 2004. "Formosa, With Love," In *Scattered: The Filipino Global Presence*, Luis Pantoja et.al, eds. Manila: LifeChange Publishing, 2004, 279-285

Aragon, Averell V., ed. *Making Missions Practical: A Compendium Of The Regional Consultation In Missions*. Davao City: Mindanao Challenge, 1990.

Baldoz, Rosalinda D. "The Overseas Filipino Workers (OFW) Phenomenon." In *Scattered: The Filipino Global Presence*, Luis Pantoja et al eds. Manila: LifeChange Publishing, 2004.

Benigno, Nena C. "Voices In The Wilderness: ACM Celebrates 10 Years Of Reaching The 10/40 Window." *The Evangelicals Today* 31, no.1 (January-February 2005): 14-16.

Claro, Robert. *A Higher Purpose*. Manila: Church Strengthening Ministries, 2004.

Dimangondayao, Lorajoy T. "Feature Report: Running With The Vision" (2003). <http://www.globalmissiology.net/docs_html/reports/vision/html>.

Dumapias, Rodolfo I. "My Journey As A Christian Ambassador." In *Scattered: The Filipino Global Presence*, Luis Pantoja et al eds. Manila: LifeChange Publishing, 2004, 313-326.

REFERENCES

Felomino, Rodrigo, Jr. "Evangelism Strategies In The Dragon Avenue." In *Scattered: The Filipino Global Presence*, Luis Pantoja et al eds. Manila: LifeChange Publishing, 2004, 209-222.

Galvez, Venus Hannah. "Ministry To Filipino-Entertainers And Japinos." In *Scattered: The Filipino Global Presence*. Luis Pantoja et al eds. Manila: LifeChange Publishing, 2004, 251-270.

_____. *Protestant Churches And Missions In The Philippines, Vol. 2: Philippine Council Of Evangelical Churches*. Quezon City: World Vision Philippines, 1983.

Javier, Eleazer E. 2002. "The Pentecostal Legacy." In *Chapters In Philippine Church History*, edited by Anne C. Kwantes. Mandaluyong: OMF Literature, 2001, 57-82.

Lim, David. "Towards A Radical Contextualization Paradigm In Evangelizing Buddhists." In *Sharing Jesus In The Buddhist World*, D. Lim and S. Spaulding, eds. Pasadena: William Carey Library, 2003, 71-94.

_____. "The Challenges of Empowering Philippine Churches for Effective Missions to China (and Beyond)." In *Asian Church And God's Mission*, Wonsuk and Julie Ma, eds. Mandaluyong City: OMF Literature, 2003a, 195-210.

Manzano, Jojo. "OMF Organizes For Cross-Cultural Outreach Inside The Philippines And Beyond." *Philippine Challenge* 19, no.2 (April-June 1998): 1, 5, 7.

_____. 1989. *From Every People*. Monrovia: MARC and Mandaluyong: OMF Literature.

Manze, Charlie. "A Case Study: Mobilizing 'Canadian-Pinoys'." In *Scattered: The Filipino Global Presence*, Luis Pantoja et al eds. Manila: LifeChange Publishing, 2004, 223-249.

Pate, Larry D. *From Every People: A Handbook Of Two-Thirds World Missions*. Monrovia, MARC, 1989.

Perry, Bill. *A Prophetic Vision For The Philippines*. Atlanta: Harvest Publishing Co, 1992.

Philippine Home Council of OMF International. *Sweet And Sour Stories From The Missionary Soul*. Mandaluyong City: OMF Literature, 2001.

Remigio, Amador A. "Demographic Survey Of The Filipino Diaspora." In *Scattered: The Filipino Global Presence*, Luis Pantoja et al eds. Manila: LifeChange Publishing, 2004

Shubin, Russel G. "The Escalating Filipino Force For The Nations." *Mission Frontiers*, (September-October 1998): 38-41.

Smith, Eric, Dean Wiebracht, and Thomas Wiseley. 2000. "Philippine
    Mission Boards And Societies." In *Evangelical Dictionary Of World
    Missions*, A Scott Moreau, ed. Grand Rapids: Baker, 2000, 752-754.
Solano, Reynaldo & Godiva Ysip. "*The Kapatiran Ng Mga Simbahang
    Pilipino Sa Singapore* (Brotherhood Of Filipino Churches In
    Singapore)." In *Scattered: The Filipino Global Presence*, Luis Pantoja et al
    eds. Manila: LifeChange Publishing, 2000, 273-278.
_____. "Filipino International Network: A Strategic Model for Filipino
    Diaspora Glocal Missions." In *Scattered: The Filipino Global Presence*,
    Luis Pantoja et al eds. Manila: LifeChange Publishing 2004, 151-172.
Tizon, Albert. "Revisiting the Mustard Seed: The Filipino Evangelical
    Church In The Age Of Globalization." *Phronesis* 6, no. 1 (1999): 3-26.
Wehrfritz, George, and Marites Vitug. "Workers for the World." *Newsbreak*,
    (4 October 2004): 31-33.
Zaide, Sonia M. "The Filipinos As Missionaries To The World." *Evangelicals
    Today* & *Asia Ministry Digest* 21, no. 11 (November 1994): 30-31, 33.
    (Also in *Asia Ministry Digest* 2.2 (1993) .

Chapter 9

Boyd, Gregory A. *Is God to Blame? Beyond Pat Answers To The Problem Of
    Suffering.* Downers Grove: InterVarsity Press, 2003.
Buddhadasa Bhikku. *Paticcasamuppada: Practical Dependent Origination.*
    Bangkok: Vuddhidhamma Fund, 1992.
_____. *Heartwood Of The Bodhi Tree: The Buddha's Teaching On
    Voidness.* Translated by Dhamavicayo, Santikaro Bhikku, ed. Chiang
    Mai: Silkworm Books, 2004.
_____. *Put-Krit Nai Tatsana Taan Putataat.* Out of print, transcribed by
    Banpote Wetchgama, 2004 .
_____. *Kristataam Laae Putataam.* Bangkok: Sukapaapjai, 2006.
Choung, James. *True Story: A Christianity Worth Believing In.* Downers
    Grove: InterVarsity Press, forthcoming in 2008 .
Jackson, Peter. *Buddhadasa: Theravada Buddhism And Modernist Reform In
    Thailand.* Chiang Mai: Silkworm Books, 2003.
Linthicum, Robert C. *Empowering The Poor: Community Organizing Among
    The City's Rag, Tag, And Bobtail.* Monrovia: MARC, 1991.

REFERENCES

McLaren, Brian D. *Everything Must Change: Jesus, Global Crises, And A Revolution Of Hope*. Nashville: Thomas Nelson, 2007.

_____. *The Secret Message Of Jesus: Uncovering The Truth That Could Change Everything*. Nashville: W Publishing Group, 2006.

Willard, Dallas. *The Divine Conspiracy: Rediscovering Our Hidden Life In God*. New York: HarperSanFrancisco, 1997.

Wright, N.T. *The Last Word*. New York: Harper San Francisco, 2005.

_____. *Simply Christian: Why Christianity Makes Sense*. New York: HarperSanFrancisco, 2006.

_____. *Evil And The Justice Of God*. New York: Harper San Francisco, 2007.

INDEX

INDEX

www.ingramcontent.com/pod-product-compliance
Lightning Source LLC
Chambersburg PA
CBHW051242300725
30355CB00035B/416